Fantasy Book Clubs: The Magic of Themes and Symbols

Lucy Calkins, Series Editor

M. Colleen Cruz and Mary Ehrenworth

Photography by Peter Cunningham

Illustrations by Marjorie Martinelli

HEINEMANN ◆ PORTSMOUTH, NH

This book is for Lucy Calkins, our dauntless leader, and her fearless sidekick, Mary Ann Mustac.—Mary Ehrenworth and Colleen Cruz

Heinemann
361 Hanover Street
Portsmouth, NH 03801–3912
www.heinemann.com

Offices and agents throughout the world

© 2015 by M. Colleen Cruz, Mary Ehrenworth, and Lucy Calkins

The authors and publisher wish to thank those who have generously given permission to reprint borrowed material:

From *The Paper Bag Princess* ©1980, Bob Munsch Enterprises Ltd. (text); © 1980, Michael Martchenko (art), published by Annick Press Ltd. All rights reserved. Reproduced by permission.

Excerpted from "Great Zimbabwe (11th–15th century)." In *Heilbrunn Timeline of Art History* (http://www.metmuseum.org/toah/hd/zimb/hd_zimb.htm/), Copyright © 2000–2015 by The Metropolitan Museum of Art, New York. Reprinted by permission.

"St. George Slays the Dragon" and "The Maiden and the Unicorn", Alinari /SEAT/ Art Resource, NY

Cataloging-in-Publication data is on file with the Library of Congress.

ISBN-13: 978-0-325-07722-2

Series editorial team: Anna Gratz Cockerille, Karen Kawaguchi, Tracy Wells, Felicia O'Brien, Debra Doorack, Jean Lawler, Marielle Palombo, and Sue Paro
Production: Elizabeth Valway, David Stirling, and Abigail Heim
Cover and interior designs: Jenny Jensen Greenleaf
Photography: Peter Cunningham
Illustrations: Marjorie Martinelli
Composition: Publishers' Design and Production Services, Inc.
Manufacturing: Steve Bernier

Printed in the United States of America on acid-free paper
19 18 17 16 15   PAH   1 2 3 4 5

Acknowledgments

LIKE ALL OF OUR READING UNITS, this one arises from a think-tank collaborative with our colleagues at the Teachers College Reading and Writing Project (TCRWP). We have to give a shout-out to some avid fantasy readers with whom we often huddle over lunch, comparing what we are reading, arguing over interpretations, and getting each other to tackle the next series: Cornelius Minor, Katy Wischow, Shana Frazin, and Natalie Louis. You have been our fantasy book club members, and your thinking runs through all these pages.

We are grateful to all the schools and classrooms that have, over the years, trusted us to dive deeply into fantasy units of study—the fourth- and fifth-grade teachers of PS 59, PS 321, PS 116, PS 29, PS 295, and PS 6 in New York City, and all of our institute and Twitter buddies around the world. So many adventurous teachers inspired their children, and now, we hope, will inspire more, by piloting and sharing how they explored novels, innovated curriculum, and coached readers to outgrow themselves. Two educators in particular were essential to this work, and you'll see the traces of their steady collaboration across these pages. They are Natalie Norris, who helped managed the pilot classrooms and student work, and Sarah Bienversie, who took her class through iterations of these lessons and whose students' work illuminates these lessons. Sarah, we never could have brought this book to such authentic production without your generosity. Thank you to the fifth-graders of Sarah Bienversie's, class of 2015!

Our team members at Heinemann have been our thought partners for years and we can't imagine writing this kind of book without their friendship and leadership. We especially thank Karen Kawaguchi, who edited this book with her usual thoughtful and expert attentiveness, and Abby Heim, who led all aspects of this work with her usual grace. It's a gift to work with you.

Many of you will know Marjorie Martinelli of ChartChums fame. We are proud to be her colleague and to have had her artistic and literary sensibilities engaged in making charts for this unit of study. As always, she manages to maintain sophisticated thinking, while creating teaching tools that help make the work memorable, as well as accessible.

Lucy, we know you'll read this, as you read every word the Project writes. It's impossible to express how fully you've mentored us, believed in us, and gifted us with opportunities. When you see in these pages references to archetypes, know that "Lucy" is an archetype for a character who shows determination in pursuit of a quest, inventiveness in the face of opposition, and courage in the face of setbacks. Look around your coterie, not just at the Project but at institutes and classrooms around the world, and you'll see "Lucy" characters following in your footsteps, doing their best to make reading intelligent, beautiful, and authentic.

On an entirely personal note, we want to thank our families. It takes enormous amounts of time—often time stolen that might otherwise have been family time—to author any text. We are grateful to our partners and children and ever hope that we may sustain you as you sustain us.

—Colleen and Mary

Contents

BEND III   When Fact and Fantasy Collide

BEND IV   Literary Traditions: Connecting Fantasy to Other Genres

An Orientation to the Unit

STUDY YOUR EXPERT and avid readers, and chances are you'll find that many of them are fantasy readers. There are a few reasons for this. One is that kids who read a lot tend to seek out series. Look at the great series written for kids, and you'll quickly realize that they're mostly fantasy. Another is that kids who read a lot also often read at high levels, and that means they quickly find that fantasy will be a better genre for them than, say, realistic fiction, in which the characters in higher-level novels begin to stray into issues that may be inappropriate, and fortunately, not that interesting to ten- and eleven-year-olds.

The important thing about fantasy novels is that they teach kids to be better readers. With their exciting plots and young heroes, these novels entice children to read, and they draw kids into series that keep them reading and lead them up levels. Think about the 400 million young readers who came of age with Harry Potter. J.K. Rowling did more than create a best-selling series. She created a generation of readers. There are underlying reasons, as well, that fantasy reading is so compelling for teens and pre-teens. As Laura Miller wrote in the *New Yorker*, "the world of our hovered-over teens and preteens may be safer, but it's also less conducive to adventure" (June 14, 2010). Kids yearn for adventure, they yearn to be transformed, to become like Harry Potter, whose ordinary life becomes extraordinary, whose private problems take on epic meaning. There is something vividly satisfying about fantasy. It fills a yearning, deep within us: the yearning to achieve significance.

Fantasy novels also teach readers to deal with complexity. These novels weave complexity through multi-faceted characters, multiple plotlines, shifting timelines, tricky narrative structures, and complicated symbolism. This unit, then, aims to help you create lifelong readers of all your children. It also explicitly aims to instill in your children an eagerness to tackle more complex narratives, the tools to embrace that complexity, and the sense of agency to do this work independently, now and in the future.

You'll anchor the unit with a read-aloud of a riveting fantasy novel for children (we suggest *The Thief of Always*), as well as a few short texts. Through these read-aloud texts, children will be introduced to the work of embracing complexity across many pages and across texts. They'll practice the work, and go on with the work of moving up levels of text complexity, through book clubs, where they will read fantasy series books. In the first bend of the unit, you'll teach students to navigate the other worlds of their novels, including the complicated settings, multiple characters, and multiple plotlines. In the second bend, you'll lead students to think more metaphorically, teaching them to explore the quests and themes that reveal themselves within and across their novels. Next, in the third bend, you will help students deepen their understanding by teaching them to deal with new challenges, such as turning to nonfiction to explain some of the references in their books, and learning to deal with ever more literary and figurative language. Finally, in the fourth bend, you will teach readers to capitalize on their expertise by investigating fantasy as a literary tradition—and studying how the thinking work developed through reading fantasy novels will pay off in other genres as well.

SUPPORTING SKILL PROGRESSIONS

Your children will probably embark on this unit in the spring of fifth grade. For many readers, this period marks a time of growth not only in understanding and knowledge but also in independence. Before embarking on this unit, you will want to reread the Narrative Reading Learning Progression for fifth grade, so that you can help your fifth-graders set clear goals. You'll also want to review those for fourth grade, because your conferring and small-group work may need to shore up foundational skills on the fourth-grade progression. This may occur even while your unit advances into the work of fifth grade and sometimes even sixth grade. You will want to provision your students with the fourth-, fifth-, and sixth-grade progressions, because some of your readers will be ready to work toward higher expectations than others, and you want to be sure your conferring and small-group work reaches your strongest readers as well as those who need extra support.

By the spring of fifth grade, the novels that your students are reading are becoming more complex. Students who read these more challenging texts will need to be ready to embrace complexity in comprehension, as well as interpretation. There will be more characters to keep track of, more tangled plotlines to follow, and more nuanced settings to make sense of. The stories they are reading will also develop more than one theme and often illuminate more than one social issue. It's going to be important that your fifth-graders learn to welcome this complexity and develop reading practices that set them up to notice the ways their novels are becoming more complicated.

No longer will students see the whole text working to support one fairly explicit and clear theme. Instead, it's much more likely that they'll need to follow different threads as they read a novel. That means they will need to recognize that the text will often have multiple main themes (some of which will be implicit, hidden between the lines). It is important that fifth-graders approach texts, expecting them to advance more than one theme and that they become alert to how themes develop across a novel. This expectation is detailed within the "Determining Themes/Cohesion" strand of TCRWP's Narrative Reading Learning Progression. This is also a critically important skill on many other high-stakes assessments. Take a minute to read across the levels in this strand below. You'll see, for instance, that in fourth grade, students trace a theme across a story, but it is in fifth grade that readers are expected to figure out more than one theme and how each develops.

Across the unit, you'll be encouraging students to analyze texts, teaching them to use language such as "The author probably included this in order to—" and "This part is important because—." This work of analyzing part of the text in relation to the whole text encompasses analysis of characterization, thematic development, structure, and author's craft. The main skill you're emphasizing is that of teaching kids to ask, "Why is this part here? What work is this doing in the story?" The "Analyzing Parts of a Story in Relation to Whole" strand of the learning progression will help you and your students tackle this work.

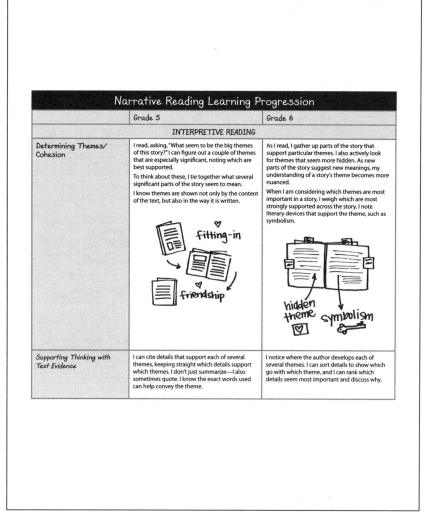

This need to embrace more complexity crosses over and relates to more than just the "Determining Themes/Cohesion" strand. This unit also supports essential character skills, and you'll see that the "Character Response/ Change" thread regularly mentions the need for students to be more flexible as they read more complex texts. This need for flexibility will relate to

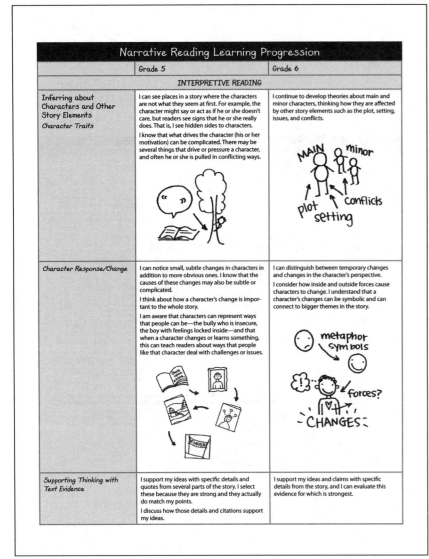

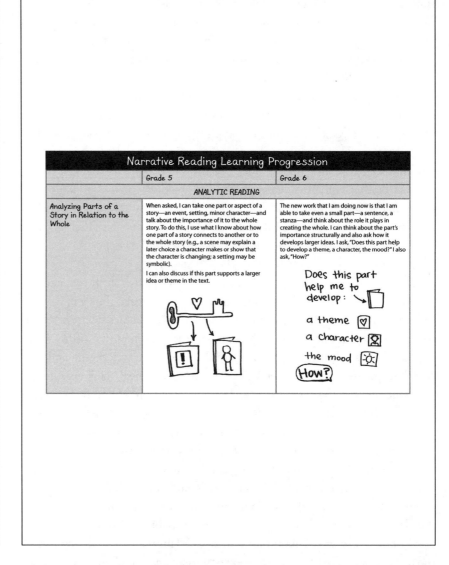

students' tracing the way that characters change, including what causes these changes and how the reader perceives change when it may be subtle. Your whole-class and small-group instruction across this unit will support students in the skills of tracing increasingly complex characters.

This fifth-grade unit will also directly tackle the "Analyzing Author's Craft" strand, paying particular attention to analyzing symbolism as a way to lead fifth-graders into deep analysis of author's craft.

Your readers will be reading several novels across this unit, and early on, they are asked to think about how the themes they encounter in one novel play

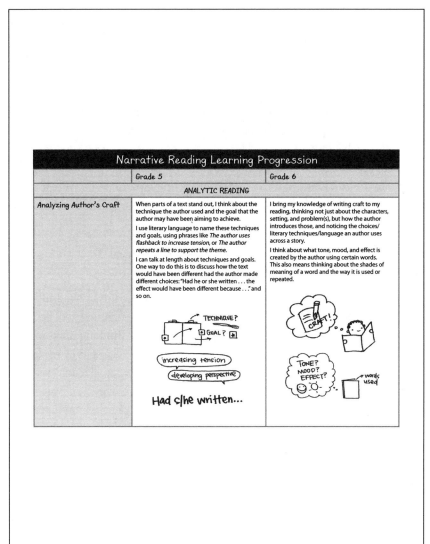

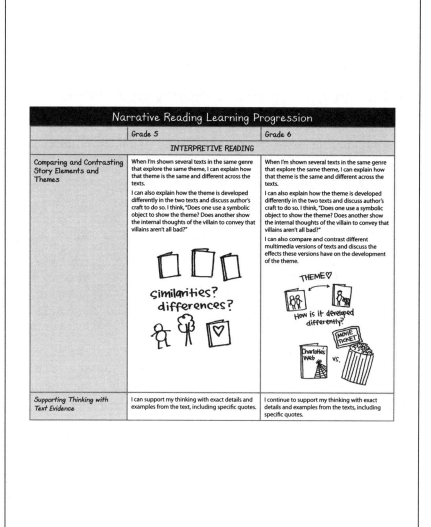

out in other texts—not merely fantasy but also historical fiction and narrative nonfiction. An important strand, then, will be "Comparing and Contrasting Story Elements and Themes," which deals with how authors develop similar themes in different narratives. The work of thinking across not just two texts they've just read but also texts they may have read at other times and in

situations will lead your readers to become the kind of readers who are alert to allusions and literary traditions, as well as to the small ways that authors differ in developing similar themes.

This unit places a spotlight on developing more active, alert readers, who question and critique texts as well as comprehend them. That means that the

"Critical Reading" strand of the progression will be helpful to you and your readers as well.

OVERVIEW

Bend I: Constructing and Navigating Other Worlds

In the first bend, you will launch your students into fantasy book clubs (or partnerships for some). Your kids will want to talk about these books, and you'll want to channel this urge to heighten their intensity and stamina for reading and for literary conversations. You will want to teach them to read with deep comprehension and to synthesize across many pages. You'll begin by alerting children to ways that fantasy novels become complicated very quickly and the work readers can do to meet these challenges. This includes doing a little work before reading. While it may not matter much if a fifth-grader picks up an easy chapter book and simply opens it to the first page to begin reading, when that reader wants to tackle a more challenging text, it's helpful to know that readers rarely start these texts cold. Often, they'll orient themselves by reviewing the information on the covers and by reading with extra alertness and willingness to reread, especially at the very beginning of the novel. Readers may find they need to keep lists, maps, or timelines, or turn to ones that may be available in the novel in the appendices. As the novel unfolds, often the central character will have a steep learning curve—and the reader needs to parallel that curve, absorbing knowledge about the place, the characters, and the potential conflicts from myriad sources—some that the main character may miss! You'll find that your readers will be fascinated by these challenges. They'll try out the work with your read-aloud text, and then practice it over and over in the novels they read with their clubs.

Part of the work of making sense of more complicated narratives, including complex places and characters, is the work of suspending judgment. So just as you taught readers to withhold judgment and be open to conflicting evidence when weighing and evaluating it, so you'll teach them to do that same work when weighing and evaluating places and people. Your readers should begin to be much more analytical and also nuanced, as they learn that people are not always what they seem, and that our first "snap" judgment may not always be either accurate or fair.

Aside from these close reading practices, your children will also tackle reading clubs with more agency. To prepare for truly independent reading lives by the time they attend middle and high school, your students will take charge of their clubs, deciding how often to meet, how much to read in between conversations, and what work to focus on. This doesn't mean you abandon your readers to their whims, letting them flounder for long periods of time or letting an achievement gap widen in your classroom. It does, though, mean that you'll explicitly teach about agency and how reading can work well without constant adult supervision. The bend culminates in an inquiry, where clubs study and celebrate the thinking work that each club is doing particularly well, and set goals to raise the level of their work in the next bend—and their next novel.

Bend II: More than Dwarves: Metaphors, Life Lessons, Quests, and Thematic Patterns

By Bend II, all your readers will be in at least their second book, and some may be in their third. That means that everything you teach now will be work they should be applying across books, and a lot of their thinking, talking, and writing should be about comparing and contrasting. You'll begin by returning to the notion of the dragon in *The Paper Bag Princess*, and you'll teach students to think metaphorically about the dragons in characters' lives. You'll also lead students to be affected by what they read—to think about their own dragons and to learn important character traits from characters in the novels they are reading. Next, you'll help children realize that characters in fantasy novels are often on quests and that those quests can be both internal and external. Expect much self-reflection during this part of the unit, as you'll see from the student work. When children first read Harry Potter, for example, they wish they could play quidditch and do magic. In your hands, they'll wish for his courage and loyalty, they'll think about what situations they've faced that call on similar traits, and they'll embark on their own quests to be ever better and braver.

You'll reinforce this teaching—that character traits, quests, and themes can run across stories, including fictional and lived narratives—by turning students to compare themes in novels to themes in history. Think about the social studies that your children studied this year (and last), and bring forth some reminders of those historical eras, events, and individuals. Then turn your students loose on comparing themes. Like us, you'll probably be somewhat stunned by their discernment and the connections they make. If you've studied the tension between colonial expansion and Native Peoples, or Revolution, or Civil Rights, you'll find your students making lightning leaps to compare characters who turn out not to be what they seem, themes that play out in history as well as novels, and heroes who step forward to lead others. It's all rather gorgeous, and it's intensely exciting to see fifth-graders analyze across texts in this hyper-metacognitive way.

Bend III: When Fact and Fantasy Collide

Bend III intensifies children's analytical work. You'll start by showing children that just as it was worth it when reading historical fiction to sometimes turn to nonfiction, it's also worth it when reading fantasy. Fantasy novels make all sorts of references to things that readers can research, from arquebuses and medieval warfare to religious and mythological figures to animal behaviors! Not skipping over these references, but instead reading to deepen knowledge, will transform your children into the kinds of readers who will excel in the future. You'll carry that work forward with their vocabulary work, teaching them not to skip over unfamiliar words, but to bring a whole toolkit of strategies for figuring out and accumulating literary, historical, and technical vocabulary.

Having lured children to read outside their novels to better understand their books, you'll then take them back into their novels, ever more deeply, beginning with a close study of symbolism. Your children will have identified symbols in their stories before this, and now you'll teach them to think about the potential meaning that symbols play in their stories, and to compare and contrast symbolism across the novels they are reading. From there, you'll move them to metaphor and allegory, teaching that many of the symbols in their novels exist outside their novels as well, and that many of their stories are part of bigger patterns and traditions.

Bend IV: Literary Traditions: Connecting Fantasy to Other Genres

Finally, in the fourth bend you'll develop children's understanding of literary traditions so that they begin to see the book they are holding as part of a grander, conceptual text set, and they begin to see themselves as scholars who are also part of long traditions (you may want to introduce robes, à la Hogwarts and Oxford). It's in this bend that you'll move your readers into more critical analysis, beginning with considering how the stories they read portray cultures and represent characters (sometimes as stereotypes). Expect your children to recall and deepen their thinking about similarities and differences in stories told in different cultures and to begin to think more actively about what work stories do in the world.

You'll teach students literary lenses as part of this work, taking them next into a study of archetypes, including the major archetypes that often occur in fantasy novels and the way that some characters break with traditional archetypes. This work will lead naturally into critical reading with the lens of representation, especially in regard to gender norms. Your readers will actively question their texts, asking about what kinds of girls are portrayed in their books, about who has power, about what kinds of resistance they see, and about how their stories reinforce or interrupt stereotypes. They'll compare and contrast representations in the books they are reading with those in film and advertising—applying some of the same analytical and critical questioning lenses they applied when they questioned authors' arguments. For some children (and adults), this will be uncomfortable work, as they reconsider childhood favorites, pass judgment on that Disney movie or that traditional fairy tale, and realize that all around them, norms are being reinforced daily through television, film, and popular music.

It will be exciting to see your fifth-graders question each other, the texts they encounter, and themselves. Look for moments when flash debates arise, and remind students to use what they learned about argument to defend positions using reasoning and evidence. If you're pairing this unit with a writing unit in literary essays, you may find that you can take that writing to new levels, teaching children to analyze not only characters and themes but also gender norms and stereotypes.

The unit will culminate with you and the children thinking about how the work they've done in fantasy will apply to other genres. If you're finishing the unit near the wrap up to summer, help children make reading plans for the summer. Choosing series will help them keep reading and join the community of lifelong readers who sustain flourishing reading lives outside of work and school.

ASSESSMENT

Your instruction will always be informed by assessments, and those assessments will be continual. You'll use running records and other observations of your students, examinations of reading logs and their writing and talking about reading, and performance assessments to track student progress. You will then use the information gleaned from these assessments to align your teaching to what your best knowledge is of what they can do, can almost do, and can't yet do.

You have presumably taken running records at the start of the year, which yielded levels of text complexity that your students can handle. Hopefully, you gave other informal running records to any students who showed signs of being able to progress up a notch during any unit. For students who recently began reading books at a new level of text complexity, you'll want to be watching for how they handle increased complexity, density, and length. Be alert especially for signs of disengagement and engagement. Watch students' reading logs for possible decreases or increases in volume of reading. You may find that you can notch some students up across this unit, as their knowledge and volume increase.

We're assuming that this unit is probably a spring unit, which means that hopefully many of your students are reading level T/U texts with approximately 96% accuracy, fluency, and comprehension. Of course, it is likely that you'll have students whose levels are well below this and some whose levels are above. Remember that during your year together, you'll be aiming to support your fifth-graders to move at least to level U texts by the end of the year, so that they are well poised for summer. Keep in mind which students you want to assess again during this unit, in hopes of moving them into a series they may be able to continue into summer.

With its emphasis on volume as well as close reading, this unit supports dramatic growth. Small-group work can reinforce this. The bands of text complexity (see Chapter 4 in *Reading Pathways, Grades 3–5: Performance Assessments and Learning Progressions*) will be enormously helpful to you as you plan your small groups. That chapter details major ways in which fiction texts become more complicated as they move up levels. With that knowledge in hand, you can help introduce new levels and series to readers, alerting them to what will be especially challenging and fascinating in their books.

You'll be able to peruse your students' Post-its and reading notebooks, and you'll probably want to assess your students' higher-level comprehension more

fully, looking specifically at all the skills comprised by interpretive, analytic reading. This unit begins with a performance assessment, available in the online resources, which is designed to highlight and support these higher-level thinking skills. The performance assessment evaluates four main skills that are critically important across this unit and on the high-stakes assessments your fifth-graders will be taking. In particular, this unit focuses on skills in the areas of these strands: "Analyzing Parts of a Story in Relation to the Whole," "Determining Themes/Cohesion," "Comparing and Contrasting Story Elements and Themes," and "Analyzing Author's Craft." Students will also do significant work in "Inferring about Characters and Other Story Elements."

More details pertaining to the assessment can be found in the Start with Assessment letter in this unit and in the online resources.

The biggest decision you will want to make right away pertains to the scoring of the performance assessment. In Chapter 2 of *Reading Pathways, Grades 3–5: Performance Assessments and Learning Progressions*, we describe ways in which you can hold a norming meeting with other teachers so that all the teachers across your grade level can collaboratively score students' performance assessments, assessing that work in roughly equivalent ways. The learning progression, combined with a big effort to calibrate your assessments, can enable you and your colleagues to come to a shared view on what constitutes good, better, or best work in particular reading skills.

But what we think is most important is that you try to turn as much of the assessment as possible over to the kids. What you are truly assessing is the black box of what goes on in a student's mind during reading, and no one is a better judge of that than the child. Between Session 2 and Session 3, you'll find a letter detailing how this work might proceed. To support your students with this work, you'll draw on the Narrative Reading Learning Progression and on student-facing rubrics, created from the progression.

A word of caution: If your students have not grown up within Units of Study for Teaching Reading and therefore have never before seen the Narrative Reading Learning Progression, you'll find their initial work on the performance assessment and their initial efforts to score themselves are very rough approximations. You would probably be more comfortable if you score their pre-assessment and then ask them to work in partners during Session 3, not to self-score but to understand how you scored them and to try revising their work. That would take a fair amount of your time, however, and if it postpones the unit or the unveiling of the learning progressions, it is probably not worth the trade-off.

Often you'll find that your pre-assessment (and the self-assessment that follows) alerts students to the thinking work they should be doing. Sometimes the reminder itself helps them begin to tackle this work with more zeal. Meanwhile, you'll be teaching a steady repertoire of minilessons that will sharpen their reading work, so that your children become more adept at reading and at self-assessment.

In this unit, your readers will be studying characters that go on quests. They'll think about how characters respond to trouble, how they overcome obstacles, and how they learn and apply knowledge in their quests. Your readers are also on a quest, one to become ever more powerful. Like the characters in their novels, it will be important that they demonstrate what Carol Dweck calls a growth mindset. Setting clear reading goals and striving to meet them will be part of this work. And like the work of the heroes in their novels, some will be best accomplished alone, and some will be done in the company of others.

GETTING READY

For the main read-aloud, we've chosen a somewhat harrowing tale that is sure to grip your students' imaginations and make them want to become the kind of readers who can read these narratives on their own—*The Thief of Always* by Clive Barker. You could also choose a series of books, such as the first three books of Dragon Slayers' Academy or the first two volumes of The Spiderwick Chronicles. The main thing is to choose a read-aloud text that you love and that will reward the teaching you want to highlight in this unit.

We do see one problem with fantasy novels for younger readers, and that is the issue of representation. There simply isn't enough representation of difference in terms of cultural identities, gender roles, or sexualities in fantasy novels in general. You'll see that in the last bend of the unit, you'll bring some critical literacy lenses to bear on the books, and we hope that will help children become aware of what's in their books and what's missing. We also suggest some short texts from around the globe as read-aloud texts to be interspersed through the unit.

For clubs, your children will need some friends to read with and some fantasy series to read. We suggest that for the most part, children form their own clubs. You will want to coach them to take into account how much they want to read, as well as what they want to read. The goal is to read whole

series during this unit. So your avid readers should club together, so they can read a lot. Talk to kids about moving up levels and how they can deliberately choose series that will help them move up levels of complexity. Do this work before the unit begins, so that kids have time to get the books. This is another way kids can show agency. Quickly show them how to order used books, how to get series with their friends on their smart devices, how to ask the local bookstore to get the books for them (and you might also ask the store to pre-order some of the hot titles). Instill the urge to not be limited by the books in the classroom library only. Avid readers find books! Get them to trade, to bring in books, to rescue them from other parts of the school. Give little book talks on the series you'd love for them to read, playing up the easier as well as the harder ones. Have in mind the series that help kids move up levels. Here are some, in particular, that may be helpful:

Series Title	Level	Author
The Secrets of Droon	(M–O)	Tony Abbott
Dragon Slayers' Academy	(N–P)	Kate McMullan
The Spiderwick Chronicles	(Q–R)	Tony DiTerlizzi and Holly Black
The Edge Chronicles	(R–U)	Paul Stewart and Chris Riddell
Books of Ember	(R–U)	Jeanne DuPrau
Deltora Quest	(R–T)	Emily Rodda
Warriors	(R–T)	Erin Hunter
The Chronicles of Narnia	(T–V)	C. S. Lewis
Rowan of Rin	(T–V)	Emily Rodda
Animorphs	(T–U)	K. A. Applegate
Gregor the Overlander	(U–V)	Suzanne Collins
Artemis Fowl	(W–X)	Eoin Colfer
Percy Jackson & the Olympians	(U–W)	Rick Riordan
Redwall	(Y–Z)	Brian Jacques
Harry Potter	(U–Z)	J. K. Rowling
The Golden Compass	(Y–Z)	Phillip Pullman

We suggest that you spend time ahead of this unit of study talking about the series that are available and helping children get these books for the clubs, either as new or used books or on their digital devices. For you want them reading not one book, but a whole series with their club. This way, the unit lures them into reading epic novels that span, especially across series, hundreds to thousands of pages. These readers will develop thematic understanding, inevitably, as fantasy novels prominently overlay their themes on the storyline. They will practice the highest level of synthesis, as they put together the clues about what kind of place this is, who has power and control, what is at stake, and how the characters fit into it all. And will they learn to revise their understanding, to wait and ponder, to rethink and reconceptualize. And then when they go to the next series or the next reading challenge, they will be better readers.

In terms of club structures, we made a conscious decision to give clubs more independence in this unit. We're assuming that it's the spring of fifth grade, that your readers have been in reading workshop for six years now, they've been in clubs many times, and they should be able to make thoughtful decisions about how often to meet, how much to read between meetings, and what to write and talk about. You will coach into clubs, but we suggest that you also research your students and give them feedback about the decisions they make and their signs of agency, rather than on how they follow directions. You won't go to middle or high school with your kids, so now is the time for them to apply what they've learned over their many years of reading instruction. You'll see, therefore, that we'll often say "if clubs are meeting today," suggesting that the decision to meet will be in the hands of the kids. Watch them, and give them some feedback if it looks as if they would be having richer conversations if they read more or if they did more writing before or after talking. This is not meant to be a "hands-off" book club unit. It's simply meant to be an opportunity for you to coach students on how ready they are for the next stage of their independence, when they will probably be sustaining their independent reading and forming social clubs around reading on their own.

❋ ONLINE DIGITAL RESOURCES

A variety of resources to accompany this and the other Grade 5 Units of Study for Teaching Reading are available in the Online Resources, including charts and examples of student work shown throughout *Fantasy Book Clubs*, as well as links to other electronic resources. Offering daily support for your teaching,

these materials will help you provide a structured learning environment that fosters independence and self-direction.

To access and download all the digital resources for the Grade 5 Units of Study for Teaching Reading:

1. Go to **www.heinemann.com** and click the link in the upper right to log in. (If you do not have an account yet, you will need to create one.)
2. **Enter the following registration code** in the box to register your product: RUOS_Gr5
3. Under **My Online Resources**, click the link for the **Grade 5 Reading Units of Study**.
4. The digital resources are available in the upper right; click a file name to download. (For any compressed ("ZIP") files, double-click the downloaded file to extract individual files to your hard drive.)

(You may keep copies of these resources on up to six of your own computers or devices. By downloading the files you acknowledge that they are for your individual or classroom use and that neither the resources nor the product code will be distributed or shared.)

PACING GUIDE FOR *THE THIEF OF ALWAYS, THE PAPER BAG PRINCESS,* AND *MUFARO'S BEAUTIFUL DAUGHTERS*

This unit uses *The Thief of Always* by Clive Barker, *The Paper Bag Princess* by Robert Munsch and Michael Martchenko, and *Mufaro's Beautiful Daughters* by John Steptoe as its demonstration texts. You may choose to use other demonstration texts, but if you decide to use these three texts, you'll want to follow this pacing guide to make sure you and your students are prepared for each session. Some minilessons will require you to read aloud text during the session. However, to keep minilessons brief and maximize club and independent reading time, we suggest that you set aside an additional block of time for most of your read-alouds.

PACING GUIDE for *The Thief of Always*, *The Paper Bag Princess*, and *Mufaro's Beautiful Daughters*

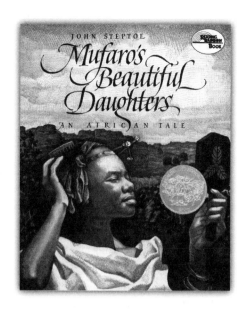

Bend I		
Session	**Chapters/Pages to Read Aloud during the Minilesson**	**Chapter/Pages to Read Aloud before/ after the Minilesson**
Session 1	*The Paper Bag Princess* (First and second pages of text.) *The Thief of Always* (Cover, blurbs, opening images at start of story)	*The Thief of Always* (Chapter 1 *before* the minilesson)
Session 2	*The Thief of Always* (Refer to Chapters 2 and 3, and read aloud Chapter 4)	*The Thief of Always* (Chapters 2 and 3 *before* the minilesson)
Session 4	Students should be able to discuss what they have read earlier in *The Thief of Always*.	*The Thief of Always* (Through Chapter 7 *before* the minilesson)
Session 5	Students should be able to discuss what they have read earlier in *The Thief of Always*.	*The Thief of Always* (Through Chapter 10 *before* the minilesson)
Session 6	None	*The Thief of Always* Stay on pace to read aloud through Session 14 prior to Session 6.
Bend II		
Session	**Chapters/Pages to Read Aloud during the Minilesson**	**Chapter/Pages to Read Aloud before/ after the Minilesson**
Session 7	Students should be able to discuss what they have read earlier in *The Thief of Always*. Have *The Paper Bag Princess* on hand.	*The Thief of Always* (Through Chapter 14 *before* the minilesson)
Session 8	Students should be able to discuss what they have read earlier in *The Thief of Always*.	*The Thief of Always* (Through Chapter 17 *before* the minilesson)
Session 9	Students should be able to discuss what they have read earlier in *The Thief of Always*. You will use *The Thief of Always* to create a timeline of Harvey's internal and external obstacles. Have *The Paper Bag Princess* on hand.	*The Thief of Always* (Through Chapter 18 *before* the minilesson)
Session 10	None	*The Thief of Always* (Through Chapter 19 *before* the minilesson)
Session 11	None	None

Bend III		
Session	**Chapters/Pages to Read Aloud during the Minilesson**	**Chapter/Pages to Read Aloud before/ after the Minilesson**
Session 12	Have *Mufaro's Beautiful Daughters* on hand.	*Mufaro's Beautiful Daughters* (entire book *before* the minilesson) *The Thief of Always* (Through Chapters 20 and 21 *before* the minilesson)
Session 13	Be ready to teach from the poem "Jabberwocky" by Lewis Carroll	*The Thief of Always* (Through Chapters 22 and 23 *before* the minilesson)
Session 14	Students should be able to discuss what they have read earlier in *The Thief of Always*.	*The Thief of Always* (Through Chapter 24 *before* the minilesson)
Session 15	Students should be able to discuss what they have read earlier in *The Thief of Always*.	*The Thief of Always* (Through Chapter 25 *before* the minilesson)
Session 16	Students should be able to discuss what they have read earlier in *The Thief of Always*. Have *Mufaro's Beautiful Daughters* on hand.	*The Thief of Always* (Through Chapter 26 (end of book) *before* the minilesson.)

Bend IV		
Session	**Chapters/Pages to Read Aloud during the Minilesson**	**Chapter/Pages to Read Aloud before/ after the Minilesson**
Session 17	Students should be able to discuss *The Thief of Always*.	None
Session 18	Show a short video clip that shows one or more archetypes that students are familiar with. One example: United Airlines https://vimeo.com/7158709	None
Session 19	Have on hand texts to refer to as you teach, including *The Thief of Always*, *The Paper Bag Princess*, *Mufaro's Beautiful Daughters*, or other texts.	None

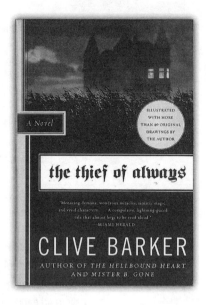

◆ START WITH ASSESSMENT ◆

ear Teachers,

You have reached what is likely to be one of your last units of the year. Congratulations. Take a moment or two to reflect on all the ways your students have already grown across this year and glory in that. Taking some time to glory in growth and to celebrate is important. You and your students have worked hard. Their efforts should be showing clearly.

By now you know how our suggestions for pre-unit work go. Our first piece of advice is to read the front matter of the book so that you can gain an orientation to the unit. Our second piece of advice is to give a performance assessment prior to the unit starting, which will help you to determine a baseline for where your students are and also get some ideas for where you want to take them during this unit. This assessment, as you remember, is designed to evaluate some of the skills that are most essential to this unit and across the standardized assessments many students take.

By now, you've likely got a sense of what helps make the assessment proceed the best it can and you've figured out with your colleagues the ways that are best for you to give this assessment. Remember that these decisions need to be made and implemented in sync with what your colleagues are doing. And of course, whatever tips and ideas you have—we're all ears. Let us know what you've done and we'll funnel what we learn into the Online Resources and share it with other schools and districts so we can all get stronger at doing this work together.

So go forward again today, making the performance assessment work for you and your children. And do make sure to take some time to celebrate the journey.

Thanks,
Mary and Colleen

Session 1

Researching the Setting

I N THIS FIRST SESSION of the first bend of the unit, you introduce kids to the complexities of fantasy, and you do it in such a way that you make these challenges seem fascinating.

The aim of this lesson is to move students past identifying a setting with a word or a phrase (it's the future, it's a place called Narnia), and into analyzing that place for its physical and psychological implications for the characters and the story. Your hope, therefore, is that their analysis after this lesson will sound more like: "It's a place called Narnia, where power seems to be held by a White Witch, and everyone is afraid. Fear seeps through the land—and it's cold and wintery, which seems related to that fear." You'll want to practice analyzing and describing the places in the stories you've read, so you can demonstrate on some novels, as you teach and confer with the kids. We suggest that you also practice with some familiar movie scenes or movie trailers, such as *Harry Potter*, *The Hunger Games*, and so on.

While this lesson is a high-level one, which aims to move readers into more sophisticated analysis, we deliberately choose to demonstrate this work on an accessible text, the alternate fairy tale, *The Paper Bag Princess*. This decision reflects two aims. One is that this high-level thinking work not be reserved only for high-level readers, so that your students' ability to do this work won't be mitigated by their reading level. The second aim is to show readers that they can do more sophisticated work on a variety of texts, not only the more difficult ones. Later in the session, you'll return to the notion of setting to investigate who has power, and kinds of power in these stories, and you'll find that again, *The Paper Bag Princess* reveals many sorts of power.

When students are analyzing the setting in this way, they are thinking across story elements. Push students to support their theories by asking, "What in the text makes you say that?" In this way, you accustom students to analyzing how part of a text relates to the whole. Also encourage students to strive for more precise and literary language. Is the setting more ominous, or utterly terrifying? Is it grim, or desolate?

IN THIS SESSION, you'll teach students that fantasy readers research the setting of a story by investigating clues about the time period and important magical elements, using covers, blurbs, and details from the beginning of the story.

GETTING READY

✔ Review the "Analyzing Parts of a Story in Relation to the Whole" strand of the Narrative Reading Learning Progression.

✔ Read aloud Chapter 1 of *The Thief of Always* prior to this minilesson.

✔ Be prepared to show a few seconds of one or two film clips from well-known fantasy movies, such as *Lord of the Rings*, *The Hunger Games*, *Harry Potter*. You might choose the opening scenes, or the trailers, all of which are easily available on YouTube (see Teaching).

✔ Have on hand a copy of the *Paper Bag Princess*, or another concise, accessible fantasy story to read aloud short excerpts (see Teaching).

✔ Introduce Bend I anchor chart, "Sophisticated Readers of Fantasy . . ." (see Share).

A note about book clubs—you'll see if you look back at the Welcome to the Unit, that we suggest clubs take on more agency in this unit of study, to prepare students to sustain their independent reading lives and their social reading lives after fifth grade. Before today, you'll want to invite children to form small groups around chosen fantasy series—perhaps they write you letters, with a few possibilities of kids they'd like to read with, and books they want to read. Coach children to consider how much they read, as well as *what* they want to read.

"Move students past identifying a setting with a word or a phrase . . . and into analyzing that place for its physical and psychological implications for the characters."

Get your avid readers to club together to read a lot. Coach other clubs to consider series that will help them move up levels. The kids should feel as if these decisions were mostly independent (what to read, who to read with), but actually, they will be highly negotiated. As children are gathering their club members and finding the books they'll need, you can quietly help any individuals join a club, you can help some readers revise their reading plans so they are wiser, and you can pause on the formalizing of clubs until you are fairly sure that they should do well together. All that work happens before today, so that today, children come with their club and their series, ready to start working together.

Researching the Setting

CONNECTION

Stir up your readers for the unit. Share your passion for this genre by giving a little keynote.

I had around me many gorgeous fantasy novels, their covers adorned with dragons, castles, and symbols. As I spoke, I gestured toward these books. "Fantasy readers, today is the day when we start our unit of study in fantasy. Some of you are avid fantasy readers, I know. Others of you are a little unsure about this. You're not quite sure how you feel about dragons, and dwarves, and epic quests where the world is imperiled. Friends, let's begin, then, by thinking about *why* we would read fantasy. Here are some reasons.

"Reason one: Because the stories are incredible. These are wild, dangerous, romantic tales, where the fate of the mankind may rest on the choices made by the main character. Everything is more important, more intense, more vivid, in fantasy stories.

"Reason two: Because when you study fantasy, really, you are studying the human condition. The stories are never really about elves and hobbits. They're about the struggle between good and evil, they're about how power corrupts, they're about the quest to be better than we are, they're about how even the smallest of us can affect what happens in this world.

"Reason three: Because if you become a powerful reader of fantasy, you're likely to become a more powerful reader of all texts. Fantasy novels are incredibly complicated. You have to figure out where the story takes place, what kind of world that is, who has power there, what the rules are. You'll enter narratives that stretch over many novels, you'll read hundreds and even thousands of pages. You'll emerge, like the characters in these stories, changed."

"I want that for you, friends. All of it. I want you to embark, from this classroom, with these characters, on wild adventures that make your head spin. I want you to feel the release that comes when you escape into other, mythic worlds, where magic happens. I want you to find stories that will spread over many books, that will keep you up at night, and fill the corners of your life with their secrets. You may or may not emerge from this study a fanatic—a dungeons and dragons player, a follower of Avatar, a reader of Manga. But you will, I am sure, know more about this wild and beautiful genre. You will, I hope, have more insight into what it means to be human. And you will, I feel sure, emerge with an increased confidence that you can tackle truly complicated texts."

Gather some favorite titles to show, either on your e-reader or some much-read print books. We find it's generative to show not only children's books, but also books you may have read in high school and college, as well as your current reading. Show kids how fantasy readers are lifelong readers. Bring out those copies of Tolkien, Hobb, and, dare we say, R.R. Martin!

You'll see here that while our intention may be for our students to become adept at reading much more complicated stories, ones with multiple plotlines, complex characters, and unfamiliar settings, what we say is: fantasy! Dragons and elves! Dwarves and hobbits! The lure of fantasy is a magical one.

Name the teaching point.

"Readers, today I want to teach you that as fantasy readers, your first task will be to figure out not just where your story happens, but what kind of place it is. One way you can do this work is to investigate clues about the time period and important magical elements, using the covers, blurbs, and details from the beginning of the story for your research."

TEACHING

Explain some of the common settings of fantasy stories and demonstrate how you use this knowledge to research the setting of a shared text.

Experienced fantasy readers expect certain kinds of settings. Often, fantasy stories are set in a medieval world, full of swords, horses, castles, dragons, and so forth—like The Lord of the Rings or Narnia. A second common setting is a futuristic world, full of reminders of this world, but different and often troubled—like The Hunger Games. And the third common setting is the ordinary world, where it seems at first as if everything is normal, but then gradually you'll notice that there is an infiltration of magic—so there is this blending of the world we know with magical elements. Harry Potter is like this."

I quickly showed bits of these films as I spoke, to emphasize their settings.

"So, knowledgeable fantasy readers know to gather up clues, right away, about what kind of place they are in. Sometimes it's a little tricky, because the story might not begin right away in the magical world. It might. *The Hobbit*, for instance, starts right off in a place full of creatures that only grow to be three feet tall, and they use carts and horses to farm, and there are wizards, so the reader knows that this place is magical. But other times, the story starts off in an ordinary place, in the here and now, and you think it's going to all happen here, and then the characters are transported. That's what happens in Narnia—Peter, Edmund, Lucy, and Susan all walk through an enchanted wardrobe, into the magical kingdom of Narnia. Whereas in Harry Potter, Harry starts off also in the ordinary world, but that ordinary world becomes magical. He doesn't go to another kingdom. He still lives in London, in the modern world. But magic enters that world and transforms it.

"Okay, readers, I've tried to jump-start your reading a bit, here, as you can tell, by giving you a little expertise on how fantasy stories tend to start. That means I expect you, from the very first moment you begin reading, to be alert for details about what kind of place you encounter in the story you are reading. Things unfold rapidly in fantasy, so you have to get oriented quickly, before a dragon arrives or you get swept through a portal to another world.

"Friends, watch how I do this work. I'm going to try to name what I do as a reader, as I do it, so you can really see the steps I follow. Then you'll have a chance to practice, on the story we read together, and of course, afterward, in the stories you'll read with your book clubs."

I picked up *The Paper Bag Princess*. "So first, before I *even open the pages*, I look carefully at the book covers. I know that with such complicated stories, I want to get all the information I can from the covers. So I'm looking to see if there's

It is absolutely worth the time it takes to create a file of video clips to use in this unit of study. Get on YouTube and gather some trailers (great for this lesson), and scenes that highlight character traits, conflict, archetypes, and quests. You'll be able to show these clips to students whenever you want. Twenty seconds of video can enliven and engage!

Teachers, you may show a few scenes of film clips from fantasy movies. The scenes give students a way to quickly compare multiple texts, and they bring all our readers, of any level, into this conversation. You can return later to look at issues of representation, gender norms, and critical literacy.

a blurb that might tell me who this story about, and more importantly, what kind of world this is. Hmm, this book has *no* blurb! That doesn't seem fair. But okay, so next, I'll look at the cover art and the title, as those can also tell me a lot. So . . . the book is called *The Paper Bag Princess*, and there is a girl with a bent crown, a huge castle-like door, and a gigantic, smoking dragon on the front cover. On the back cover there is another image, of the same dragon breathing cataclysmic fire over the head of the girl. Hmm . . ."

I opened the inside of the book. "Inside, the story starts like this."

> *Elizabeth was a beautiful princess. She lived in a castle and had expensive princess clothes. She was going to marry a prince named Ronald.*

I looked at the page, saying, "And there's a picture of a snotty-looking prince, with his nose in the air, and a besotted girl, staring at him with hearts flying around her. The room looks like a castle, with arched windows, stone walls, and old wooden chairs. And their clothes are definitely medieval (that's from the Middle Ages, like you'd see in the time of King Arthur). Okay, so I definitely see from the furniture, the buildings, and the clothes, that this story happens in a place that is medieval." On the next page, it says:

> *Unfortunately, a dragon smashed her castle, burned all her clothes with his fiery breath, and carried off Prince Ronald.*

"Aha! So there is magic here, too, this is not historical fiction, from the actual Middle Ages. A dragon has entered. That is definitely a magical creature. He has even magically managed to smash Elizabeth's castle, and burn all of Elizabeth's clothes, without harming her at all."

I put the book down. "Okay, readers, I think I know enough now. But what matters is that I've learned about the physical time and place—and even more importantly, I'm getting a sense of what *kind* of place this is, its *psychological* implications. It is pretty clear that this story begins in a medieval place. It has castles, old-fashioned clothes, and princesses. And, it is magical. There are dragons. There are *no* subways or buses, or laser guns, or spacecraft. And, the story started right away in this magical kingdom. And, I know all this, because I carefully considered the pictures and text on the covers, the clues about daily life, and the appearance of any magic. It's also, though, a place of sudden violence, where people's lives are ripped apart, and they can find themselves alone, facing horrid challenges without any support. It's a land that seems charming at first, but turns out to be unsafe."

In more complicated stories, the setting is literally setting up the reader—it incorporates the mood or atmosphere, and it often incorporates some of the conflict for the character, so it is definitely worth paying attention to! It might seem as if the setting in The Paper Bag Princess *is simply—some kind of place in the Middle Ages where there was a castle and a princess. But if you consider the psychological implications, it's more than that. It's a place where sudden violence happens. It's a place where no one is safe. It's a place where people are isolated, and often suddenly alone.*

ACTIVE ENGAGEMENT

Set up children to work together to research and think about clues from the story you read aloud.

"Readers, let's give you a chance to practice this work together. I'm going to return to the first chapter of *The Thief of Always*. I saw when we were reading it, that your jaws were practically hanging open as the story unfolded. Like me, you were entranced, and shocked, with how much happened, and how wild it was. In fact, most of your conversation was simply retelling to each other what you *think* happened. You seemed as unsure as Harvey was, about what kind of trip he was really going on."

I picked up *The Thief of Always*. "Friends, we dove right into the story, so that everything happened fast, and without any warning. When Harvey was moping around his house, and when Rictus suddenly appeared, we barely had time to consider if he were real or magical. This time, let's see if we could have gathered more clues, a little earlier. Then we'd have a deeper understanding of what kind of place Harvey is living in."

I held the book up so that everyone could see it. "Readers, I'm going to show you the covers, and read you what's on the back blurb. This time, follow my example in using the strategy of really researching the time period and the magical elements within the story by paying extra attention to the covers and the start of the story, including the images."

I held up the cover, and paged through the opening images, in front of the children, letting them see the details, especially the rather grim details. I read aloud a few key excerpts.

Give children an opportunity to turn and compare their analyses.

"Readers, I can tell you have a lot to say, already, about the clues that a reader could gather here about what kind of place this is, before he or she even opens the book. Turn and tell your partner all of what you might surmise, just from the cover and beginning so far."

They did. I encouraged them to use specific and literary language, saying for example, that the images looked "ominous" and the place "duplicitous."

I put the book down. "Whoa, I can't believe how much better prepared we would have been as readers if we had done this analysis first! I could hear you talking furiously. Readers, I heard you say that from the blurb, our research tells us that Harvey lives in a modern world, but it's a world where magic happens. We find out that there are characters with magical powers—and that some of them are evil. Then the very first images give us a picture of what some of those characters look like—and let us know this can be a scary place, full of dark magic. This isn't a place full of happy fairies—it's a place full of menace."

LINK

Send your students off, reminding them to research the settings as they begin their stories.

I put *The Thief of Always* down, saying, "Readers, this work is going to be very important now for you as readers. The novels you're choosing are complicated. The places will be unusual and significant. You will want to use the strategies you know to be alert to details about these places, and their physical and psychological implications. So not just today, but whenever you pick up a complex novel, you'll want to research the place carefully, using the covers, the blurb, and all the details in the beginning of the story. Off you go, readers. I'll be eager to see you do this work, and listen to your conversations, when you'll have a chance to share your research on the stories you are reading."

One thing that is really interesting about reading strategies is how you may use them for a time, then you may not need them so much, as you become very confident with some levels of text. Most fifth-grade readers now ignore the information from the covers, beyond how it entices them to choose the book. But then, as they tackle even more complicated texts, they need those strategies again.

Making Sure Essentials Are in Place

WHILE THIS UNIT AIMS TO INCREASE STUDENTS' AGENCY, you also want to make sure that they get started wisely. Sometimes a very quick intervention, in the form of calibrated feedback, can make a world of difference. You might, therefore, tell your students that you are going to spend the first few minutes researching them, by looking over their shoulders at their books and notebooks, and then you'll give them feedback as needed.

Coach into bands of text complexity.

As you look at the choices students have made, consider how to respond to these choices. Note the level of text students have chosen, and especially for students who

have chosen series that will move up levels within the series, you might gather them quickly and let them know that one thing that will happen in their series is that the stories will gradually begin to get more complicated. Tell them that they should be able to use what they've learned about the characters and places at the beginning of the series, to help them navigate this complexity—but that they should also be alert to ways that their stories are becoming trickier, and they should bring these complications to their clubs for consideration. You might consider offering some cards to clubs, that lay out some of the more fascinating ways that their texts will become more complicated—so clubs can be alert and looking for these complications.

NOPQ Dragon Slayers' Academy, Spiderwick

- Characters face more than one problem.
- Problems don't get solved easily, they unfold over many pages.
- Some problems aren't solved at the end of each book—they continue across a series.

RST Deltora Quest, City of Embers, Warriors

- The place is complicated, full of challenges.
- Some troubles are outside of the characters' control.
- The character's flaws may interfere with his or her quest.

UVW Narnia, Lightning Thief, Gregor

- Some characters are not what they seem.
- Characters' change, so that their traits are less stable.
- Solving one problem sometimes causes others.
- The minor characters and what they want can become very significant to what happens.

XYZ Harry Potter, Redwall, Golden Compass

- The setting may have many parts and places, and these are harder to get to know.
- There may be specific vocabulary that is used in this place, that you need to learn.
- It takes longer to get to know characters—their histories are presented in bits, and they hide their feelings more often.
- Some problems seem unsolvable.

Taking into Account the Complexity of the Setting

"Readers, can I have your eyes on me for a moment? La Von was just noting something that I think might be important for a lot of you. His club is reading Narnia, and he's gotten to the point where Lucy has gone through the wardrobe into Narnia. La Von is noting, rightly, that his book has more than one setting. So far, he sees three important ones. It has London, which is being ravaged by war and planes and bombs. It has the country estate where the kids are sent, with its quiet, grand house full of mysteries. And now it has Narnia, which is a magical place. A lot of your stories will be like that—they'll range across more than one setting, and for each one, you want to figure out what *kind* of place this is. You may want to figure out how you're keeping track of these changes in setting—and more importantly, what matters most about these places, which will be interesting to talk about with your clubs."

Make sure kids' reading plans are ambitious and reachable.

You will have approved kids' book choices before today, so you shouldn't have to check that children are matched to books. You may, though, want to research how much kids are planning to read, how often they are planning to meet, and the work they've set for themselves. Ask questions such as: "What thinking and writing work has your club set itself for its first meeting?" "What's your overall plan for making your way through this series?" "When do you need to be done with the first book?"

Make sure they'll have read enough, and done enough work, for that club meeting to be worth it, and for them to sustain the volume of reading they need. You might suggest for some clubs that they make a quick calendar of the weeks of the units and the books in their series they want to read across those weeks. Remind them to be realistic—to plan for events such as away soccer games, upcoming family events, and so on. By now, you want to emphasize that the health of their reading life isn't about obedience, it's about agency—they need to read as much as they can, when they can, which means looking ahead to events, making adjustments, and giving each other the encouragement they need to thrive.

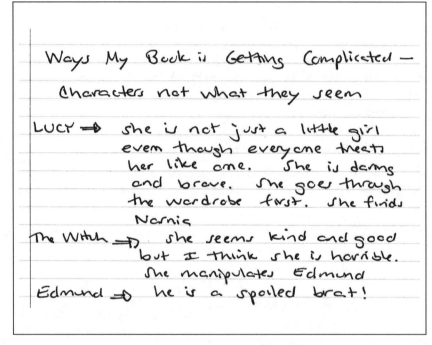

FIG. 1–1 La Von uses bands of text complexity to think deeper about characters.

Considering Who Has Power in These Places

Ask children to figure out who has the power in their novels, and find evidence to support their ideas.

"Readers, for today, will you come together for our share, and bring your notebook and books? Sit with your club." I waited a moment for children to convene.

"I've been looking over your shoulders as you've been doing some jotting as you read, and listening to the quick conversations some clubs have already had. By the way, I applaud that some clubs decided to read for the whole time today. Often you need to read more, to have more to say.

"I think there is another question you can ask as you research the places in your fantasy novels, which will be intriguing. That question is 'Who has power here?' And then you might add: 'How do you know?'

"La Von, I see you nodding already, I bet you're thinking about who has power in Narnia, and what kind of power you see so far . . ." I turned to the rest of the children.

"Go ahead, try out that inquiry question, and see where it takes your club. Take a second to think and possibly jot . . . then turn and compare your thinking."

They did so, talking eagerly about the power to bewitch that the White Witch has in Narnia, and the power to do magic in Harry Potter. Meanwhile, I began an anchor chart.

> **ANCHOR CHART**
>
> Sophisticated Readers of Fantasy . . .
>
> - Research the setting. (What kind of place is it?)
> - Ask about power—who has it, evidence, kinds of power.

WRITE DOWN YOUR BEST THINKING ABOUT SETTING

Readers, it's important that you remember you are reading not alone, but with and for a club. That means you want to consider the reading work that will make your club conversations rich. Today you studied a variety of ways to investigate the setting, including considering which places are most important in your series, how those change, and who has power there.

Tonight, think about what quick writing about reading you might do to document your thinking, and do that. You might begin a timeline of power. You might consider a flowchart of the settings, or a chart. Choose one strategy, and then do your writing about reading.

The main thing is, make sure your best thinking doesn't get lost. Be ready to share with your club when you do meet.

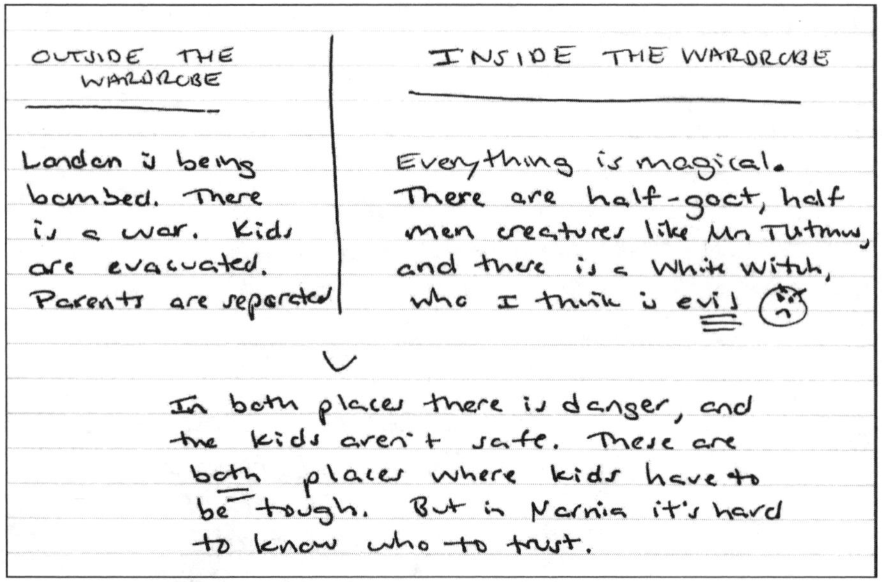

OUTSIDE THE WARDROBE	INSIDE THE WARDROBE
London is being bombed. There is a war. Kids are evacuated. Parents are seperated	Everything is magical. There are half-goat, half-men creatures like Mr Tutmu, and there is a White witch, who I think is evil 😠

In both places there is danger, and the kids aren't safe. These are both places where kids have to be tough. But in Narnia it's hard to know who to trust.

FIG. 1–2 La Von reflects on the settings in Narnia.

Session 2

Learning alongside the Main Character

ONE OF THE MOST INTERESTING CHOICES that J. K. Rowling made in creating Harry Potter, was to have him begin as a character who knows little about anything. He has literally been kept in a cupboard under the stairs. Just about everything Harry learns—the history of magic, the special powers he has, the struggle between Voldemort and others, he learns in front of the reader. What this means is that the reader has the opportunity to learn alongside Harry. For the first book, at least, neither the reader nor Harry have prior knowledge—they learn simultaneously.

A lot of historical fiction and fantasy novels are structured this way. It's a writerly trick, a craft move that lets an author fill readers in on important stuff they need to know while staying within the narrative. Lots of engaging nonfiction for kids uses the same trick. Picture the children's nonfiction series, The Magic School Bus. The characters find themselves inside of, say, the human body, they are confused and ignorant, they learn a lot of stuff about the human body, and they emerge more expert, as does the reader. Of course, it only works if the reader bothers to learn. Just as Jack in The Magic Tree House is forever noting what he's learning about lions and ninjas, readers too need to think of themselves as on a learning journey.

Today you explicitly point out some ways that authors educate their characters and their readers, and you offer children some signposts they can be alert for. Watch how your readers do with this work, and use your conferring and small-group time to help them. It's a skill that directly helps readers tackle harder fiction, and it's closely related to learning new information from nonfiction as well—it's about absorption.

IN THIS SESSION, you'll teach students that fantasy readers expect to learn alongside the main character, and are alert to clues that characters are in the midst of important learning experiences.

GETTING READY

✔ Prior to this minilesson, read aloud *The Thief of Always*, Chapters 2 and 3. You will refer back to Chapter 3 in this session (see Teaching).

✔ Be prepared to show a quick video clip from Narnia (search the terms "The Lion, the Witch and the Wardrobe—Lucy Meets Mr. Tumnus" on YouTube, or find a video of your choice of a character learning from others) (see Connection).

✔ Have chart paper ready to write "Signposts of Learning Moments for Characters" (see Active Engagement).

✔ Read aloud *The Thief of Always*, Chapter 4, page 32 to the middle of page 36 (see Active Engagement).

✔ Start some tools to accompany *The Thief of Always*, such as a visual timeline, a character list, and/or a map of your read-aloud text. They should look quickly sketched. Have them on hand (see Conferring and Small-Group Work).

✔ Print or pull up on a device the student notebook samples in Figures 2–1 and 2–2 to use as mentor texts (see Conferring and Small-Group Work). 🖐

✔ Prepare a chart entitled, "Clubs Take Charge of Themselves by Asking . . ." (see Share). 🖐

Learning alongside the Main Character

CONNECTION

Tell a story about your reading experience, where a main character seems confused by his or her environment.

"Readers, one thing that happens in harder fantasy is that often the author tries to help the reader by providing information through the mouths of characters. You'll note, for instance, that a character will ask about a legend, or a historical incident—and an experienced readers knows to think, 'Aha! I'm supposed to pay attention here.' Anytime that one character describes some incident, legend, or history, you're supposed to learn about it too. Tutmus tells Lucy about Narnia. Gandalf tells Frodo about the history of the ring of power. Dumbledore tells Harry about Voldemort's history. Alert readers sit up at these times, and take notes. Or sometimes the main character has a dramatic learning experience. The main character comes away with new realizations. As readers, we are supposed to get these realizations, as well—we're on the same learning curve as the main character.

"Right now, for example, see if you can list everything you learn from Mr. Tutmus, the faun in Narnia . . ."

I showed the video clip of Lucy meeting Mr. Tutmus, where he explains that she is in Narnia. The children jotted and then compared their notes.

 Name the teaching point.

"Readers, today I want to teach you that in complicated stories such as fantasy novels, often the main characters begin without a lot of knowledge, and they have a steep learning curve. As alert readers, when the main character is told important information or has dramatic new experiences, you can see those moments as opportunities for you to learn hand in hand with the main character."

Colleagues, you'll find yourself using short video clips again and again in class if you assemble these ahead of time on your laptop or iPad. On YouTube, search for "Lucy meets Mr. Tutmus," and you'll find the scene you want to show your children. The joy of these videos is they mitigate reading level, they move quickly so you can show a whole scene in a few seconds, and they engage students immediately. We find it easiest to keep a file of clips so we don't have to rely on an Internet connection, which is sure to be down, slow, or filtered when we want to use it in class.

TEACHING

Demonstrate in your read-aloud text how you learn with the main characters as they ask questions, hear explanations, and have new experiences.

"Let me show you want this looks like. I see you reading *Dragon Slayers' Academy*, *Harry Potter*, and *The Lion, the Witch and the Wardrobe*, for instance. So I know this will help you. In the stories you are reading, indeed in most fantasy stories, often the main characters are a little bit like outsiders. Wiglaf doesn't know much about Dragon Slayer Academy yet, Harry doesn't know much about magic or Hogwarts, and Lucy definitely doesn't know much at the beginning about Narnia. And so, these characters are not only on an adventure quest—they're also on a learning journey.

"Characters in fantasy stories often go to new places, as they embark on quests, or journeys. That means characters get many opportunities to learn about these places. In a way, by making the characters a little ignorant, the author helps *us* learn. So instead of being frustrated that our main characters aren't more expert, we can build our expertise at the same pace that they do. We listen for when characters ask questions, we pay attention to the answers they get, and we try to learn rapidly.

"Readers, I've read a lot of fantasy, and so I expect that I have to learn alongside the main character. I don't get frustrated—Instead, I try to be extra alert to moments when the main characters ask questions, listen to explanations, or have new learning experiences. I need to almost read those moments like a nonfiction reader would, keeping notes in my mind (or in my notebook) about what I learn. In more complicated stories, you'll notice how often the main character has a pretty steep learning curve, that we're supposed to join in on.

"Let me show you what this looks like. Basically, I want to show you how there are certain moments in the story, in which you can almost feel the author saying to you 'Listen up, this matters!' Readers, often those moments are marked by the main characters visibly trying to learn. Sometimes their learning isn't totally successful—in complicated stories it takes a long time to learn everything. But it's like you can see them *trying* to learn.

"For instance, think back with me to Chapter 3 of *The Thief of Always*. Let's go back to it, and watch how alert I am to anytime the main character asks direct questions, or gets to hear any kind of explanations.

"Readers, recall that I said that experienced readers expect to be extra alert to any time the character asks questions, hears explanations, or has new learning experiences?" I ticked these off on my fingers. "In all of Chapter 3, Harvey is confused about what is going on, about what's real or not real, and it means we're uncertain too. Then, there is this moment when Mrs. Griffin gives him some direct information. 'Nothing's perfect,' she says, when Harvey admires the house. Then when he asks, 'Why not?'"

> *"Because time passes," she went on, staring down at the flowers she'd cut. "And the beetle and the worm find their way into everything sooner or later."*

Interestingly, when a reader takes in the information from the back covers of their stories, she often begins the story knowing more than the main character does. In a way, that lets her read with a kind of birds-eye view, alert to those learning opportunities which will bring the main character along her learning curve.

Go back to the book here, and reread, aloud. Use your body language and tone of voice to emphasize a sense of confusion, then gradual awareness. Remember that the greatest read aloud teachers are those who exaggerate both their voice and body language, and also their response to the story. Like these teachers, remember that you are both bringing the story alive and demonstrating what an engaged reader looks and sounds like.

I reread the line. I thought visibly, reread it, then I let my face light up, and suggested, "Oh . . . she's telling him that time is passing at this house. That makes me worried—Harvey should listen to her, because it's like she's trying to warn him, don't you think?" Lots of nods.

"Readers, do you see how I was extra alert as soon as I realized this might be an important learning opportunity for Harvey? I could tell that a question like this would probably reveal important new information, so I was ready to learn. I may even have learned more than Harvey did! That's actually a really cool moment in a story, readers, when you realize that the author is giving you clues, and that you are inferring ahead of the character. What matters, is that as soon as I realized that a significant conversation was about to happen, I was alert and ready—which is why I now know so much more."

ACTIVE ENGAGEMENT

Remind students of text markers that indicate the character is learning, such as direct questions, explanations, and unfamiliar experiences. Set them up to try this work on a text excerpt of the read-aloud.

"Readers, what often happens is that the story moves along, and there are fast parts and slower parts, and there are parts where it's almost all action. And then, there are parts like the one I just reread, where it's pretty much all conversation. I hope you see that readers expect to learn something from conversations, especially any conversations the main character overhears, or ones in which direct questions are posed. In a fast-moving story like *The Thief of Always*, there will be important conversations even in the middle of action. But you'll know, if you see the main character asking direct questions, listening to explanations or stories, or having new, unfamiliar experiences, that you should be alert to learn alongside the character—those are all signposts of learning moments."

I jotted on the chart paper:

> ### Signposts of Learning Moments for Characters
> - Direct questions and answers
> - Explanations or stories
> - Unfamiliar experiences

"Let's give this a try. I'm going to read aloud the next part of the story, which is Chapter 4. So far, during read-aloud, we've mostly been adding to our timeline of events as we read during read aloud, and talking about the characters, as we would at the start of any story. This time, though, can you be extra alert to any clues such as the ones I just jotted, and be ready to tell your partner about the moments when you learned at the same time that Harvey visibly learned something new? We'll start right after where we finished, which was just as Harvey went to sleep for the first time in the house."

In Notice and Note: Strategies for Close Reading *(Heinemann, 2012), Kylene Beers and Bob Probst introduce us to the idea of literary signposts that can help students take charge of their questioning and annotating of literary texts. Essentially, the authors teach kids to be alert for a group of commonly occurring moments in stories that are worth noticing, and they help students find those moments and develop rich thinking around them. We have found the* Notice and Note *Signposts to be incredibly productive in our high school classrooms especially. Here, you do similar work, teaching children that there will be predictable moments that are worth finding and thinking about in their books.*

I picked up the story where we had left off, and read aloud Chapter 4 (page 32 to middle of page 36), until Wendell tells Harvey about Lulu, ending with "Her brain's turning to mush."

Ask students to turn and talk—and then summarize what they said.

I looked up. "Wow, readers, I could see you taking lots of notes. Every time Harvey asked a question, or Wendell or Mrs. Griffin explained something to him, I saw you pick up your pencils. That's what I mean about being alert to the questions and explanations. Why don't you compare your learning with what your partner learned in this part? Turn and talk."

After students talked for a few moments, I summarized some of what they said. "Readers, I heard you talking about how long Lulu has been in this house, and how much time might be passing. Some of you thought maybe Mrs. Griffin was giving Harvey another warning, when she talked about everyone having someone watching them. I wonder if Harvey caught that? Sometimes, there is this odd thing that happens, when you realize that maybe you caught even more from a conversation than the character did."

LINK

Give your students a moment to talk about the learning curve of the main character in their book. Then encourage your students to use their pencils as they read, and send them off.

"Before you go off to read, friends, why don't you take a moment to tell your partner about the learning curve of your main character. Is your character far along on this learning curve, or just getting started? You'll have a chance to do lots of thinking about their learning, as you read, but this will help you get ready for this work."

If you actually call on the kids to share their insights after having already given them time to talk in partnerships and build those insights, you'll be in the lesson forever. So listen to the kids while they talk in partnerships, take notes, and then share some of their insights. This lets you add onto their practices as well, adding in literary terms and language, organizing their examples, and essentially, as Donna Santman describes in Shades of Meaning: Comprehension and Interpretation in Middle School *(Heinemann, 2006), handing over academic discourse to the children through your consistent modeling.*

Setting Up Reading Notebooks and/or Writing about Reading to Engage Deeply

YESTERDAY, you worked with readers particularly around the kinds of complexity they might encounter in their novels, such as more minor characters who play significant roles in the story, unreliable and changing characters, and multiple plotlines. Today, therefore, it makes sense to nudge your book clubs to think carefully about what work they'll do in their reading notebooks that will help these readers engage deeply with these aspects of their books. It can help to have on hand some models of notebook pages that can serve as mentors. We've included some here, that you can print from the online resource for this unit.

It's important to keep track of multiple characters and their characteristics.

It's probably been awhile since your readers needed to keep charts or lists of characters to remember them. Yet in fantasy novels, this work can become important again, as there may be many characters, and some of them, while only referred to fleetingly, may play important roles. Examples include Poseidon in *The Lightning Thief* or Aslan in *The Lion the Witch and the Wardrobe*, who don't appear until near the end of the book, but are referred to much earlier. Visit clubs that are reading these kinds of books, and remind them that they may want to keep a list of characters, including those with magical or divine powers. Encourage them to jot, think, and talk about the characteristics of these characters, and their potential significance in the story. You might show them some examples of notebook pages, such as those you see in Figures 2–1 and 2–2.

Try to make sense of the place and know how the geography might matter.

In many fantasy stories, the geography of the place matters to the story—part of the quest that a character goes on is related to the obstacles of the setting. You might, therefore, remind your clubs to see if the author has provided a map of the place. Open up *Lord of the Rings*, or *Deltora Quest*, for example, and you'll find a sketch of the place, with some of the physical attributes laid out, and sometimes some of the dangers. Your club members might find it helpful to make their own sketch of the place in their stories, if the setting plays an important role. Set your readers to figuring this

> Percy Jackson The Lightning theif
> Percy is a boy in sixth grade and it
> seams that every year he goes on a
> feild trip he seams to get in
> trouble or do somthing wrong. He also
> has this thing where to him it
> feels like just a secound but it's
> realy a minute or two to us. Percy
> gets realy mad and pushes a girl
> down and one of the teacher aids
> take him to musem to 'talk' but
> she goes all crazy and turns
> into what we thought was
> Maduca. Then percys teacher
> throws him his ballpoint pen
> wich turns into a sword in
> mid-Air and percy swings the
> sword at maduca and she
> turns to dust, but he thougt
> he killed her but we dont
> think Maduca if it is her,
> dies that easy.

FIG. 2–1   Aly tries to figure out what her character knows and doesn't know so far.

out together with their club, and to keeping whatever kind of map will help them chart the territory their character encounters. You may want to show them that these maps can be symbolic—they can chart the dangers, not just the territories.

Inferring Ahead of the Main Character

"Readers, as you are reading, I want to give you one more tip about learning alongside the main character. And that is—sometimes you will actually infer ahead of the character! It's like you want to shout at the character, 'Don't you realize?!' Like when I was reading *Twilight*, I wanted to shout at Bella, 'Bella, they're vampires, don't you get it?!' And when we were reading *The Paper Bag Princess*, the way Ronald had his nose up in the air and was ignoring Elizabeth on the first page, made me want to shake her and say, 'He's no good for you!'

"The truth is, readers, that sometimes the author gives you clues that let you make these grand inferences before the character does. Then as you keep reading, you can be alert to when the character finally catches up with you—if she or he ever does!"

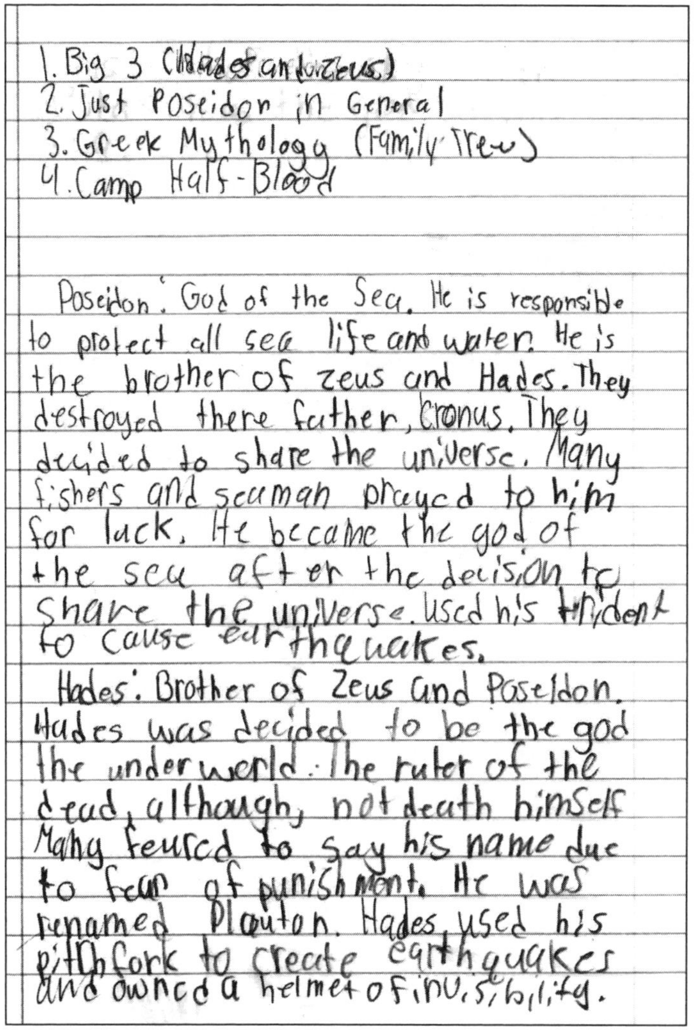

> 1. Big 3 (Hades and Zeus)
> 2. Just Poseidon in General
> 3. Greek Mythology (Family Tree)
> 4. Camp Half-Blood
>
> Poseidon: God of the Sea. He is responsible to protect all sea life and water. He is the brother of Zeus and Hades. They destroyed there father, Cronus. They decided to share the universe. Many fishers and seaman prayed to him for luck. He became the god of the sea after the decision to share the universe. Used his trident to cause earthquakes.
> Hades: Brother of Zeus and Poseidon. Hades was decided to be the god the underworld. The ruler of the dead, although, not death himself. Many feared to say his name due to fear of punishment. He was renamed Plauton. Hades used his pitchfork to create earthquakes and owned a helmet of invisibility.

FIG. 2–2   Maya keeps an extensive list of characters, including keeping track of gods and goddesses in her novel. Even as children tackle new, higher-level work, it will be essential to attend to monitoring for sense, which in longer, denser novels and series often includes keeping track of many characters, some of them historical or mythological.

Fifth-Graders Need to Set Their Own Agendas for Clubs

Channel students to take responsibility for their own independent reading lives.

"Fifth graders, will you gather with your club back at the meeting area? Bring your novels and your reading notebooks." I waited a moment for them to gather.

"Readers, it used to be that you were told when to meet with your club, and maybe even what work you should do. But those days need to be behind you now. For the rest of your life, you will be in charge of your independent reading. If you want to be in a book club—you have to start one! If you want to do smart reading work—you have to figure out what that work should be. Sometimes you can turn to a mentor—someone who reads a lot. I'm trying to play that role for you in this unit. I've read a ton of fantasy, and some of you are fantasy experts who have read a lot of fantasy, too! You've been in clubs for years, so you know what's gone well and what hasn't.

"So right now, will you meet with your club, and will you do some serious thinking together about these questions?" I unveiled a list I had charted, and motioned to them to get started.

"You make plans. I'm going to jot some notes, so I have an idea how you're going about it all."

 ## NOTE WHERE AND HOW YOU LEARN NEW INFORMATION

As you read tonight, note any places where you learn important new information. When you find these, take a moment, and notice *how* you learned this information. Did another character teach you and the main character? Did the main character make a discovery? Did you learn something the character didn't? Jot at least two Post-its or quick entries, so you'll be able to share with your club.

ear Teachers,

Today will feel familiar to you and to your students. By now you've seen the power that comes from students having the opportunity to get feedback on their work and to form goals and action plans that can carry their work to new heights. You've seen the energy and the resolve. And so have your students.

As you've done in previous units, we suggest that today you set aside time to engage students as active agents of their own reading development. By studying the rubrics and learning progressions next to their own work, by looking at exemplars and trying to determine where their own work falls in comparison, students can understand what the expectations are for their work. And, they can determine what their goals and action plans are for the future. Of course, they'll need some strong coaching to help them do this and that's where you come in. Remember that one of your greatest jobs as a teacher is to help students to know where they are now, where they need to go, and how to get there. The goals and next steps should be transparent for students so they have a crystal-clear sense for what to do next. There is an enormous feeling of empowerment when you are in charge of your own learning. You feel ownership and determination, a readiness to do whatever it takes to improve. Remember that the goals for students should feel worthy—not completely out of reach but offering work that likely cannot be mastered in the span of one workshop. You'll want to support students in assessing themselves with accountability to the rubrics and exemplars, creating worthy goals for themselves as well as the action plans that will help them to reach those goals. What is most important is that as students move forward, they can ask themselves, "What is going well for me? And how can I push myself to do more to meet my goals?" It's this constant questioning, a constant seeking to be stronger, an embracing of mistakes as a chance to learn and to do more that leads to the mind-set of growth and of being a lifelong learner. It's how a person goes from good to great at anything.

Remember at the start of the first unit, we described the story of Lucy who crept through the wardrobe into Narnia and found herself on a great adventure. You'll no doubt recall that our heroine in the story made many decisions and was in charge of her own journey. Today is all about making sure that students know they are in charge of their own learning journeys, not just on this one day, but for their whole lives. You are the hero/heroine of your own great learning adventure, you want to convey. It's up to you to shape that adventure.

☀ Remember that the Online Resources will be a resource to you. You'll find a more detailed description of how today's important work might go, as well as relevant rubrics, learning progressions, and exemplars.

To lifelong adventures in learning!

Thanks,

Mary and Colleen

Session 3

Keeping Track of Problems that Multiply

THIS FIRST BEND OF THE UNIT focuses readers' attention on unraveling complexity in their novels. You want to ensure that children don't read these novels the same way they read much simpler ones. That is, you want children to notice the minor characters, keeping track of their influence in the story. You want them to see how the settings in fantasy novels often change, and place new obstacles in front of characters. Today, you will alert students to how the books they are reading have multiple plotlines. The easiest way to see those plotlines is to see how many problems characters face, and how those problems often continue to unroll across the whole novel.

This work will set some of the children's prior notions of problem-solution structure on its head. As kids get older, the books they are reading are less and less focused on "one problem, one solution," and more about "problems . . . more problems . . . some of which get resolved and some don't." In *Because of Winn Dixie*, Opal can't solve the problem of getting her mother back, or her father's loneliness and withdrawal, just as later, in *The Bluest Eye*, Pecola won't solve the problem of institutionalized racism. It's important to teach children, then, to notice not just the big or most personal problem, which may be solved, but also the other problems that arise in the novel. Often looking at some of these unsolved problems gets to the heart of the story.

You'll see that in the lesson, we focus on a transcript of one club's discussion of the problems in their novel. We chose to focus on the problems in Dragon Slayers' Academy, an extremely engaging series that combines great narrative complexity with readability (the series is a level N–O). That decision is strategic, reflecting the urge to make sure that lower level readers are celebrated, and to show that readers can do high level reading work in these books. To get this kind of transcript from your own students' work, you can help a club rehearse a bit—or you can borrow the transcript in this lesson, passing it off as kids from a prior year or in another class.

IN THIS SESSION, you'll teach students that as fantasy readers tackle more complicated books, they use charts, timelines, and other graphic organizers to help track and analyze multiple problems and plotlines.

GETTING READY

✔ Prior to this session, read aloud *The Thief of Always* through the end of Chapter 7.

✔ Bring a transcript of a club conversation to use in today's teaching, along with a sample chart titled "Tracking Problems and Solutions/Changes." Before class, you may want to prompt a club to produce the kind of conversation you think might be useful to your class and then transcribe that club's discussion—or you could appropriate the club conversation provided here as an example (see Teaching).

✔ Gather some student notebook pages with Post-it notes to use as exemplars in Gallery Walk. Alternatively, print or pull up on a device the student notebook sample in Figure 3–1 to use as mentor texts (see Active Engagement and Share).

✔ Display and add to Bend I anchor chart, "Sophisticated Readers of Fantasy . . ." (see Link).

Keeping Track of Problems that Multiply

CONNECTION

Tell a personal story about a time when problems began to multiply.

"Readers, have you ever set out to solve a problem, and then it seemed as if problems just kept multiplying? Like once I set out to rescue these kittens, only to have them immediately develop life-threatening emergencies that led to late night visits to the emergency clinic, and then I found out I was allergic to cats, so it was a series of solving one problem and then facing another and another!

"Or remember, at the end of the first *Harry Potter* novel, Harry does find the sorcerer's stone. But when he found it, he also found Lord Voldemort, who was released from his years of not having a body, and became a sort of evil spirit, who would come back in the next book. So Harry solved one problem, only to have another arise."

 Name the teaching point.

"Readers, today I want to teach you that as you tackle more complicated books, you will run into multiple plotlines. You will find it helpful to use charts, timelines, and other graphic organizers to track multiple problems and plotlines, and to gather data as scientists do, in charts and tables that allow close analysis."

TEACHING

Share a transcript of a club conversation, that demonstrates the many problems that arise in complex stories. Invite students to analyze this transcript.

"Readers, yesterday I was listening to the Dragon Slayers club talk about the end of the first book in the series they're reading, Dragon Slayers' Academy. I got so intrigued by their conversation that I wrote it down. I think that it illustrates some of these issues of more complicated stories—that there will be more than one problem. I'm going to put the transcript of their conversation up here. Can you put on your reading researcher lenses, and see what this conversation suggests to you about the notion of multiple plotlines and problems? You might want to do some jotting, so I'm glad you've got your notebooks."

Whenever you make allusions to lessons in books that carry over into life, and vice versa, you deepen the likelihood that students will transfer what they are learning in these texts to other situations.

If your students are reading books at and above level R–T, chances are that the stories they are reading have multiple plot lines and unresolved problems. Even in Dragon Slayers' Academy, Wiglaf faces many problems especially across the series.

I put the transcript up for students to see:

Michael: I can't believe Wiglaf killed the dragon!

Jose: I know, that was all he wanted—to kill a dragon, so he could get gold for his family.

Sam: But now headmaster Mordred has stolen his gold anyway! So he killed the dragon for nothing.

Michael: I know, and he feels bad about it too. Now Wiglaf has a new problem–he doesn't like killing dragons.

Sam: But the dragons don't know that. And I notice the next book is called *Revenge of the Dragon Lady*.

Michael: Well, that's a new problem for Wiglaf.

Jose: So the book ends and Wiglaf is still poor. And now he has a new problem—he's at a school for dragon slayers, and he's a dragon-liker. And the dragons hate him.

Michael: And what about Wiglaf's friend Eric, when is he going to impress everyone? He's so desperate to kill a dragon, but it was Wiglaf who did it.

Sam: Actually, Eric's problem is that he's a girl. Wiglaf is a secret dragon-liker, and Eric is secretly a girl. I read ahead. Her problem is worse than Wiglaf's. And it stays worse for longer. And Angus has problems too. He's Mordred's nephew. That stinks. And he can't stay away from sweets.

Jose: At least Mordred's happy, because he has gold now.

Michael: Nah, Mordred will always want more gold. You can tell. He's greedy, and greedy people are never satisfied.

Jose: Snap! These folks have a lot of problems.

"Readers, I see you have some notes and ideas. Why don't you turn to your partner and share your research. What did you notice about the issue of multiple plotlines and problems? Turn and compare."

They compared their thinking. Then I gathered them back.

"Readers, it's kind of amazing, isn't it, how much is happening in Dragon Slayers' Academy, how many plotlines and problems arise? And we definitely saw that by the end of the story, only some problems were resolved. Michael, Jose, and Sam are having some rich conversation about the different problems in their first book."

Introduce a way to chart these problems, and show an example.

"Readers, yesterday, when I pulled alongside this book club, I recommended that they invent some kind of chart or other graphic organizer to keep track of the problems arising in the book. They could also use that chart or organizer to track

We adore the Levels N–O series, Dragon Slayer's Academy, for the way it raises social issues relevant to kids' lives, introducing young readers to medieval settings, and both teaching and breaking with archetypes. If you haven't read this series, do!

Clearly, this transcript closely matches the teaching point. A hint—you can set up some students to produce the kind of teaching tool you think might be useful to your class. This means that you might gather a club and do some preteaching beforehand, and then transcribe some of their work as they discuss their reading. Tell them, "I really want to highlight some new work for the class. Will you give it a try? Here's what you'll need to do . . ."

how those problems get solved or change—and which new problems arise across the book and even into the next book in the series. Let me show you a simple chart that this club made, for instance. Why don't you take a look and see what you notice about problems here. Give a thumbs-up when you see some pattern or have an idea."

Tracking Problems and Solutions/Changes

Character	Problem	Solution/Change	By the End
Wiglaf	Needs gold	Kills a dragon	Mordred takes the gold
	Was poor	Can't keep gold	Still poor
	Wants to kill a dragon	Kills a dragon	Finds out he hates killing dragons. Also, dragons want revenge.
Eric	Wants to impress everyone by killing a dragon	Goes with Wiglaf and finds dragon	Can't figure out how to kill dragon, and Wiglaf gets the glory
	Is a girl	Dresses as a boy	Still hasn't told anyone

I waited for some thumbs up, then I said, "Readers, you could imagine how this quick chart would really launch a long and deeply analytical conversation, can't you? These quick charts and timelines are great starting places for detailed conversations. They don't take long to make—it's not that much writing over time—but they help you make your book club conversations more substantial because you've done so much collecting of data, and have created opportunities for real thinking."

ACTIVE ENGAGEMENT

Bring your students to a recent chapter of the read-aloud text to practice this work. Begin keeping public records/charts to support the read-aloud.

"Readers, we should think about the records we've been keeping around *The Thief of Always*. A lot is going on in this story, and we don't want to drop anything. For instance, we're at the end of Chapter 7 now, and let's just consider, not what's happened, but how many problems we can name, for Harvey and/or his friends. Let's try that for a moment—turn to your partner, and list all the problems that you can discern, so far in this story. I'll try to catch what you're saying and jot it up here.

Teachers, you can imagine how we could teach our readers that it might be helpful to do separate charts for separate characters, once they have this much information. The main point, though, is that to analyze evidence, kids need to collect it, just as they do in their science labs. Analytical thinking comes from paying attention to detail and seeing connections among details. You might find out what kind of data charts kids are using and creating in science, so you can develop shared language for analytic thinking.

After a moment, I interrupted. "Whoa readers, I'm going to interrupt you. It's too hard for me to catch everything! I've jotted that Harvey doesn't know what the rules are in this house. He also doesn't know how long he's really been there. He's worried about the fish in the pond, and if they're prisoners of some kind. And there's the haunter—he's sure the place is haunted. And some of the problems he has, we're more worried about than he is—like if his parents really know where he is."

"Yikes! Readers, this story is so complicated, with so many problems emerging for the characters, that it will be helpful to organize a little writing to keep track of these problems, and how they change, as the Dragon Slayers' Academy club did. I'm not sure we're doing enough writing about our read aloud novel—so if some of you have a moment and want to help make some tools such as lists, maps, timelines, charts of these problems, let me know. Give me a thumbs up if you want to come up at lunch or after school, and help with some of these tools for maybe fifteen minutes or half an hour?"

Don't underestimate kids' willingness to come help with classroom inquiries and tools. When you put all the work on yourself of making every chart, every learning tool, it can become overwhelming. Meanwhile, a few of your kids would love to help—so invite them, set them working, let them do some of this work while you get to other classroom tasks. You're teaching them to work on behalf of themselves and others.

LINK

Set students up to make thoughtful decisions about the work they'll do.

"Readers, you need to make some thoughtful decisions about the work you'll do. You're learning some new skills, and sharpening others. You've got some work you've done for homework that you probably want to share with your club, and now you've got some new possible thinking work. So you have to make some decisions—and our anchor chart might help you make some of those decisions. I gestured to where I had added our recent work:

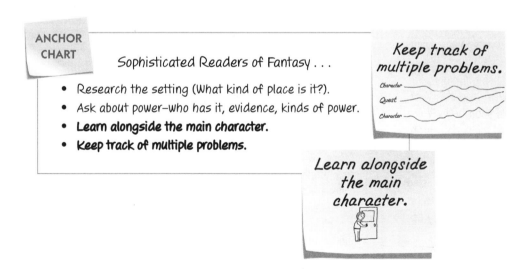

FIG. 3–1 Aly begins to think deeply about what she knows about the major and minor characters and their problems.

"Before you go off, why don't you take a second to just check in with your club, to set your work. Will you be meeting today? What is the best work you can do?"

Weighing and Evaluating Problems for Their Significance to the Character, Plot, and Theme—and Using Argumentation Skills to Develop New Thinking

AS YOU CIRCULATE TODAY, you'll want to do some spot-checking that children are reading at a strong pace, getting through dozens of pages each day. You also may want to ask to see some notebook pages and/or Post-its, to see how kids are using their writing about reading efforts to develop some thinking, get some lines of inquiry going, or make sense of tricky parts of their books. Set aside any strong examples, that might help other students, so you can use those in your share.

Then, you may want to visit with individual clubs, and do some guided work with them, on moving from discerning multiple problems in their stories, to thinking about their significance to the character, the plot, or the themes. This work is often best done in small groups, where you can embed the work in the book kids are actually reading. It will go best if you know the book, but if you don't, remember what you know about bands of text complexity, and assume that the problems in the books they are reading *are* multiplying, and that it will be interesting to figure out which problems matter most. In the back of your head, you may also have in mind some of the skills that are assessed on the PARCC/SBAC exams, where kids are often asked to weigh and evaluate aspects of a text, not just identify.

For instance, I sat with the club that was reading *The Lion, the Witch, and the Wardrobe*. Club members were almost done with the novel, and would soon be in *Prince Caspian*. I suggested that they take a few quiet moments to record the various problems that had come up in the novel. As they did so, I left to double check how reading, and writing about reading, were going for other children. When I came back a few minutes later, this club showed me some of their charts. Club members had listed problems such as Lucy's brothers and sisters never believing her, Edmund lying to his siblings, the eternal winter that had struck Narnia. I suggested, then, that they ask themselves:

Which of these problems is most important in the story?

How is it important? Does it affect a character? The plot? A theme?

After a moment, La Von led by saying that the long winter was the biggest problem, because all the animals were suffering in it. Sarah, though, responded that while it looked like the problem of the winter might be solved in the battle, the problem of Lucy's siblings treating her like a little kid would go on. When you hear your readers do this kind of thinking work, where they are poised to defend different ideas, rather than encouraging them to simply commit to one, you can return to kids' argumentation skills. Suggest they jot down the best evidence that supports their idea. Set them up to defend these positions in a flash debate. I helped this club remember its argumentation skills, and set up club members to debate their positions, knowing that this argument work would force their analytical thinking. I also suggested that they try to explain how each problem was important to a character, plot, or theme. La Von, then, began to jot that the long winter was really about the plot—it was the big conflict.

MID-WORKSHOP TEACHING
Using Flash Debates to Defend Positions

"Readers, I want to call your attention to some work that the Narnia club has been doing. The club realized that club members had different ideas about which problems were important in their story—and why. So they set themselves up to defend their positions in some quick flash debates.

"Here's what's so smart about the work the Narnia club just did. First, they took the time to outline their thinking individually, and realized they didn't think exactly the same way. Second, instead of just agreeing, they remembered their argument skills, and decided to clearly define their positions. And the third point is that those arguments helped them come to some new thinking about how each problem was important to a character, the plot, or a theme. So today or on any day, you might want to try that work. Don't just nod, say it like you mean it: '"Let's develop and defend these positions!"'"

A Gallery Walk of Some Notebook Pages

Ask students to look at exemplar notebook pages to get ideas to try for their own books.

"Readers, I've put out some notebook pages on some tables here. If you take the time to look at them and talk to your club about them, you may find some work here that you want to try. So now, take a few Post-its and a clipboard. Walk around, looking closely, and jot some notes. Ask yourself, 'What work here would make sense for my book or my club?' Then find your club and share. If you need to, bring your club to look at a page."

Students circulated, looking at the examples I had put out. Then they found their clubs.

"I like the way these pages are places to keep your Post-its. I never know what to do with them," Sarah said.

"Maybe you want to make some headings for them, and reorganize them under some ideas?" I suggested.

SESSION 3 HOMEWORK

 MAKE YOUR OWN CHART OR TOOL TO ANALYZE PROBLEMS IN YOUR STORY

Tonight, if you haven't already done so, jot some kind of chart or tool that will let you analyze some of the problems in your story. You might make a table, for instance, or a list. Then, do some ranking of these problems—put numbers or stars next to the ones you find most important, and write a sentence or two about why that problem is most important. Is it important to the characters? To the plot? To a theme? Your chart doesn't have to be fancy. The goal is to develop new thinking.

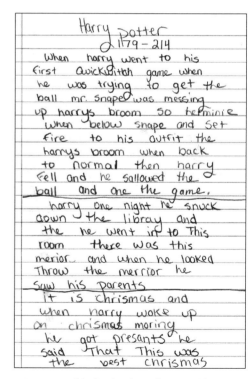

FIG. 3–2 Addi thinks about how problems multiply for Harry Potter.

Suspending Judgment
Characters (and Places) Are Not Always What They Seem

IN THIS SESSION, you'll guide students through an inquiry to explore what they can learn about characters if they study them over time, delving deeply into their formation, motivations, and actions.

GETTING READY

✔ Review the "Inferring About Characters" strand of the fifth-grade Narrative Reading Learning Progression.

✔ Prior to this session, read aloud *The Thief of Always* through the end of Chapter 10.

✔ Be prepared to show a quick video clip (search the terms "Harry Potter and the Deathly Hallows, Part 2, Snape's Memories, Part 1") or be prepared to retell that part of the story (see Teaching and Active Engagement).

✔ Display and add to Bend I anchor chart, "Sophisticated Readers of Fantasy . . ." (see Link).

✔ Display chart titled "Weighing, Evaluating, and Ranking Evidence" (see Conferring and Small-Group Work).

ONE OF THE QUALITIES of a more sophisticated reader and thinker is the ability to suspend judgment—to withhold that urge to snap to an opinion. In the new science standards, this skill is linked to weighing evidence—to looking at data for both sides, to looking hard at what the data says, not what your preconceived notions suggest. It turns out that this is a hard skill for adults to master as well as kids. We tend to make snap judgments and to hold on to them. It's hard for us to reevaluate a relationship, a colleague, an idea. So the skill you're emphasizing in today's inquiry lesson is one that is important, not just in reading books, it's important in life.

The tricky part of this skill is recognizing that it is just that—tricky. To withhold judgment, you have to recognize how quickly most of us do judge, and you almost have to train yourself to say, "Wait, there is probably more going on here." You have to look at that character or person and say, "I may not like her now, but maybe there is more that I can't see yet." (Now you see how tricky this is!) The work your students did in critical reading of arguments will help. There, they learned to expect things to be complicated, and to wait before coming to decisions. If you review the strand, "Inferring About Characters and Story Elements" in the fifth-grade Narrative Reading Learning Progression, you'll see that fifth graders are asked to analyze characters' motivations, changes, and issues, that all of these develop over time in their novels—and that they are specifically coached to notice how characters are not always what they seem at first.

We suggest you start this lesson by looking at characters most kids will be familiar with—they'll know them from the Harry Potter films, even if they haven't read the books. Another way to start would be to tell a story about a time when you misjudged someone. As you do this work, you'll see that we suggest you gather evidence that is conflicting—that leads you to sort and rank, to weigh and evaluate. Again, this work echoes work readers did in nonfiction, and that's deliberate. The work of weighing evidence, of revising our thinking, of remaining open to new possibilities, is the work of reading any text, including the texts of our lives.

Suspending Judgment
Characters (and Places) Are Not Always What They Seem

CONNECTION

Tell a brief story of reconsidering a character who seemed good or evil.

"Readers, last night I was rewatching one of the Harry Potter movies, and I was thinking about how detestable Professor Snape is. He's cruel, he's powerful, he's nasty—he *is* that word that J. K. Rowling uses all the time to describe him—*malevolent*!"

I paused as if pondering. "But the thing is, I've read all the Harry Potter novels, and I know that Snape is not *truly* evil. He's more complicated—as if he's bad in small ways, but better in the big ways. He's *flawed*. It's rather fascinating. It made me think about how to understand Snape, you have to be willing to reserve judgment and see how this character develops over time. I think that's true about a lot of characters."

"So today, I want to guide an inquiry in which you consider what you can learn about characters over time, instead of coming to quick conclusions—and being willing to rethink along the way!"

Name the question that will guide the inquiry.

"Our work for today is to answer this question: 'What can we learn about characters if we study them over time, delving deeply into their formation, motivations, and actions?'"

TEACHING AND ACTIVE ENGAGEMENT

Invite children into an inquiry, using a shared text to explore character traits.

"Let's do some of this work together. Some of you are actually reading Harry Potter now. And for some of you, these fabulous stories might be part of your summer reading. They are *so good*! Since we haven't all read these books, let's take one moment, and those of you who know who Snape is, turn and explain to others around you. Just focus on Snape at the beginning. If someone doesn't know about Hogwarts, explain briefly what it is and Snape's role there. If you all know that, dive into

---

◆ COACHING

You'll know the popular culture texts that your children are "on" about. Virtually all children know Harry Potter, *so we often use that text to illustrate points, but you might choose a Pixar film or one from Disney (* Frozen *comes to mind) to make this point.*

> At first the White Which seem very kind to Edmund. She gives him sweets and lets him ride in her sleigh. She does speak a little sharply to him though. But it turns out she is horrible. She tries to KILL ASLAN!
>
> She CUTS HIM UP WITH A KNIFE. SHE IS HORRIBLE!

FIG. 4–1 La Von has a change of heart about a major character! Look for these examples of students responding to your instruction, or even doing the work *before* you teach something. You can use this work as examples in your teaching.

Snape's relationship to Harry's parents. Go ahead, turn to three or four people near you, and compare your knowledge of Snape."

I gave children a minute to talk and then gathered their attention back. "Now we all know that Snape is Harry's professor at Hogwarts. He's the Instructor of the Dark Arts, which sounds ominous! He also was a student at the same time as Harry's parents—he knew Harry's mother, in particular. He seems cruel and nasty to Harry. Let's do an inquiry, to see if those are all of Snape's traits."

I pulled up a video clip showing how Harry goes back into Snape's early memories, and we see Snape being tormented as a boy. "Readers, let's look at this bit from the story—it shows a scene where Harry goes back into Snape's memories, and we see Snape as a boy, trying to make friends and being bullied. Can you watch this bit, and research Snape's traits? The question you want to be asking is: 'What character traits do you see in Snape?' You'll want evidence to back up your ideas, so jot notes if you're a note-taker while reading. I'll also pause the video sometimes for you to jot for a second, as there's a lot to notice."

Remind children to rank their ideas and evidence.

As we watched the clip, some children took notes. I paused the clip occasionally. As I did so, I voiced over. "Remember, you'll want to back up your ideas with evidence. You also want to rank your traits and evidence. What character traits are emerging most strongly? What details in the story best support your ideas?"

The children then turned and compared their thinking. Then I gathered them again.

"Readers, I want to give you some feedback. What you're doing well is, you're noting that Snape displays a variety of character traits. It's clear to you that he's not only one way. You're also supporting your ideas with evidence—like one of you said that Snape was *imaginative*, and you gave the example of how he sent a butterfly in order to make friends with the girl."

Ratchet up the level by investigating reasons *why* characters are the way they are.

"Here's what I want to try now. I want to take it to the next level, and it will be a little tricky. So far, you gathered evidence for some traits. Now, can you see if you can try to gather some clues about *why* Snape is the way he is? The question you have in mind, then is: *Why* does Snape develop these traits? This will be harder, because you'll have to infer. You'll have to try to figure out how some of the smallest details suggest reasons that Snape is . . . lonely . . . or unhappy . . . or perhaps even cruel later. So you're not looking so much for evidence, as reasons and motivations. Let's try it—we'll watch again."

We watched the clip again, and as we did so, I voiced over at times, looking over kids' shoulders at their notes. "Oh, I see some of you thinking that Snape was lonely, and that's why he wanted to make a friend so badly . . . and some of you are considering his poor clothes and sort of unwashed air—and maybe that's also why he's lonely. Powerful inferring!"

I gave children an opportunity to compare their thinking.

There's an art to introducing a scene with a brief angled retelling—it helps orient kids to the work you're doing, and also gets them more ready to read. You might also consider pre-teaching this with a small group. If you have kids with IEPs, for instance, give them a chance to try this out ahead of time, and then they'd be able to jump into this work with the class. Remember that you can pre-teach to increase readiness, rather than re-do to catch kids up.

Reminding kids to rank ideas and evidence ratchets up analytic thinking. (It also implicitly teaches skills that will be rewarded on high stakes exams.)

When you want kids to do more inferring, especially about small details that a reader has to combine in order to see what they suggest, it helps if you demonstrate. In an inquiry, though, you don't want to do the work for the kids. Voicing over lets you informally demonstrate, acting as if you see/hear kids doing some of this work. Hearing it, more kids will actually do it!

Sum up, reiterating the power and newness of this work for them as readers.

"Readers, you did two important things just now as readers. You expected that characters were complicated, and you gathered evidence for various, and even contradictory traits, like kindness and cruelty. You also thought not just about evidence for their traits, you were willing to delve deeply into the formation of these traits, which means you reconsidered why characters are the way they are."

LINK

Send children off to read, encouraging them to make choices with their club about when and how to add this work to their club's reading work.

"As you go off to read, add this work to your repertoire. It's the work of suspending judgment while you gather information and evidence and analyze them. Be ready to reconsider characters, to continually observe and analyze them, and to be open to rethinking. Of course, you and your club need to decide if this is work you're doing today, of if you already had work that you need to accomplish. I'm going to add this work to our anchor chart. (We will talk about suspending judgment about *places* in the mid-workshop.) Why don't you add it to the thinking work you're doing?

ANCHOR
CHART

Sophisticated Readers of Fantasy . . .

- Research the setting. (What kind of place is it?)
- Ask about power—who has it, evidence, kinds of power.
- Learn alongside the main character.
- Keep track of multiple problems.
- **Suspend judgment about characters and places.**

Suspend judgment about characters and places.

"Off you go. If you need a moment to meet with your club to set up your work, or to revise it, take that now before you leave. If you already know what you're doing as readers, go to it!"

Weighing, Evaluating, and Ranking Evidence

IN THE NONFICTION READING UNIT, you undoubtedly noticed that some children struggle to weigh, evaluate, and rank evidence. When asked which is the stronger argument, they will choose the side that has the *most* details to support it, instead of the *most meaningful* details. The same problem will arise when these readers are evaluating characters—they'll list all the scenes that show Snape is a jerk, and not realize that while there is only one scene that shows how unhappy and bullied Snape was, that scene is crucial to understanding him. You'll want to research this problem a bit. Part of the problem seems to be an urge to value quantity of details over quality. Another part seems to be a reluctance to rethink and to see multiple sides of characters. Keep in mind that it's not always lower-level readers who struggle with nuance. Sometimes strong readers are also quick to come to opinions, and reluctant to rethink.

If you find some students who are struggling with this kind of weighing and evaluating, you might introduce some helpful tools. For instance, you might gather one or two students, and show them a chart such as this one, which asks kids to rank their details with a number for strength. If the kids jot their details on Post-its, they can then create a kind of continuum of these details, ranked by strength. In this case, you might discuss with the children how, while there are two details to support Snape being mean, while there's only one to show he's heroic, the mean details aren't as important as the heroic one. Then invite students to try this same work out with their characters.

Weighing, Evaluating, and Ranking Evidence

Trait	Detail	1–5 Strength (5 = "most important")
Nasty meanness	Snape speaks sharply to Harry about having his book–being unprepared for class.	1–It's not really such a big deal. It just shows he's annoyed.
Nasty meanness	Snape won't call on Hermione even though she raises her hand.	1–He's mean to Hermione but she is annoying.
Heroism	Snape agrees to do whatever Dumbledore asks, even if he has to kill him.	5–It shows Snape's inner side, how he is willing to sacrifice himself.

MID-WORKSHOP TEACHING
Reconsidering Places as Not Always What They Seem

"Readers, can I have your eyes on me for a moment? I want to remind you that it's not just people you want to revise your opinions of—you might also want to be careful about believing in *places*! For instance, in *The Thief of Always*, the house seems, at first, like a magical place of happiness, where kids get everything they want. But gradually you start to suspect that the house, indeed the whole place is darker than that. You might see that in your novels too—places can be more than one way, or not what they seem at first, just like people!"

Relating New Evidence to New Possible Themes

Invite children to begin capturing initial ideas about themes.

"Readers, we've been looking mostly at ways to tackle the complexity in our books—characters and places that are more than one way, problems that multiply and don't get solved, moments when you're supposed to infer important information as a reader. As you keep track of all these details, I want to encourage you not to wait to begin to think about how all of these details relate to the themes in your book.

"Our Dragon Slayers, for instance, were thinking about how many problems Wiglaf has, and how he ends up with new and different problems at the end of the first book. That led them to talk about a theme of the book being that sometimes it's hard to see our real problems. They went back and reread a bit with that lens, and they're finding all sorts of details that seem important now—like how friends matter more to Wiglaf than gold, he just doesn't know that yet, or how he doesn't want to kill anyone, he just thinks he needs to be brave.

"I bet in all of your books, you've got some ideas about the themes, and that some of those themes are related to characters being complicated, or to the setting, or to the problems. So right now, so you don't lose that thinking, can you take a moment to jot down the themes that seem most important to you? Do it quietly, then it will be interesting to compare with your club."

After a moment, I gestured that readers should join with their clubs. "Go ahead, compare your thinking."

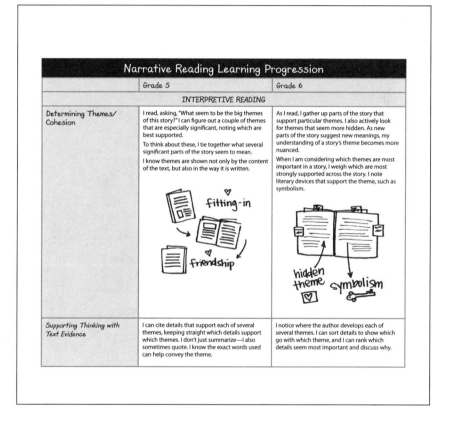

Narrative Reading Learning Progression		
	Grade 5	Grade 6
	INTERPRETIVE READING	
Determining Themes/ Cohesion	I read, asking, "What seem to be the big themes of this story?" I can figure out a couple of themes that are especially significant, noting which are best supported. To think about these, I tie together what several significant parts of the story seem to mean. I know themes are shown not only by the content of the text, but also in the way it is written.	As I read, I gather up parts of the story that support particular themes. I also actively look for themes that seem more hidden. As new parts of the story suggest new meanings, my understanding of a story's theme becomes more nuanced. When I am considering which themes are most important in a story, I weigh which are most strongly supported across the story. I note literary devices that support the theme, such as symbolism.
Supporting Thinking with Text Evidence	I can cite details that support each of several themes, keeping straight which details support which themes. I don't just summarize—I also sometimes quote. I know the exact words used can help convey the theme.	I notice where the author develops each of several themes. I can sort details to show which go with which theme, and I can rank which details seem most important and discuss why.

PREPARE TO DO YOUR BEST CLUB WORK

Readers, tomorrow you'll be showing off the best thinking/writing/talking work of your club. Tonight, take some time to work on your reading notebook, to think about what your club might want to discuss tomorrow, and to mark up your books so you are ready to quote and cite. You may even want to call some club members tonight to make some detailed plans. I'm sending home as well the Learning Progression you used to assess your thinking a few days ago. Glance down it and see if it gives you ideas for ways to raise the level of your thinking.

Reflecting on Learning and Raising the Level of Book Clubs

ear Teachers,

To mark the end of this bend, we suggest that you have a day where children reflect on their prowess and progress, and set goals for how to outgrow themselves. The day will essentially be a kind of inquiry and celebration, to mark children's growth as fantasy readers and children who can sustain literary conversations. Last night, children's homework was to prepare for this day. You will want to let your readers know that they'll be showing off with their club—showing off their writing about reading, their conversation, and their new, best thinking—and how much they've read. When children know they are showing off or being assessed, they prepare their best work, better than they might do if caught unawares.

The structure we recommend for this class is a partial fishbowl. That is, set up the period so that after a few minutes to prepare, for the first half, one half of your clubs are in a book club talk, while the other half is researching them, and that for the second half, they flip. You might suggest some particular lenses, such as:

- how the club uses its conversation to make sense of tricky parts of the book
- how the club conversation leads to big ideas
- how club members quote and cite specifically from the text
- how the club entertains multiple ideas and evidence and weighs or ranks these
- how the club's writing about reading is useful for developing thinking.
- how the club is demonstrating grade-level work via the learning progression.

For their inquiry work, set each club up to sit around another club, notebooks open, ready to research. They should have their learning progression on hand, and your teaching charts should be visible. The question they are researching is: "What reading and thinking work is this club doing particularly well?" As the clubs discuss and do research, you can play a couple of important roles. One is to be the avid researcher, saying aloud some of the things you're noticing, as a way to mentor your students. "Oh, I love the way they're adding to Sarah's map right during their club discussion—so they won't forget that point, and to help Sarah add to her thinking." Or perhaps, "Wow, it sounds like they decided on their own to also watch the movie—I can tell by the way they're comparing it to the book."

A second role you can play is to video record some of these discussions, so that you can play some snippets at the end of the period. Kids are good at analyzing video performances—perhaps from watching so many athletic competitions. Suggest that they watch some of these snippets and give a kind of TV announcer voiceover, naming the moves various kids make during the "game." If you need a couple of book club videos, you can find several on our website, at http://readingandwritingproject.org/resources/units-of-study# ("watch a small group conversation to see students tracing a theme across and within *Bud Not Buddy* and *Tiger Rising*," which can be found among the videos under "Reading Literature").

Invite readers, as well, to suggest any notebook pages they admired during their research for a "wall of fame" board, or some kind of bulletin board or site where kids can see how other kids are using their reading notebooks. If you're in a tech-friendly classroom, this might be a good time for kids to take pictures of great pages, so they'll have them on their iPads or phones. It might be a great time to think about next steps for notebooks—should kids be thinking about digital tools such as Notability or Evernote? Where are kids on the continuum toward efficient, innovative notebooks?

After clubs have had time to research and share their results, you may want to suggest that each child, individually, open up his or her notebook and reflect on how they've grown as a reader so far in this unit, and what work they admired today that they want to strive towards. Emphasize the role that preparedness and agency played in student success today, and suggest that they want to not only set goals, but also think about how they want to reach those goals. Some may want to develop a digital notebook. Others may want to read more. Others may want to think harder about smaller details. The most important thing is that kids take some time to reflect, to set some goals, and to develop some thinking about how they want to reach those goals.

Meanwhile, you might want to do the same. Jot some notes about what you've seen kids get better at. Compare their work to the learning progression. What were you pleased at during today's book club talks? What growth do you hear in their thinking or see in their notebooks? How much independence have kids shown? Remember that celebrating kids' growth is celebrating your teaching. We don't do enough of that—look for those insights kids had, those great moments in their conversations, and realize—you're hearing the soundtrack of your teaching!

Yours,
Colleen and Mary

Here Be Dragons

Thinking Metaphorically

IN THIS SESSION, you'll teach students that readers know that in fantasy stories, characters face different kinds of dragons—some are literal, while others are metaphorical dragons symbolizing conflicts faced by those characters. Experienced readers look to how these conflicts develp into themes.

GETTING READY

✔ Display an image of the Carta Marina to show your students. A link is available in the online resources, http://en.wikipedia.org/wiki/Carta_marina. You may also want to show students an image of the Hunt-Lenox Globe, the first map to include the phrase, "Here Be Dragons" (see Connection).

✔ Have *The Paper Bag Princess* on hand (see Teaching).

✔ If, after Session 3, some students made some charts of the many problems that characters face in their books, it would be helpful to have those on hand (see Active Engagement).

✔ Display and add to the anchor chart for Bends I and II, "Sophisticated Readers of Fantasy . . ." (see Share).

✔ Be prepared to jot notes as clubs talk about how to improve their discussions. You will create a list similar to "We Have So Much to Think/Talk/Write About! Clubs Might . . ." (see Share).

I N THE FIRST BEND OF THIS UNIT, you focused students' attention on noticing complexity. Robert Scholes, in *Protocols of Reading* (1991), notes that readers get out of reading what they put into it. So far, therefore, you've tried to make sure that your readers are alert to the subtle nuance of detail, to the way that authors layer details to suggest meaning, to the way that details might conflict and readers need to entertain uncertainty even while trying to figure out what is really going on in their novels. This work has been all about deep comprehension of more complex narratives.

In this bend, you'll move your readers to deeper interpretation. Your hope is that because they've been doing so much work not only paying attention to detail, but sorting and ranking those details, that when they return to interpretation (they've done interpretation work before, of course), that they'll do so with greater nuance. Today, you'll remind students that the problems characters face are often metaphors. While Elizabeth faces a real dragon, all characters—all people—have dragons in their lives. Some are real dangers, that they have no control over but still try to overcome. Others are struggles inside them, that if they can come to see, they can conquer, the way Elizabeth conquers her feelings for Ronald.

This is one of those lessons that has great potential for interconnectedness between reading and writing. If your students will finish the year with a memoir writing unit, you might want to remind them that it's not only fictional characters who have dragons in their lives that are worth thinking about. It's also a lesson on thinking metaphorically—of realizing that many of the conflicts and lessons in books can be thought of as being true outside of the book as well.

Here Be Dragons
Thinking Metaphorically

CONNECTION

Share a story that demonstrates metaphor, such as the "Here Be Dragons" term on old maps, which symbolized the host of unknown dangers that travelers might encounter.

"Readers, in some of your social studies books, you might have seen old maps drawn by the first mariners who charted the oceans. I love these charts because they are so gorgeous and mysterious and symbolic. When they wanted to show that someplace was dangerous, for instance, they might write 'Here Be Dragons' on that area. The Latin words for that were *Hic Sunt Dracones*, which were first written on a famous globe called the Hunt-Lenox Globe, in 1503.

"Or the cartographers or mapmakers might show sea monsters lurking along the coast. There is this beautiful map that I adore, called the Carta Marina. It was created in the sixteenth century, and it shows dragons attacking boats, and all the mythical dangers one would encounter if you ever dared to leave the familiar shores of your homeland."

Readers, what's fascinating about these charts is that the dragons and sea monsters depicted on them are symbolic. Long ago, mariners probably saw giant squid, and then drew them on their maps as sea monsters. But mapmakers also put dragons on maps to show that the explorer was approaching a place that was unknown and dangerous. They showed dragons in places where earthquakes happened. They marked the borders of unknown terrain with *Hic Sunt Dracones*. 'Here Be Dragons' has come to be a symbolic expression meaning 'Look out, there's trouble!'"

 Name the teaching point.

"Readers, today I want to teach you that in fantasy stories, characters face different kinds of dragons—some are literal, while others are metaphorical dragons symbolizing conflicts faced by those characters. Experienced readers look for these conflicts, and consider whether some of them are becoming themes in their novels.

TEACHING

Demonstrate the difference between real dragons and metaphorical dragons. Foster the idea that all characters have dragons.

"To illustrate this thinking, let's go back to a favorite story."

Children love to pore over primary sources and old documents, especially ones as beautifully illustrated and enticing as these old maps. There is a beautiful book, Maps, *by Aleksandra Mizielinska and Daniel Mizielinski, that you may want for your classroom. It is filled with maps that use pictographs—tiny, symbolic illustrations—to show natural resources, dangers, and human impact. There are also glorious images online at Google Images. Do a search for medieval maps, and you'll find dozens of images that demonstrate the metaphorical way people thought about and illustrated unknown dangers.*

I picked up *The Paper Bag Princess*. "Remember *The Paper Bag Princess*? Well, in this story, Elizabeth literally faces a dragon. When I think about the big problem that Elizabeth has, it's that a dragon has smashed her castle and taken Prince Ronald away. And of course, readers, Elizabeth conquers this dragon. She finds the dragon, tricks him, and exhausts him, and she completes her quest by rescuing Prince Ronald.

"But readers, *The Paper Bag Princess* is a more complicated story than just this simple quest. If all that happened were that Elizabeth rescued Prince Ronald, there wouldn't be any significant character change, and the story wouldn't be that memorable for us. But Elizabeth does change. So readers think with me for a moment. Ask yourself: 'What other "dragons" does Elizabeth face—what other conflicts or troubles does she have, besides the actual dragon?' When you have some theories, thumbs up."

I waited to see thumbs up, then invited children to compare their theories with a partner. Then I summarized their thinking.

"Readers, I hear you saying that Elizabeth has other dragons—like being homeless, and having to depend on her own resources. And then there's Ronald! When Elizabeth gets to that cave and rescues Ronald, she finds that Ronald is just as much of a monster as the dragon was. At least the dragon was polite, even if he did want to eat her. Ronald turns out to be monstrously cruel."

I opened the book to the page, saying, "Remember, Elizabeth has finally made her way through danger and death, through burnt forests and fields of horses' bones, to this cave." I read aloud this excerpt again:

> There was Prince Ronald. He looked at her and said, "Elizabeth, you are a mess! You smell like ashes,
> your hair is all tangled and you are wearing a dirty old paper bag. Come back when you are dressed
> like a real princess."

"Readers, I agree with you. I come to this part of the story, and here's what I think. 'Aha! *Hic Sunt Dracones*! Here Be Dragons! This is Elizabeth's real dragon! Ronald is her dragon—he's the thing that she needs to conquer. He's the problem she has to get past. His cruelty and indifference, his snobbery, his way of ignoring, demeaning, and humiliating her—that's her dragon. If I were a medieval cartographer and making a map of this story, I would show Ronald as a dragon inside the cave, to symbolize 'Look out—here's trouble!' Also, when I think about Ronald being one of Elizabeth's problems, or conflicts, I realize that maybe . . . this author is teaching that it's important to make wise choices about relationships!"

Summarize as a series of replicable steps, including thinking about dragons in real people's lives.

"Readers, do you see how we did this? We thought *metaphorically*. We moved to thinking about dragons not as real, but as *metaphorical* dragons that characters face. When you do this, readers, you can begin to think deeply about the dragons in all characters' lives, and in your own lives as well. Ask yourself, for a moment: What are your dragons?" I paused, as if considering my own dragons. "I have a few, readers. You'll know them from writing workshop. I bet you do, too. Then you can think about what facing these dragons teaches you."

Your students have thought about themes before, of course. By posing the notion of troubles as "dragons," you are moving children to think metaphorically—to name not only actual troubles a character may face, but also the notion of trouble as a force in our lives.

Teachers, this is a powerful move to make as a reader, to begin to truly think metaphorically. It's one reason to read The Paper Bag Princess *with any grade! There is something about the literalness of the dragon imagery—the way it symbolizes danger, that seems to help young readers move into metaphorical thinking gracefully, across reading and writing. Ask your kids about the dragons in their lives and see what stories emerge.*

Dear Ms.Binuersie

    I've read the first, seound, and now the third book in the series <u>Percy Jackson & The Olympians</u> by Rick Riordan. What the books have been about is Greek Mythology, and the titan God and the Gods and Godes's. As the book goes on Percy learns that it's not just myths, this stuff is real. He and his friends take on a big responsibillity by going on quests and fighting monsters. As Percy is about to leave school for Summer break and go back to camp Half Blood, something happens and Percy's friend Tyson saves him, with the help of Annabeth.

    The three go back to camp. Tyson has never been to camp and he's never really had friends either. Tyson is an orphan that Percy's school adopted as a community service project, so basically the school had him there to make the students feel better about themselves. When they get to Camp, Posidon claims Tyson as his son, and when

they enter the camp (which has a protection border that keeps monster and kindly ones from entering), the mist (something that can make humans and demigod see only what their mind can process) fades and we discover that Tyson is a cyclops. Tyson is a very emotional, lobeing, caring, protecting, hard working and determand Cyclops! Percy is really kind of embaressed that he has a big guy like Tyson as a brother. Tyson doesn't even mind that or he doesn't seem to notice it all too much. Also Tyson is as persislante as a mosquito.

    Tyson is a very generous cyclops. Tyson is a son of Posidon, the god of the sea, just like Percy. Tyson is very kind and forgiving. Tyson, in a way is clueless. When Percy tells him that all the Greek myths are real Tyson doesn't seam suprised at all. Tyson teaches me that sometimes people are harsh, but that doesn't mean you should let it get to you (or be your dragon), just

give them time and wait it out.

    Another very important lesson Tyson taught me is to be persistant. In the secound book of the series, <u>The Sea of Monsters</u>, Tyson went down in the boiler room and tried to stop all the pressure so it didn't cause the boat to explode. Unfortantly it did and Tyson went with it, but little did we know, Tyson's friend, Rainbow, the hippocampus, was following their boat the whole time and saved Tyson from drowning. Tyson followed Percy and Annabeth and he didn't give up, he just kept on going, and trying.

    Even thought I'm reading a fantasy book, I still learned some very valueable life lessons, when someone is mean to you or hurts your feelings, don't let it get to you. Also, if you are doing somthing, believe in yourself, be determined, be persistant, like Tyson.

Your Strong reader,
Alyece

FIG. 6–1 Alyece writes about the "dragons" her character faces and the lessons these events teach her.

ACTIVE ENGAGEMENT

Give your readers a chance to try thinking metaphorically about characters' dragons, in the read-aloud text and/or their own stories.

"Readers, now it's time for you to try this work. One way to do this thinking is to look back over your notes for the series you're reading in your club, and to reconsider the many problems that a character faces—and then to see if some of them add up to some big emotional 'dragons'—places in the character's emotional life where you might say, 'Here Be Dragons!' Or you might choose to focus on Harvey in *The Thief of Always*. We're right at the point in the story Harvey was turned into a vampire, and he terrified Wendell. He's also found out that they can't leave the house, that Mr. Hood

Teachers, you'll find that any public records you've made, such as charts and timelines of the multiple plotlines and problems in your read aloud text, are incredibly helpful. Having tools at hand that help us to recall important parts of the story means that students can move more easily from recall work, to thinking deeply about characters.

has them prisoner. So you could also talk about Harvey's dragons. Use all your materials, readers, and when you begin to have some ideas, turn and talk with your partner."

Recap their conversations, elevating students' responses to include minor characters and inner troubles.

After partners had been working and talking for a few minutes, I called them back. "Readers, I heard some fascinating conversations. Clearly it's productive to ask the question: 'What are this character's dragons?' Some of you focused on Harvey—and I also heard some of you focus on Wendell, who is one of the minor or secondary characters. That's some nice reading work. A lot of us wouldn't have thought about him. Sam theorized, for instance, that Wendell's biggest dragon is . . . greed! Sam and his partner talked about how Wendell keeps being unable to escape, because he's greedy for the food and the presents that the house gives him. Isn't that interesting? That sometimes our dragons are *inside* us? So a character's biggest dragon could actually be his character flaw."

LINK

Inspire your readers to think about the dragons in their own lives, as well as the lives of their characters.

"Readers, today you learned to think metaphorically about the dragons that characters face. You learned that these dragons could be troubles they face, that they have no control over, or they could be troubles—flaws—that are inside characters. You also learned to think about how facing these dragons might be related to themes in your stories. Finally, you learned some Latin. *Hic Sunt Dracones*. Let's go off to read, and perhaps you'll be noticing in places, that *Hic Sunt Dracones*! Add this to your repertoire. If you need a moment to plan your work with your club, take it now. Decide how far you're reading, when you're meeting, and what work you'll do." I gestured toward our chart "Clubs Take Charge of Themselves" as a reminder.

Looking for the Subtle Theories, and Grounding Them in Specific Text Details

WHEN YOU CONVENE SMALL GROUPS, it's worth thinking not only about *what* you want to teach these students, but *how* you want to teach them. That is, will your method be demonstration, guided practice, or explaining and giving an example—common methods you've seen in these units of study. Another method you pull out of your sleeve during book clubs is to join a club and be an active club member. This method allows kids to be in the presence of an interested, prepared, knowledgeable club member, who has graceful conversational moves up his or her sleeve. Often, you joining a club for a bit can dramatically raise the level of engagement and intellectual rigor. And it's a lovely moment for you, to be a real reader among other readers.

This method often makes sense with some of your strongest readers, whose thinking you can challenge when you read the same book they do. On this day, I asked the *Lightning Thief* club if I could join them. They were on Book 2 of their series by now and were talking across Books 1 and 2. I'd read this series and so I listened with interest as the club talked about possible "dragons" they saw in the books. The club was jumping from idea to idea, and so I said, "Wait, you're going fast, let me just try to say back what you've said so far about the characters. So . . . for Annabeth, I heard you say that her relationship with her dad is her dragon. She seems haunted by it, every time it comes up. And you talked about how Percy seems to have a few dragons, right? Some of you talked more about his guilt. Others of you talked about his feelings about his father—that he seems to feel abandoned, and that makes him want to prove himself."

These ideas were perhaps a bit obvious for this group. I tried a more subtle one. "What about Grover?" I asked. "He seems to have some secret dragon that we don't totally understand yet—he often mentions that something terrible happened on his first quest, but we don't know more because every time he mentions it, he says that he can't talk about it!" The club readers nodded. That's when I made my teacher move. "You are all nodding, but is it really true—does Grover have some secrets? We should go back to the book and see if we can find some evidence for this theory."

Soon we were all avidly looking for and talking about these theories. Before our time ended, I gave a tip that you may want to give to your students, as well. I said explicitly, "You know, from now on, guard against just 'nodding.' If everyone agrees, then maybe you should look for a more subtle, harder-to-see theory. Or maybe you should say something like, 'Where in the text do you see that? What's the most important evidence for that theory?' Nodding makes it seems as you agree exactly, but the truth is, you might be thinking slightly different things, or you might have different evidence. So it's always worth it to get to a finer grain of detail."

MID-WORKSHOP TEACHING
Characters' Perspectives Can Limit Their Understanding

"Readers, I was just talking with La Von for a moment about Elizabeth, in the *Paper Bag Princess*. He was saying that it was interesting how Elizabeth, in the beginning, couldn't really see what a jerk Ronald was. I'm quoting him now—La Von said, 'It was like Elizabeth's princess clothes were a cage, and she couldn't see out of it.'

"Isn't that insightful? La Von is showing us that sometimes, characters' perspectives limit their understanding. This might be true in your stories as well—some of your characters might have blinkers on—like they can't fully see everything. Give me a thumbs up if that might be true for one of your characters . . ." I waited a moment. "Jot down that thinking, before you forget. I bet you might want to think about it more tonight, or with your club."

When Your Club Has So Much to Talk About and Think About, How Do You Bring It Together?

Channel club members to think about ways to make their club work more effective.

"Readers, can you gather in the meeting area with your club and all your materials?" I waited a moment.

"I've gathered you here, together, because you're reaching a time when you going to face a significant challenge as a club—it's kind of like you have a dragon, and it might eat you up." Seeing their mystified faces, I motioned to all the materials children had brought with them. I also pointed to our anchor chart.

ANCHOR CHART

Sophisticated Readers of Fantasy . . .

- Research the setting (What kind of place is it?).
- Ask about power—who has it, evidence, kinds of power.
- Learn alongside the main character.
- Keep track of multiple problems.
- Suspend judgment about characters and places.
- **Read metaphorically by**
  - **Considering the "dragons" characters face**
  -
  -
  -

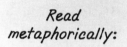

Read metaphorically:

- Consider the "dragons" characters face

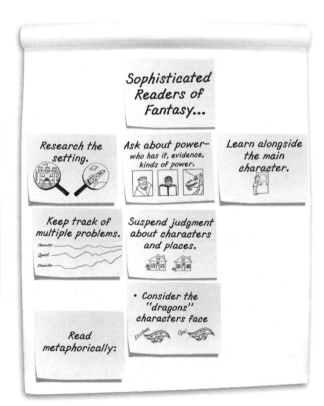

Sophisticated Readers of Fantasy...

| Research the setting. | Ask about power— who has it, evidence, kinds of power. | Learn alongside the main character. |

| Keep track of multiple problems. | Suspend judgment about characters and places. | |

- Consider the "dragons" characters face

Read metaphorically:

"The problem you're beginning to face is . . . you have too much to say! There is simply so much to talk about and not enough time for it all. You want to talk about the characters, you continue to have ideas and interesting notebook pages about the setting, you've got small details that might be important, and big ideas you want to go back and get evidence for. So how do you do it all? I bet you have some thoughts on this. Think for a moment. How will you bring all this thinking, writing, and talking together?"

I waited for them to think. Then I gestured for them to talk to each other, while I gathered some notes.

After a few moments, I put my notes up for them to see.

"Readers, here are some ideas you came up with. There is a lot of smart thinking here. Can you look this list over, and then choose something from here that will make sense for your homework tonight? Think hard about the challenges your club is facing, and what you want to try next. Some of these overlap."

We Have So Much to Think/Talk/Write About! Clubs Might . . .

- Email each other or talk outside of class
- Divide some stuff up–get partnerships going on different things
- Read bigger chunks or meet less often so we focus on big things
- Finish half a book before talking, or even the whole book!
- Find out what kind of stuff we each like to talk about most
- Use our notebooks to have silent conversations about some stuff

---

SESSION 6 HOMEWORK

SET SPECIFIC HOMEWORK FOR EACH MEMBER OF YOUR CLUB

Tonight, make plans with your club members and set homework for each member. Be specific. Write down your homework in your notebook. Tomorrow, we'll take some time to check how it went—asking if you did important work, if you did it well, if it helped you and your club come to new thinking. It's really important that you become the kind of learner who pushes forward yourself, not waiting for someone to tell you what to do. Show off your independence tonight.

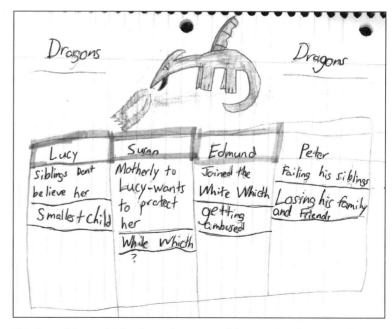

FIG. 6–2   Tristan thinks about the personal dragons his characters face.

Readers Learn Real-Life Lessons from Fantastical Characters

IN THIS SESSION, you'll teach students that insightful readers mine fantasy stories to discover themes and lessons that might apply to their own lives.

GETTING READY

✔ Prior to this session, read aloud *The Thief of Always* through Chapter 17. Be prepared to discuss Harvey's decision to return to the house to rescue the children (see Teaching).

✔ Display and add to anchor chart, "Sophisticated Readers of Fantasy . . ." (see Active Engagement).

✔ Prior to conferring with children, study the example of a chart for tracking themes and related evidence, "Themes in Dragon Slayers' Academy" (see Conferring and Small-Group Work).

✔ Have on hand the "Narrative Writers Use Techniques Such As . . ." visual checklist (see Conferring and Small-Group Work).

✔ To prepare to teach this lesson, think about and compose an example of a textual lineage (a list or timeline of the books that have mattered to you). You can also find an example on our online resources (see Share).

✔ Provide paper and markers to students so they can create their own textual lineage charts (see Share).

I F ON SOME QUIET, SUMMER EVENING, you want to curl up in a chair with a beautiful book about reading, turn to Francis Spufford's *The Child That Books Built*. He tells the story of how as a youngster, he read the Narnia series over and over. All other books, he relates, were just filler until he could read *Narnia* again. Until, that is, he read *The Hobbit*. Then he mixed Narnia and Hobbit. Spufford describes how he learned to read from these books. He learned to figure out tricky words, to study characters over many pages, to suspend disbelief again and again. He also learned how to *live*. From Lucy and Bilbo he learned about courage. From Aslan and Gandalf he learned about wisdom. From Edmund and Thorin Oakenshield he learned about frailty.

When children read at a young age, they soak up not just the stories they read, but the lessons the characters teach as well. It's one of the most beautiful aspects of reading—that you can learn from characters in books just as you learn from people in the real world. Today, you highlight this truth for your readers. You'll especially emphasize that while fantasy novels often have fantastical plots, the life lessons they teach are anything but fantastical.

One note—for a state exam, children *won't* be asked about themes and lessons that matter to them personally. They'll be asked to discern which are most true across the story—which are best supported, not which are most significant to the lives they live. We note this because we follow Louise Rosenblatt's belief that real reading is transactional—that meaning is made between the text and the reader, and that each reader will find a particular meaning in a text more important than another reader might. If you are near the time of your state tests, you'd want to think less about what matters to readers, and more about which theme is best supported across the whole of the text—a logical, if somewhat impersonal lens. We emphasize this lens in the conferring and small-group work, if you want to reinforce it.

Readers Learn Real-Life Lessons from Fantastical Characters

CONNECTION

Tell a story about a fellow reader who speaks of books in terms of their themes and life lessons.

"Fifth-graders, yesterday I met with my book club, and we were considering which book or series we might read next. Most of us wanted to read a new book, but one of us wanted to reread *Lord of the Rings*. You probably know the movies if not the books. They're about Frodo, the Hobbit, and the quest to rid Middle Earth of the ring of power and the evil rule of Sauron.'

"I asked this club mate, Nate, 'Why do you want to reread this story? After all, you know what happens with the hobbits, and the elves, and so forth. What makes this story so important?'

"Nate stared at me. I thought at first that I had hurt his feelings, that he wasn't going to answer. But he was just building up steam. When he did speak, the words came out in a torrent. 'This story isn't about hobbits and elves. This story is about the struggle between good and evil. This story is about how power slowly eats away and corrupts. This story is about how the physically strong can use their gifts to protect others. This story is about how even the smallest and physically weakest can find moral strength to defeat evil. This story is about how love drives us to be better than we are.' Nate stared at me. 'That's why I keep reading this story,' he finally added. 'It's teaching me how to live. And I'm not an elf.'

"Readers, you can imagine that this was a humbling moment for me. I realized that Nate was learning more from the books we were reading than I was. He was actively thinking about their big life lessons!"

 Name the teaching point.

"Readers, today I want to remind you that fantasy stories might have fantastical plots—but they are also about themes and life lessons. Insightful readers mine these stories for lessons that might apply to their own lives."

♦ COACHING

Whenever you refer to books other than the read aloud, it's often helpful to hold up the book cover, or, if it's also a film such as The Hobbit, *or* Lord of the Rings, *to have up on your screen a clip from the trailer. These quick visual cues act as reminders to children of the characters, or give you a chance to point them out quickly as you talk. They also stir children's interest in being a lifelong reader, as they'll know these books are waiting for them!*

TEACHING

Recall some familiar fantasy tales and retell them in terms of themes and lessons. Then demonstrate how you consider which of these might apply to the life you lead.

"Readers, fantasy novels are incredibly helpful in teaching us how to read this way—to mine for themes and lessons. The trick of it is let go of the fact that the plot is fantastic, and to ask yourself—what lessons do these characters learn, or teach, that could be important to my life?

"For instance, when I consider *The Thief of Always*, I know that I'm never going to find myself imprisoned in a magical house. I'm never (I hope!) going to find myself changed into a hungry vampire. But that doesn't mean there aren't things I could learn from Harvey and what happens to him. So . . . the question I ask myself is . . . what lessons might Harvey teach me? You might ask this question of yourself, as well . . ."

I pondered visibly, and I nodded as students' hands went up.

"Readers, I'm not going to call on you now—keep your thoughts in mind, and see how they compare to mine. I'm thinking about the moment when Harvey decides to *go back* to the house, not only to get back his years, but to rescue the other children. I remember being struck, at that moment, by how incredibly brave he was. He was kind of selfish, or self-centered at the beginning of the book, but now, at that point, I thought about how he had changed—he wasn't just thinking about himself. Now, in my own life, is that an important lesson?" I pondered over that question. "Well, I think the most important part is realizing that you can make mistakes, and still pick yourself up and do better. Like Harvey makes a lot of mistakes at the beginning, but now he's beginning to be better. That's helpful for me—give me a thumbs up if that lesson might be helpful for you too—that you can make mistakes but still pick yourself up and do better?"

Lots of thumbs went up. I nodded.

ACTIVE ENGAGEMENT

Set children up to consider, rank, and analyze themes and life lessons that are particularly relevant to their lives.

"I know you've got your own ideas about life lessons that you're learning from *The Thief of Always*. And I bet there are some big life lessons or themes that seem particularly important to you personally, in the series you're reading with your club.

"Let's take a moment for you to try this work. You already know a lot about tracing themes and lessons in stories. Right now, will you think across a few of the themes or life lessons you've come across in your reading that seem particularly important to you, and choose one to describe to a partner? Be ready to really explain why that lesson might be important in your life."

If you've never had the pleasure of reading Alfred Tatum's books, Reading for Their Life: (Re)Building the Textual Lineages of African American Adolescent Males *(Heinemann, 2009), or* Teaching Reading to Black Adolescent Males *(Stenhouse, 2005), you should invite a colleague to study them with you. Tatum talks extensively about making reading relevant to the lives kids actually live. Part of this work involves what he calls documenting one's "textual lineage." This means tracing the books that have mattered most to you and figuring out what you have learned from them. Here, you delve into that work, striving to guild deeply personal connections to books with your children.*

I gave children a few moments to jot and think, then motioned for them to turn and compare.

Rosie said, "I'm thinking about how Percy, in *The Lightning Thief*, learns he can be incredibly brave, even though he's afraid."

Her partner, Julia, added in, "That's actually a lot like Harvey. It's not that they're not scared. They're both scared, like when Harvey is being chased by that vampire thing, or when Percy battles that monster on the arch—but they don't want their friends to get hurt, so they try to be brave."

I motioned to Christian, who was talking about Wiglaf in *Dragon Slayers' Academy*, to join them. "I think, from listening to you, that Wiglaf learns some similar lessons about being brave . . . maybe you should compare those?" He scooted over to join Rosie and Julia, and they began talking.

After a few moments, I gathered them back.

I said, "I'm adding what you just worked on to our anchor chart."

When children are comparing their thinking during the active engagement, sometimes you want to listen with the lens of how they are doing with what you've just taught them. Is it sticking? Are they trying the work you wanted them to, or for whatever reason, are they doing different work? Other times, you can quickly assess their focus, and then listen for children who might talk productively together, and motion them into little groups, or set them up to meet later. Attentiveness to the content of their talk inspires high levels of engagement. That attentiveness makes children feel visible.

ANCHOR CHART

Sophisticated Readers of Fantasy . . .

- Research the setting (What kind of place is it?).
- Ask about power—who has it, evidence, kinds of power.
- Learn alongside the main character.
- Keep track of multiple problems.
- Suspend judgment about characters and places.
- Read metaphorically by
  - Considering the "dragons" characters face
  - **Applying life lessons learned in fiction to their own lives**
  -
  -

- Apply life lessons learned in fiction to their own lives

LINK

Review the choices readers might make, emphasizing their need to consider what work they want to accomplish.

"Readers, I heard a lot of you saying things that you might want to write down before you forget. Why don't you take a moment to think about the choices you might make today as a reader. Will you open up your notebook and do some fast writing about how the book you're reading is influencing you? Or will you try some of the work we started yesterday, thinking about the dragons that the characters face—and perhaps you want to bring in today's lesson and compare those to your own? Or will you continue some of the work we began earlier—some of that might be especially important if you're starting a new book." I motioned to our anchor chart.

"Go ahead, think about the work you most want to accomplish, then turn and compare with your club. Make sure you're clear about what work you want to accomplish before meeting again."

Weighing and Evaluating Themes and Life Lessons with Different Lenses

YOUR READERS have done a lot of work during their reading lives with lessons and themes. When they were younger, they mostly waited until they had finished a story to think about the lessons it taught. Now your readers should be in the habit of thinking about themes and lessons early in the story, and reading with those themes in mind. As you coach your readers today, you might choose to remind them of a few lenses to have in mind as they weigh and evaluate themes. You may also find you need to coach students in weighing evidence.

Consider which themes seem most important to the author by thinking across the story.

As clubs research themes and life lessons in their stories, one lens they can use is to consider which themes seem most important to the author (a skill highly rewarded on state tests). To do this work, readers often jot down two or three possible themes they see in the text. If you were most interested in meanings which seem personally significant, at this point, readers would consider the text of their lives, and think about that. But to think about which theme or themes seem most important to the author, or in the story, you rank usually using two main qualities. One quality is the strength of the theme across the story. That is, if the theme only seems to appear in one part of the story, it's not as significant to the whole story. So jotting down evidence for each theme, and then weighing it by how much it goes across a story, is one way to evaluate the overall strength of the theme. Another is to consider the overall strength of each piece of evidence—sometimes it feels as if the author is almost putting words in bold, telling the reader an important lesson or theme.

It's often helpful to have children list the themes they are finding, and then put Post-its or a list of evidence under each theme. This will help you coach them in two ways. First, it will help you see how children are doing with matching evidence to themes. Some children struggle to sort, and this exercise will help you see if any of them need some guided practice simply sorting evidence. Second, you'll then be able to coach children

to consider the overall strength of their evidence for each theme. The Dragon Slayers Club, for instance, laid out three main themes. When they listed their evidence for each though, it was clear that the evidence for their first theme only appeared at the start of the story, and that they only had a little evidence for their third theme. However, their second theme was true across the story and had solid evidence to support it.

Themes in Dragon Slayers' Academy		
It's important to help your family.	**Real friends help each other.**	**Not all our wishes turn out to be good.**
• Wiglaf has a lot of brothers and sisters and they need money. • Wiglaf goes to DSA to get gold. • He wants to kill a dragon to get gold for his family.	• Erica and Wiglaf help each other tackle the dragon. • Angus and Wiglaf keep Erica's secret. • Wiglaf and Erica help Angus deal with his uncle Mordred.	• Wiglaf is upset he killed a dragon.

Compare themes across stories, including how they are developed.

Your readers are reading series, and many clubs will be on their second or third book by now. You might coach these readers, therefore, to remember what they know about comparing themes across stories. Suggest that one or two club members write down the themes they've found in the first book, and other club members jot down the themes they've found in the second and/or third books. Then, have them 'play' these

Post-its by putting them in the middle of their table, and asking if any of those themes hold true across more than one book. You can get children started on this work, then leave them to visit another group. When you return, where you will probably need to coach the children is in thinking about how these themes are developed. That is, are they precisely the same in each book or are they slightly different? To do this work, it can be interesting to not only list evidence, but also take into account the techniques authors use to develop a theme. You might want to return to the "Narrative Writers Use Techniques Such As . . ." visual chart, as a guide—or cut one up into small cards, that kids can use.

The Narnia group, for instance, was ready to think across novels in their series. When they laid out themes in the first two novels, *The Lion, The Witch and the Wardrobe* and *Prince Caspian*, they settled on one that they found compelling in each story: People find hidden strengths in times of trouble. (To get to a theme like this, kids often need to first say the theme more as a word or phrase, such as "strength" or "courage." Then ask them, "What does the author suggest about that quality?" Using the narrative technique cards, the club began to think not only about specific details in the text, but *ways* or *techniques* the author employed to develop this theme, and they were able to have a sophisticated conversation about not only theme, but how an author develops theme, as shown below.

Narrative Writers Use Techniques Such As...

Flashback & flashforward	Multiple plot lines	Inner thinking
Dialogue	Revealing actions	Multiple points of view
1st person narrator	Reader knows MORE than the character	Description
Metaphor	Tone	Symbolism

People Find Hidden Strengths in Times of Trouble	
The Lion, The Witch and the Wardrobe	**Prince Caspian**
• Dialogue—Aslan tells Lucy that she needs to not depend on her brothers and sisters, but look inside herself for strength.	• Inner thinking—Caspian thinks about what kind of prince he wants to be, when he is planning his return to Narnia.
• Multiple points of view—When it switches to Edmund, you get to see him. learning to be strong—when he defies the White Witch.	• Flashback—When we see how Caspian's father was murdered, it makes the trouble stronger—and how strong Caspian will need to be.

MID-WORKSHOP TEACHING **Readers Learn from Mistakes Characters Make, Not Just Their Achievements**

"Readers, I was just talking with the Narnia club, and they reminded me that in their novels, the reader often learns big lessons from the mistakes the characters make. For instance, Edmund, one of the boys in the story, starts out by betraying his brothers and sisters, and Narnia, for the sweets and attention the White Witch gives him. As a reader, you watch him do this, and you keep thinking, 'No, Edmund, she's a witch! You need to trust the people who love you, not the people who flatter you!' Ultimately, one of the interesting themes of Narnia is going to be about trust—about how people earn trust through their actions. And it's the mistakes characters make early on, that reinforce this lesson, as they learn from those mistakes.'

"You might find this in your books, too—to be on the lookout for moments when you can learn from mistakes characters make, so you don't have to make the same ones!"

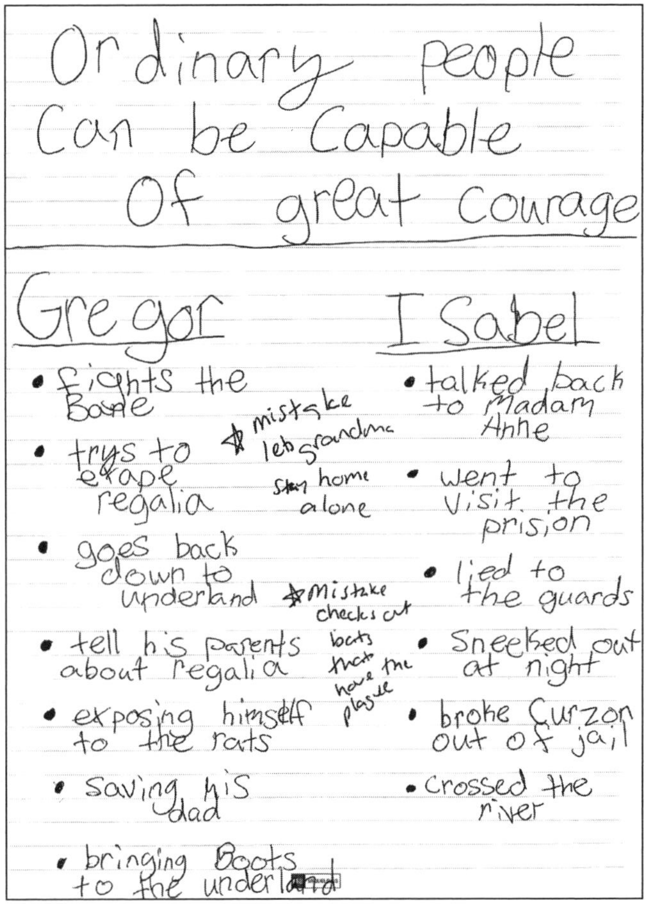

FIG. 7–1 Julia thinks about character's mistakes as well as strengths.

Reflecting on Textual Lineages—the Books that Have Mattered to Us and Why

Invite students to think about books that they remember best—and then create their own textual lineage charts.

"Readers, can you gather back at the meeting area please, with your notebooks and something to write with?" I waited a moment for students to gather. Then I unveiled my sample textual lineage.

"Readers, you've been doing a lot of thinking about the lessons that the stories you are reading are teaching. This isn't the first time you've done this work, either. You did it in fourth grade and third grade, and I bet, when you were very young, you probably thought about things Frog or Toad did, and you thought, 'That was a mistake!' or 'That was smart!' You were absorbing lessons even then."

I pointed to my sample. "Readers, there's a famous researcher, Alfred Tatum, who suggests that readers think hard about the books that have affected them, and record these so they carry them with them as a lasting legacy. He calls this work 'textual lineages.' A lineage is like a family history—only this would be a book history. It's fascinating to think about which books you most remember and why—and it fits beautifully with the work you're doing now. So I thought this might be interesting to do, right now. Shall we?" I noted their cautious nods, and gestured towards the markers at my feet.

"You don't have to make yours look just like mine. You might make a timeline or a chart, or a list—whatever way you most want to show the books that you remember most, and what they've meant to you. Let's take some quiet moments to do this work. Then, when you're ready, if you're ready, tap your partner or someone in your club, and share."

Dear Morgan,

I am reading the book series 'Percy Jackson: The Olympians.' When I started the first book The Lightning Theif, I thought the book was about a kid in sixth grade who had dyslexia and ADHD. Although it is a story about a boy named Percy who finds out his father is a god. Percy goes to a camp called Camp Half-Blood, where he is claimed by his father Poseidon, the god of the sea. Now percy must fight monsters to fulfill his prophecy. There are many life lessons, but I think that Percy has taught me that things aren't always as they seem. This lesson can be taught because Percy would have never been suspected a DemiGod, but he clearly is. At times, Percy himself thought maybe he really didn't belong, when he did. This could also be the lesson Ordinary People Can Be Capable Of Great Courage. In the first book when Percy is clueless about his father, he has to face his first monster,

a fury. Percy had to be brave. The second lesson would be Don't think just do. Percy had to learn the lesson because he and his friends had to think up plans quickly, and Percy has to know to not think of what would happen, he just knows to do.

Percy taught me that things aren't always as they seem. In the book, monsters seem like ordinary people, but the are Monters. I connect to this because when I meet new people or friends, they may seem mean at first, but they eventually are really nice people. I can also connect because, as I said before, Percy is not the person he thaight, and I think that I connect because I'm not the person I thought I was a few years ago.

Percy also taught me to not think, just do. Percy doesn't always have the chance to think before he does something. I connect to this because in dance, I have to just do. There are many risks I have to take when doing things like lifts and falls, but if I thought about the risks, I probably wouldn't dance.

In conclusion, I think that I connect with Percy, because of the challenges we've faced and lessons we've learned.

Sincerely,

Maya

FIG. 7–2   Maya writes to a classmate about the life lessons she learns from a fantasy character.

YOUR TEXTUAL LINEAGE—WHICH BOOK MATTERS THE MOST?

Readers, today in class you thought hard about themes and life lessons in books, and you reflected on the books that have mattered most to you. If you didn't get a chance to finish your textual lineage (the books that you most remember, and why they matter to you), finish that tonight for homework. If you did, think about which book matters absolutely the most to you, and jot a quick entry about why that book—why does that one matter to you? Was it the life lessons you learned? You might write a notebook entry, or even a letter, about the book.

Quests Can Be Internal as Well as External

IN THIS SESSION, you'll teach students that most fantasy stories follow a quest structure, and to achieve deeper understanding of the story, it's valuable to investigate both the external and internal quests of major characters.

GETTING READY

✔ Prior to this session, read aloud *The Thief of Always* through Chapter 18.

✔ Prior to this minilesson, choose a student to share her interpretation of *The Paper Bag Princess* during the share. Rehearse with this student to prepare her for the share (see Share).

✔ Prepare a character timeline of the internal and external obstacles faced by Harvey in the *Thief of Always* (see Teaching).

✔ Display a chart, "Thinking about External and Internal Quests" (see Active Engagement).

✔ Display and add to anchor chart, "Sophisticated Readers of Fantasy . . ." (see Share).

ONE CHALLENGE children face is recognizing common text structures and articulating the effects of those structures (such as using flashbacks to provide backstory, or jumping forward in time to show resolution). From colleagues such as Paul Deane, Cognitively Based Assessment *Of*, *For*, and *As* Learning (CBAL), and the Educational Testing Service (ETS), we've come to understand that dealing with structure is one way to deal with more difficult text. As narratives become harder, one way they get harder is that the story no longer has a problem-solution structure, and time moves in uneven and sometimes nonlinear ways. So teaching children to notice, think, and talk about structure helps them become more at ease with one of the most important aspects of narrative.

Fantasy is a genre that particularly rewards inquiry around structure. Most fantasy novels are set up around a quest structure, in which the character sets out in search of something, faces a series of obstacles, and ultimately achieves his or her goal. Learning to recognize and anticipate quest structure gets young readers to notice structure at all, and they enjoy the sense of expertise this insider knowledge gives them. After all, part of becoming expert in a genre is learning the qualities of that literary tradition, so that students come to the text with more knowledge about how things might unfold. With this knowledge, readers are better able to predict events because even if they don't know this story, they know stories like this. Readers can see how that insider knowledge will help them tackle more difficult books.

If you think that recognizing quest structure is itself sufficiently challenging for your readers, you could modify this lesson to introduce the notion of quest structure, and teach children some simple methods for timelining or outlining the quests in their novels. We suggest, though, that you take this work one step farther, and that you lead children to investigate the internal as well as external quests their characters are on. Most of your readers (with luck) are reading at R–T and above by now. That means that the characters in their series will have significant internal obstacles to overcome. Percy Jackson needs to understand and overcome his feelings about his father and his uncertainties about his magical heritage. Harry Potter is on a quest to better understand his parents and their legacy to him. Wiglaf ultimately ends up on a quest to *appear* as if he is slaying dragons while not actually killing any. The internal quests of these characters will be as fascinating as their external quests for magical objects, defeating dragons, and so on. As with the lesson you taught yesterday on life lessons, your hope is that your readers will come to realize that they too, have internal quests they can pursue.

"Teaching children to notice, think, and talk about structure helps them become more at case with one of the most important aspects of narrative."

One note: today's share invites a child to share her interpretation of *The Paper Bag Princess*, as a way to model how structure and theme are often linked, that is, when a reader begin to analyze structure, it often leads her to theme. You might, therefore, rehearse with a student, to ready him or her for this share. Or, of course, you could demonstrate this interpretation work yourself.

Quests Can Be Internal as Well as External

CONNECTION

Set students up to think about patterns in fantasy novels or movies, especially in terms of obstacles that characters face.

"Readers, I want you to think about the fantasy novels you've been reading, and any fantasy movies you've seen, such as *The Hobbit*, or *Narnia*. Can you think about *how these stories go*, and see if you see any patterns in the obstacles that characters face? Does the characters always accomplish what they want right away? Do they stay home or are they forced to leave? Think for a few moments, and when you have something in mind, give a thumbs up."

I waited a moment until thumbs were up. "Go ahead, compare with someone near you. What patterns are you noticing about how these stories go? Like maybe they face a series of dangers, or maybe they're always traveling, or maybe they look for some kind of magic object, or something else."

I listened in as students spoke.

"Readers, I hear you talking about how often characters seem to leave their homes and go on a journey. And you also talked about how they don't just face one problem, but also a series of problems. What you're really talking about is how these stories are *structured*. Most fantasy stories follow a quest narrative structure. This means that the hero is given a quest, which means he or she must journey to achieve something, like Percy is searching for Zeus's lightning bolt, or Wiglaf must slay a dragon—literally! Or maybe the character sets his or her own quest, like Elizabeth deciding to follow the dragon, or Harvey deciding he must return to the house that kept him prisoner, to free the other children."

 Name the teaching point.

"Today I want to teach you that experienced fantasy readers know that most fantasy stories follow a quest structure. What's often most interesting to these experienced readers, then, is to investigate the internal quest as well as the external."

Often as you prompt children to consider an inquiry question, you can toss out some casual "starters" that help children begin this thinking. Mentioning the kinds of quests that might be coming up in their novels, without unfolding all aspects of them, will help your children feel a sense of familiarity with what you're asking them to investigate, even if the vocabulary of "quest structure" will be new. David Rock notes that any new vocabulary is perceived inherently as a threat, so mitigating it by first building familiarity can help more children process your instruction successfully.

TEACHING

Demonstrate steps in investigating quest structure, including creating a timeline of obstacles, both external and then internal.

"Let me show you what I mean. Once you know to expect a quest structure, you'll begin to see it everywhere. Sometimes the quest involves rescuing a captive or a sacred object, as with Shrek or Sinbad. Other times the quest may ask the hero to destroy a villain or a dangerous object, as with The Lord of the Rings and Harry Potter. And the other common quest narrative is that the hero has gotten into another world or place, and the quest is the journey out of there, as with Narnia and *Alice in Wonderland*.

"So one thing that can be interesting is to recognize that the character in your novel is probably also on a quest. He or she is probably trying to accomplish something big, and he or she is going to have to overcome a series of obstacles to accomplish this task. To do this work, think of Harvey and how he wants to rescue the children and destroy Mr. Hood. Now think of all the obstacles he has to face."

I put up a timeline of Harvey's external quest and the obstacles he must face.

"Often, just thinking about the quest itself is interesting. It calls your attention to some of the smaller obstacles and gets you thinking about how they might be connected to a character's greater task. But I want to show you one more thing. It's *also* interesting to consider the character's *internal* quest. To do that work, think for a moment about the obstacles that are *inside* Harvey—what does he find hard? I shared the bottom half of my diagram, revealing Harvey's internal quest."

"It's fascinating to think about both these quests, isn't it? An inexperienced reader wouldn't even know that his or her fantasy followed a quest structure. A more experienced reader would see that structure. And an even more sophisticated reader, like you, might see an internal quest as well as an external one. Let's see. . . ." I pondered the two timelines. "I'm thinking that perhaps Harvey has to deal with the obstacles that are internal, to be successful at his external quest. Does that make sense to you? I wonder if that might be true for your characters too." I waited for nods as we pondered this possibility.

ACTIVE ENGAGEMENT

Invite children to quickly jot one of the quests a character is on, and to discuss it with a partner.

"Let's give you a chance to try this work out on one of the books you've been reading. So, to do this work, remember that readers think of the main character, and what he or she is most trying to accomplish. To think about the external quest, readers then consider that task not as just one problem, but as a series of smaller obstacles, and see if that helps you see more about

We tend to introduce academic terms after children understand and recognize them. For instance, getting children to see that characters in their novels face a series of obstacles could lead them to name the associated series as a quest. Other times, it's helpful to give children the vocabulary almost as a conceptual lens and invite them to look for evidence of that new concept.

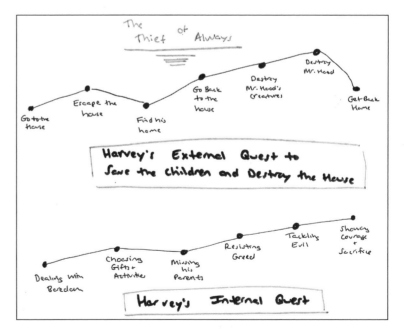

FIG. 8–1   Here you see not only a timeline, but a kind of EKG, or the story mountain, of a character's internal and external quests.

how the story is structured and what the character faces. To think about the internal quest, readers consider what's inside the character that gets in the way—what internal flaws or conflicts do they need to overcome?" I revealed the chart I had ready.

Thinking About External and Internal Quests

⇒ **For external quests, readers think about:**

- The big problem or goal

- A series of smaller obstacles

⇒ **For internal quests, readers think about:**

- What's inside the character that gets in the way?

  • Internal flaws to fix or get around

  • Conflicts to overcome

"Go ahead readers, take a moment, and see what happens if you try to sketch one of these quests. Choose any character, and either external or internal or both."

After a minute, I motioned to them to compare sketches with their partner.

"Readers, I hear you talking about your books in new ways. You sound extremely sophisticated, and you also are seeing new things. I heard Sam say something like, 'In *The Lightning Thief*, Percy's internal quest is more important than his external. Because while he wants to find Zeus's thunderbolt, it's really even more important that he make peace with his feelings about his father.' That's sophisticated thinking, and Sam got there by thinking about quest structures."

When you quote children in class, you can elevate both what they said and how they sound, by using a highly academic, polished tone, and exaggerating the power of their words. Just as you when you read kids' writing aloud, you make it sound even grander, when you "replay" children's comments and conversations, you can similarly aggrandize it.

LINK

Remind students to add this work to their repertoire of interpretation approaches. Suggest they make a quick plan with their club.

"Readers, when you are thinking about what interpretation work you want to do with your club, this may be interesting work to pursue. You have a lot of different kinds of thinking you might do. You might be thinking metaphorically about the dragons in characters' lives—that thinking might intersect in interesting ways with this work on internal quests. Or you may be weighing and evaluating various themes, within and across novels. And of that might lead to some fascinating discussions in your club.

"Take a minute to review your plans with your club, then off you go!" I added this work to our anchor chart.

> **ANCHOR CHART**
>
> ### Sophisticated Readers of Fantasy . . .
>
> - Research the setting (What kind of place is it?).
> - Ask about power—who has it, evidence, kinds of power.
> - Learn alongside the main character.
> - Keep track of multiple problems.
> - Suspend judgment about characters and places.
> - Read metaphorically by
>   - Considering the "dragons" characters face
>   - Applying life lessons learned in fiction to their own lives
>   - **Considering internal as well as external quest structures**
> -

> • Consider internal as well as external quest structures

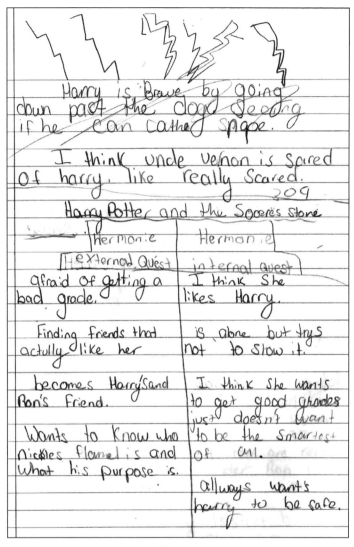

FIG. 8–2   Isabella tries to sort out external conflicts as ones other characters know about, and internal ones as private.

Managing the Social and Intellectual Work of Clubs Independently

YOUR CLUBS ARE IN VARIOUS STAGES OF INTERPRETATION, and they are meeting on different days, at different times. This means that you'll want to be checking in regularly to make sure that students are making wise choices. Some clubs may need help negotiating how often they are meeting, and how many pages they are getting through. Even if all was well at the start of the unit, because this may be their first independent endeavor at managing the social and intellectual work of their own reading clubs, they may need some occasional coaching.

Some predictable table conferences you may need to have, then, include the following.

If clubs are writing so much that they are barely reading, then . . .

Even with the best of intentions, sometimes children will get so excited about the charts and timelines they are making, and the entries they are writing, that they don't notice that their reading has slowed to a crawl. You'll know this has happened when you look across children's reading notebooks and you see glorious maps and sketches, but in the series, they are still reading Book 1, or they are barely starting Book 2.

Often a quick reminder is all it takes—but at this point in fifth grade, you'll want to alert them to a problem and see if they can figure out how to solve it, instead of offering them your solutions. So you might say, "When readers become avid at writing about reading, as you've become, sometimes they drop out of the reading zone. So if you know the reading zone is about 40–60 pages (in and out of school total) each day, how could you figure out if you're slipping, and what steps might you take to get back in the zone?" Chances are, children will figure out that they may need to step slightly back from so much writing and sketching, and spend more time reading. They may appoint a club member to keep track of their reading, set more ambitious goals in terms of page numbers, or do more writing on the weekends and less during the week.

If clubs are getting stuck because they don't have the next book in their series, then . . .

It sounds like a small thing, but a lot of young and adolescent readers get stuck if the next book in a series is not easily accessible. They may read out of order or even abandon the series, which means they also abandon the higher-level thinking of tracking a character over hundreds of pages.

You have two ways to help solve this problem. One is to simply solve it for your students. You might keep track of how clubs are proceeding in their reading, and notice if you need to beg, borrow, or buy the next few books in a series for certain clubs. You might put out a "desperately needed" note to parents asking for a few urgently needed titles.

Another way to approach this problem is to ask the kids to help solve it. We've definitely found that kids who have learned to obtain their own books are more likely to shape their own independent reading lives in middle and high school. So you might help kids take charge of the practical aspects of getting books by suggesting they organize a bake sale and use the proceeds to order used books online. Perhaps you could teach them to ask for interlibrary loans, or to write letters to parents requesting books.

If all members of a club aren't thriving, then . . .

As an adult, you may have been in a book club dominated by a member who talked loudly and often, or you may have noticed that some members barely spoke across the whole discussion. Kids are often more sensitive to this issue than adults are. Spending years in reading workshop means they are trained to make connections to each other's thinking, and to elaborate, recap, and question. It's still worth checking in to evaluate the overall health of the book club and its members. One method that Donna Santman, author of *Shades of Meaning: Comprehension and Interpretation in Middle School* (Heinemann, 2005) uses is to sketch the interactions, using arrows to show the movement of talk from one person to another, and look for patterns.

Santman also often suggests using "talk cards" to help children get into a discussion. Similar to sentence starters, these cards are also related to *when* in a talk students might talk. For instance, it's easier to begin a discussion than it is to follow and jump into a quickly moving one, especially for English language learners. Using red cards for initiating discussion, blue for connecting, and green for summing up can help children plan their participation, and can help them study their interactions. Here are some you might use now, for instance:

To Start a Discussion . . .	To Connect Within . . .	To Recap or Summarize . . .
Let's start with what we decided to pay attention to as we read . . .	*Some important evidence for that could be . . .*	*To summarize, we spoke about . . .*
Let's go over what we did for homework first . . .	*Let's review the evidence for a moment . . .*	*So the new thinking we came to is . . .*
Let's focus on the idea . . .	*That also makes me think . . .*	*So what seems most important here is . . .*

MID-WORKSHOP TEACHING   Noticing that Other Structures in Stories Often Give Readers Crucial Information

"Readers, some of you have been noticing other structures in your stories—especially flashbacks, where you go back in time and sort of parallel narratives, where you follow one character for awhile and then another. Whenever you notice these, it's worth asking: 'Why might the author have done this?' 'What was accomplished by including this flashback or this shift to another character?'

"Often, the author is giving you crucial information, perhaps about a problem that you'd only know about if you went back in time in the story, or perhaps an obstacle that is arising through another character. In any case, it's great that you are noticing these structures, and it's almost always worth thinking about what work they do in the story. Often in fantasy, you'll see a quest developing in the past and moving into the future."

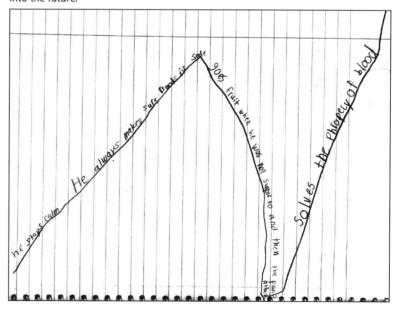

FIG. 8–3   Morgan thinks about Gregor's quest.

Understanding How Quests Change Characters: Linking Structure to Theme

Ask one student to share how she connects a character's quest to the story's theme.

"Readers, come sit with your clubs and listen in for a moment." I waited briefly. "As you consider this work, you may notice that quest structures might be related to the themes you're seeing in your books. When characters go on journeys—emotional ones and real ones, they often learn big lessons. So be alert to where you see some of this work coming together. Sarah, for instance, was talking about Elizabeth in *The Paper Bag Princess*. Listen to Sarah explain her thinking about the quests, and when you feel like she's beginning to also talk about theme, give a thumb up."

I motioned to Sarah to share her thoughts, and gave her the book. She said, "Well, Elizabeth follows the dragon in order to get Ronald. She makes a journey, and on the journey she overcomes several obstacles set by the dragon. Like first she has to find him, then he wants to eat her, and he doesn't want to let her into the cave where Ronald is . . . so that's her big quest."

Sarah flipped through the pages so the class could see the book as she spoke. "Today, though, I thought about the inside quest Elizabeth is on. Like she is on a quest to find her true love. And her first obstacle, maybe, is that she thinks she's supposed to be with a prince, but Prince Ronald is a jerk and doesn't notice her." She showed the picture of Ronald ignoring Elizabeth. "Then her second obstacle is when she finds him, he's mean to her. So now her bigger obstacle isn't finding Ronald—it's getting rid of her feelings for him. She learns that she doesn't need a prince to be happy." Thumbs began to go up around the room.

"Say that again, Sarah," I said. "Say it like this: 'So on her quest, Elizabeth learns . . .'"

"Elizabeth is on a quest to find her prince," Sarah said. "But on the way, she learns she doesn't need a prince to be happy."

I looked around at others. "How many of you think this might work in the book you're reading for your club—that the quest might be leading to a theme? And is it the internal or external quest or both? Give me a thumbs up if you've got something to say to your club about this idea.

"I've summarized what you just worked on and added a point to our anchor chart."

I waited a moment, then motioned to children to explore their thinking with their club.

USING A QUEST FROM YOUR STORY TO HELP DEVELOP A THEME

Readers, today in class you explored internal and external quests, and how those may relate to themes in your stories.

For homework tonight, choose one of these quests (internal or external) for a story you've been reading. Then write a few sentences explaining how understanding that quest helps to develop a theme or life lesson in your story.

Be sure to use some examples from the book to demonstrate the quest structure. Also, remember to explain your theme in a full sentence (so not just "friendship," but "Harvey learns that people will be strong to save their friends").

Comparing Themes in Fantasy and History

IN THIS SESSION, you'll teach students that knowledgeable readers assume that some themes are so universal that they appear in more than one book and across history, as well. These readers use their knowledge of history to compare how these themes develop.

GETTING READY

✔ Prior to this session, read aloud *The Thief of Always* through Chapter 19.

✔ Have on hand some historical narratives, such as *The Story of Ruby Bridges* or *I Am Rosa Parks* (see Connection, Teaching and Active Engagement, Conferring and Small-Group Work).

✔ Prepare a chart with some of the historical characters students have studied and their troubles and accomplishments (see Teaching and Active Engagement).

✔ Provide half-slips of paper with universal themes written on them to each club (see Teaching and Active Engagement).

✔ Prepare a chart with some common universal themes (see Teaching and Active Engagement).

✔ Display Figures 9–1 and 9–2 as examples of student writing about thematic patterns (see Teaching and Active Engagement and Conferring and Small-Group Work).

✔ Display and add to anchor chart, "Sophisticated Readers of Fantasy . . ." (see Link).

✔ Be prepared to jot themes related to novels your students are reading (see Share).

✔ Review the "Comparing and Contrasting Story Elements and Themes" strand in the fifth-grade Narrative Reading Learning Progression.

✔ Have handy copies of the Student Assessment Tool (child-facing rubric) for this unit.

T ODAY'S LESSON will work best if your students have been studying issues and themes in history in their social studies class. We're guessing you *are* their social studies teacher, so if you have any charts that record the big essential questions and the big ideas that your class has tackled this year in social studies, now would be a good time to get those out. If you're in our writing units of study, children explored big ideas in Westward Expansion earlier this year, and chances are they've studied Civil Rights since then. So themes such as "people often struggle for resources or fight for land," or "people often have to fight for their rights," or "working together makes people stronger" have probably come up already. It doesn't really matter what content you've been studying.

You'll inspire children to think across historical themes and those in the novels they're reading. This is a precursor to the work they'll do as more informed readers, when they begin to consider the time and politics in which the novels they're reading were set. (It's not accidental that Narnia was composed during WWII, during an epic struggle between forces united to enforce a reign of darkness and opposing forces determined to resist that reign.)

It's just possible that some of your clubs may be ready to make those connections today. The main goal, though, of today's work, is to expand on the work children have done prior to this, which is to explore how themes live in more than one story, and to take that to exploring how themes may live in historical narrative as well as fictional ones.

This is ambitious intellectual work. Depending on how deep your children's knowledge of history is, expect that they'll be better able to support their theories with specific evidence from their novels than from history. If you've been engaged in a deep social studies unit though, with good chapter books, including narratives, have those available, so that clubs can flip through them and remind themselves of possible themes. A few good picture books (if you've been studying civil rights, a few narratives of Rosa Parks and Dr. Martin Luther King, for instance), might be helpful.

Comparing Themes in Fantasy and History

CONNECTION

Share observations that themes are appearing again and again in stories.

"Readers, Maria and Sam came to me yesterday with something they were noticing. They were noticing that it wasn't just that a lot of the books in their series had similar themes or life lessons—a lot of the books you've been reading do, including ones like this." I held up *Number the Stars* and *I Am Rosa Parks*. "You've seen this before, of course. In your interpretation book clubs, you explored themes that appear in more than one book, and last year, when you read historical fiction, I know you did some similar work.

"Children, what's interesting about this is that we're reading novels that are fantasy—they're made up, they have magic in them! Yet we're seeing similar themes to ones that came up in realistic and historical fiction.

"It's all made me wonder, children, if perhaps some of these themes aren't even universal just to books—maybe they're big themes in the world, too. So I thought we might do an inquiry today, to explore this question. To do that let's begin with an assumption."

 Name the teaching point.

"Readers, today I want to teach you that knowledgeable readers assume that some themes are so important, so universal, that they appear in more than one book, and across history as well. Sophisticated readers, then, are alert for these themes, and they bring their knowledge of history to what they're reading to compare how these themes play out."

TEACHING AND ACTIVE ENGAGEMENT

Invite children to explore universal themes that may relate to both their fantasy novels and history.

"Readers, I know you've studied history in a lot of ways. You learned about Copenhagen and what happened there in WWII during your study of *Number the Stars*. You read other historical fiction and studied the history of that era. You studied the American Revolution, the Civil War, and the civil rights movement. You know the story of Ruby Bridges and

When you refer to work from prior years, it can be really helpful if you actually use the name of the read-aloud text, or hold it up. That kind of physical reminder means that children who are just nodding to be agreeable actually do remember what you're referring to. Do some quick investigation into what were the major read-aloud texts children encountered in prior years, and you may want to have these books on hand. You'll also encourage children to think and talk across texts more, when you and they can physically point to books they've read before.

This is a sophisticated teaching point. If you need to create bridges to academic language here, you might gather some students before the lesson and say something like this. "Sophisticated readers think about the themes that are coming up in the stories they're reading, and they wonder if some of those themes might come up in true stories too, like this story of Ruby Bridges." Using specific examples, and more social language, may help more students grasp sophisticated ideas.

the story of Rosa Parks. What I'm saying, then, is that you know a lot about historical characters just as you know a lot about the fictional ones you're studying now.

"Just for a moment, turn and remind each other of some of these characters' accomplishments. What quests were they on? What dragons did they face?"

I hand out half-slips of paper with themes written on them to each club. "Readers, I'm handing your club a slip of paper with some of the universal themes you've been discussing."

"For our inquiry, ask yourself first: which of these themes have you seen in your book and also in history?"

"Go ahead, I can see you're dying to discuss with your club. First, ask yourself which of these plays out most strongly in your series. So rank these themes. Then see if you can narrow down to one that you also have seen in history—a period of history that you actually know something about!"

I gave clubs some minutes to work and circulated among them, helping them make wise choices, reminding them of history they had studied and the characters they knew. For some clubs, I passed out familiar picture books, such as *I Am Rosa Parks*, for them to peruse as reminders. When they had all chosen a theme to focus on, I gathered their attention again.

Recap their work so far as a series of steps. Invite children to try comparing how these themes play out across fiction and history.

"Readers, what you've done so far is to remind yourself of some themes that have appeared again and again in your reading. Then you've done some ranking of these themes by discussing them with other readers who've read the same book. Then you asked yourself, 'Of the themes we've seen the most, do we also see any of those in history?'

"Let's take it one step further. Now that you and your club have narrowed down your choice, try to bring what you know about that history, including the important characters and events, to compare how that theme plays out in your book and in history. Let's see what new insights you come to. For now, why don't you focus on one theme and one historical era or character."

As children talked, I circulated, sometimes gathering their examples to highlight, other times jumping in to help move the discussion along.

Your students will find it helpful if you have a chart on hand with the names of some historical characters, along with their accomplishments and time periods, which reflects the work students have done in social studies. Grant Wiggins has noted again and again that many children need simple cuing systems to recall and apply prior learning. Find out what they studied in fourth grade as well as fifth, and prepare a chart, timeline, or list that will help raise the level of their work.

Common Universal Themes

Kids grow up fast in times of trouble.

Even ordinary people or minor characters can affect events.

Ordinary people can be capable of great courage.

When people band together they can build power to change.

Where there is power, there is also resistance.

Humans are capable of great evil to each other, and great goodness.

Summarize: quoting children; elevating their discourse; providing an example of what this work sounds like.

"Readers, you're doing some beautiful work. I love how you're bringing what you know about history to bear on your book club discussions. Sam's group, for instance, talked about the theme, 'Where there is power, there is also resistance.' They've been reading Harry Potter, and they talked about how the stronger Voldemort and his evil henchmen get, the stronger Harry and his friends become. It's like they find more power to resist, as they see how dangerous Voldemort is booming. *Then* they compared Harry becoming strong when things got bad, to Washington and his troops finding strength during Valley Forge. That was a dark time too, and as men froze and starved, and some men died, they became even more determined to finish their war for independence."

LINK

Remind students of the reason for doing this work at all, and send them off.

"Readers, what's so beautiful about the work you just did is it reminds us that we can learn from characters in books just as we can learn from characters in history and in our lives. All of those are sources of strength for us. Today and every day when you're reading, then, remember that the comparisons you make and the patterns you see across books, history, and your life *matter*. They'll be sources of lessons, comfort, and inspiration.

"I'm adding this important point to our anchor chart."

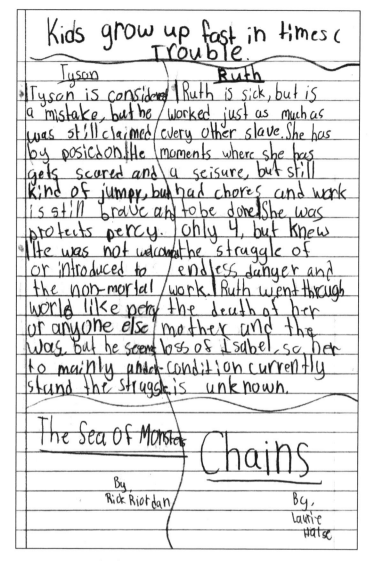

FIG. 9–1 Maya thinks about themes across fantasy, historical fiction, and history.

Historical Character	Accomplishments	Quests	Dragons
George Washington	• Unified the American Army • Beat the British	• To win out against the British – a bigger army	• Cold & hunger in Valley Forge • Getting men to believe in the fight
Rosa Parks	• Getting Civil Rights passed CIVIL RIGHTS ACT of 1964 BECOMES LAW!	• For equality (buses, schools) • Desegregation	• Segregation • Racism • Ignorance DRINKING FOUNTAIN WHITE COLORED
Harriet Tubman	• Freed slaves • Underground railroad BE FREE OR DIE	• Get to the North • Escape the South/ Slavery N	• Hatred • Branding • Lynching • Slavery

Sophisticated Readers of Fantasy . . .

- Research the setting (What kind of place is it?).
- Ask about power—who has it, evidence, kinds of power.
- Learn alongside the main character.
- Keep track of multiple problems.
- Suspend judgment about characters and places.
- Read metaphorically by
  - Considering the "dragons" characters face
  - Applying life lessons learned in fiction to their own lives
  - Considering internal as well as external quest structures
- **Comparing themes in fantasy and history**

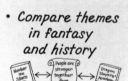

• Compare themes in fantasy and history

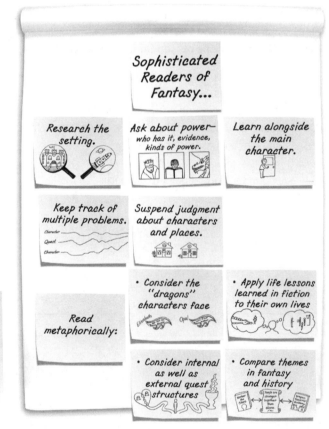

"Now, off you go to read! I'll be eager to hear about the new thinking you're doing."

I motioned to a few students. "Some of you probably need to meet with your clubs for a minute to make some plans. Be sure to decide if you're meeting today and if you want to talk about this new work, or if you're already 'on' about something." I gestured to our anchor chart.

Bringing Story Schema to the Study of Narrative Nonfiction, and Historical Lenses to the Study of Novels

THIS IS ONE OF the days when you can predict that if you want your students to fully access the work they began in the lesson, some will need extra support. You can also predict that some of your students will be ready to run with this work, and will be ready to take it to higher levels. Thinking of your clubs and your knowledge of your students not only from reading workshop, but also from social studies units of study, you might be prepared to support and extend today's lesson.

Bring story schema to the study of biographies and historical narratives.

You might, for example, want to gather one group of students and do some interactive read aloud focused on the art of thinking about narrative nonfiction through the lens of story. I gathered a small group of four students around *The Story of Ruby Bridges*, making

sure I had at least one fluent reader in the group. We had read this story earlier in our Civil Rights unit, but I suggested that that we read it again, thinking about the story through the lenses of "quests" and "big themes or life lessons." "Let's divide into partnerships," I suggested. "Partnership 1, can you be responsible for thinking about quests in this story? Will you jot some notes as you're listening, compare your thinking, and be ready to share? Partnership 2, can you be responsible for thinking about big themes or life lessons? And will you do the same? Jot some notes, compare your thoughts, be ready to share. I'll begin reading, and then I'll turn it over to you. You'll have to help each other know when to pause, so you can jot some notes, and when you want to talk to a partner."

I began to read, pausing after only a few pages, saying, "I can tell you've got some thoughts. Go ahead, I bet you want to jot and then talk to a partner." I waited until they had jotted for a moment and were talking to each other, then gathered them back to share their thinking. Soon the group was eagerly comparing their thoughts on quests for justice, quests for a safe school, quests for learning, and Ruby's internal quest to be brave and to be a role model, with their thoughts on big themes such as "Even children can play a big role in social justice." I helped them with the logistics of planning for reading, jotting, talking, and managing their time. Then I left them to it, suggesting that they pause eventually to record their big ideas to see if any of them played out for their club novels, as well.

Bring historical lenses to interpretation of novels.

Next, I gathered the Narnia group. For them, I had rescued a basket of our WWII and Holocaust books that they had used in social studies. I placed these in the center of the club. "Readers," I said, "I think you may be ready to take this work one step farther. What you've done so far, is you've thought about big themes that are in your novels. You've compared them to themes that have come up in true stories, like the stories of Ruby Bridges or Rosa Parks. You can also think about what was going on in history *when your books were written*, and think about how your novels might be tackling some of those historical themes."

(continued)

MID-WORKSHOP TEACHING   **Creating Records of Our Thinking so Other Readers Can Borrow It**

"Readers, Christian just reminded me of something important for our community. He was complaining (I winked at Christian) in the nicest way, that he just realized an idea he has been trying to explain is one that Julia and Rosie had also been working on. Christian reminded me that when readers come up with some big thinking, like ideas for themes that they have seen in a lot of books we're reading, it doesn't do any of us any good if that thinking is private!

"So readers, if you or your club comes up with an idea that you think other readers would want to borrow, can you figure out how to make that idea public? Maybe you want to put it up on the wall, and you can start a corner of ideas for universal themes. Or maybe you want to email your thoughts to your classmates. As sophisticated fifth-graders, you're engaged with a whole reading community that is bigger than your club, so take this on, okay?"

I gave the club my iPad, which was open to the Wikipedia page on the conception of Narnia. "It says here that kids were being evacuated to the country in England, and they were separated from their families. London was being attacked by the Germans, being bombed and destroyed." I waited a moment, watching kids' faces. "I bet that gives you some ideas for intersections between what was happening in history and what was happening in this series." I waited for nods, then motioned to the basket of picture books and chapter books about World War II. "Here's what I want to suggest. I'm going to suggest that you flip through some of these books, reminding yourself of some of the big events and characters of World War II and the Holocaust, which you've studied a bit before. You'll remember from studying history around *Number the Stars* last year, and our work in social studies. Jot some notes as you go. Then when you're ready, why don't you share your thoughts as a club, thinking deeply about how events in history might be echoed in your novels, and especially, any big themes that might be true then. Does it feel like you could do this work without me?"

Satisfied with their nods, I left them to it. You'll have kids like this in your class who are eager to do more, to be challenged intellectually, and to pursue independent inquiries.

Percy Jackson & The Olympians	When people band together they can build power to change
	Annabeth
	Annabeth has to work with Tyson, who is a cyclops, and Annabeth doesn't have a good past with cyclops, but Percy insists upon it. Annabeth also has to work with Percy, who Annabeth is fine with now, but wasn't too sure when they first met, given they're parents past, but when the three of them work together they act in such a way that is simply heroic.
	Sophia **Sophia's war**
	Sophia has to work with Mr. Townsend and comunacate with him about the information that she discovers and she is telling him very valueable information. Sophia also has to get her information to Mr. Townsend in a safe and sucure way, in widch they both have to work together to keep it that way. When Sophia gives him the information, that puts the rebels one step ahead of the British.

FIG. 9–2 Aly compares themes in fantasy and historical fiction, learning big life lessons.

Considering How Characters' Perspectives Might Shape the Themes They End Up Demonstrating

Invite students to think about characters' perspectives and how they might relate to themes.

"Readers, I have a challenge for you. The Narnia group has been researching historical perspectives, like those of children who were evacuated from London during World War II. They've been thinking about how those perspectives might help shape some of the themes in their stories." I gestured to where I had jotted these themes, and underneath them, a certain historical perspective.

Themes

- Kids in war grow up fast.
- Danger brings out the best and the worst in people.

Perspective

- Kids who were evacuated from London during WWII.

"Think about those ideas for a moment. Think about how the perspective of children who are evacuated might help develop one of those themes."

I waited for a moment, then motioned for them to talk with a partner, listening in so I could highlight a few points.

"Readers, I here you saying that the perspective of kids who have been evacuated will help develop the theme of how danger shapes us, because they're *living* in that danger. Their perspective as they experience those dangers will show whether it brings out the best or worst. For example, it brought out the best in Lucy, but the worst in Edmund."

I motioned to the books on their own laps. "Readers, I'm guessing that this thinking isn't true just for the Narnia readers. Will you take a moment and think about the perspectives of characters in your stories? Consider how those perspectives might help develop certain themes. Go ahead, think, and when you're ready, grab your club to compare your thinking."

WRITE ABOUT A BIG IDEA ABOUT CHARACTERS, QUEST STRUCTURES, OR THEME

Readers, today you did some big thinking about themes in novels. You've also done big thinking before this about characters and about quest structures.

Tonight for homework, choose one of these and write a paragraph, a notebook entry, or a letter that shows your best thinking about a big idea you have about characters, structure, or theme. Do your best thinking work, and be ready in class tomorrow for us to look at these entries closely. Take home as well your Student Assessment Tool and rubrics to help you with this work.

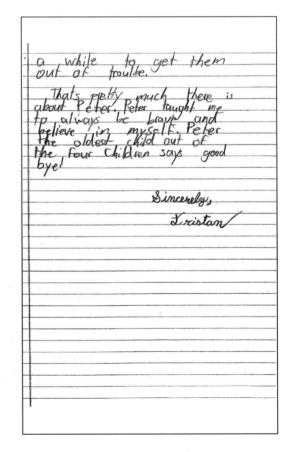

Dear Julia,

I am reading the book The Chronicles of Narnia The Dawn Treader. In this book there is a character named Peter. Peter is the oldest child out of the four main children. Peter and his siblings Edmund, Susan, and Lucy travel into a wardrobe that leads to Narnia. In Narnia a lot of mysterious things are there. In Narnia animals can talk and/or understand humans. I think that Peter taught me to be brave all the time and I also think he taught me to always believe in myself no matter what.

Peter is always brave and always believes in himself, Peter never gives up. When Peter was fighting the White Witch he never gave up he kept on fighting but, afterwards he told every one that he single handedly

take down the White Whicth when Aslan, Edmund, Susan, and Lucy all helped.

The Chronicles of Narnia The Dawn Treader is just the fifth book out of seven. Peter is in six of the books. Peter is always courages when he is in battle. Peter is brave and has no fears so far. Peter is sort of selfish because he take all the glory for defeating the White Whicth and become the High King whe Edmund, Susan, and Lucy just became normal kings and queens. Peter and his siblings take down a lot of bad guys like the White Whicth and Lord Miraz. Peter and his siblings also encountered the great lion, Aslan who shows up once in

a while to get them out of trouble.

Thats pretty much there is about Peter. Peter taught me to always be brave and believe in myself. Peter the oldest child out of the four children says good bye!

Sincerely,

Tristan

FIG. 9–3 Tristan writes to a classmate to sum up his thinking about character, themes, and quest. Go, Tristan!

Session 10

Self-Assessing Using Learning Progressions

ear Teachers,

We suggest that today you revisit your work on assessment literacy with your students. Remind students that readers can evaluate and raise the level of their work themselves, when they have in mind the qualities of strong work. In particular, your readers have been working on developing sophisticated thinking about character, structure, and theme. To prepare for today's lesson, last night's homework required children to come in today with one strong entry in their reader's notebook that represents their best thinking about character, structure, or theme. They also brought home the Narrative Reading Learning Progression for these skills.

Your goal today is twofold. One is to help children raise the level of their work immediately. The more long-term goal, though, is to inculcate a habit of self-assessment, so that your children go forth as learners who have agency over their own success. Chances are that in their future classes, your students will receive a lot of assignments, sometimes without a lot of instruction. If they've learned that they can investigate or even just reflect on what strong work looks like before they begin working, and then again as they revise their work, they'll be much better positioned to excel.

To get ready for today's lesson, you'll need a few things. Your children will need at least one notebook entry that represents their best thinking about character, structure, or theme. You will also need a few entries about theme or character in *The Thief of Always* for your read-alouds or for the Performance Assessment text. When we say *entry,* we mean a notebook entry that is a paragraph-long sample of writing about reading. You will need one sample that you will evaluate against the learning progression in your minilesson. That entry needs to be flawed in obvious ways so that children can see where to improve it. You will also need one sample, at a lower level, for your small-group work—also flawed in obvious ways. Finally, you'll want an exemplar that demonstrates the qualities listed in the learning progression. If all of these entries use a familiar text, and all of them do theme work, it will be easier for the children to compare them. If you're pressed for time, you can use the examples that accompany the pre-unit Performance Assessment, as these are already available for you and will be familiar to the children. These are found on the online resources or you can make your own with some markers and paper.

MINILESSON

For your minilesson, then, you might start with a connection that reminds children of the work that top athletes do when they want to excel. You might, for instance, play a video of Shaun White practicing his tricks as he gets ready for a snowboard competition. Or invite children to think of any experience when they revised their work by holding it up against an expert's. Children will usually talk about listening to musical performances as they ready themselves for their own performance, or studying videos of their own performances and comparing them to top-notch athletes.

Use children's familiarity with that kind of "improve your own performance" effort and energy for that kind of agency to show that they can do that same work academically. For your teaching point you might say, "Today I want to teach you that you don't have to wait for someone else to give you feedback on your thinking. You can evaluate it yourself. Often, when students want to excel, they pause in the midst of their work to ask, 'Is there anything I could do better?' and they hold their own work up against a mental model of strong work."

Your demonstration will be important in this lesson. This isn't the first time, even in this unit, that students have self-assessed. Yet, each time is an opportunity to teach children to be more discerning. If you make the work seem too easy, then children don't hold themselves to a high enough standard. Have on hand a snippet of writing that represents your thinking (or you can say it's a child's work, just not a real child in this grade or class), for instance, about theme. If you are making your own sample, make sure that this writing about reading has some of the qualities that are on the learning progression for fifth grade, but not all, and exaggerate that lack so kids can really see it. For example, don't include any specific quotes, and only mention one theme. Then, be sure to have the child-facing rubrics on hand. Together with the children, evaluate your sample, and come up with one or two ways to raise the level (finding specific quotes as evidence, exploring more than one theme), and then add something right then and there to revise.

Narrative Reading Learning Progression		
	Grade 5	Grade 6
	INTERPRETIVE READING	
Inferring about Characters and Other Story Elements *Character Traits*	I can see places in a story where the characters are not what they seem at first. For example, the character might say or act as if he or she doesn't care, but readers see signs that he or she really does. That is, I see hidden sides to characters. I know that what drives the character (his or her motivation) can be complicated. There may be several things that drive or pressure a character, and often he or she is pulled in conflicting ways.	I continue to develop theories about main and minor characters, thinking how they are affected by other story elements such as the plot, setting, issues, and conflicts.
Character Response/Change	I can notice small, subtle changes in characters in addition to more obvious ones. I know that the causes of these changes may also be subtle or complicated. I think about how a character's change is important to the whole story. I am aware that characters can represent ways that people can be—the bully who is insecure, the boy with feelings locked inside—and that when a character changes or learns something, this can teach readers about ways that people like that character deal with challenges or issues.	I can distinguish between temporary changes and changes in the character's perspective. I consider how inside and outside forces cause characters to change. I understand that a character's changes can be symbolic and can connect to bigger themes in the story.
Supporting Thinking with Text Evidence	I support my ideas with specific details and quotes from several parts of the story. I select these because they are strong and they actually do match my points. I discuss how those details and citations support my ideas.	I support my ideas and claims with specific details from the story, and I can evaluate this evidence for which is strongest.

For the active engagement, have children get out the entry they composed for homework last night and start evaluating all the parts of it, using the Learning Progression tool. It helps if you have colored pens, or small attractive Post-its, for kids to mark up with their own work. Swag helps! We suggest that you encourage readers to use a larger Post-it to fix up their work right then and there, revising to bring part or all of it up a level.

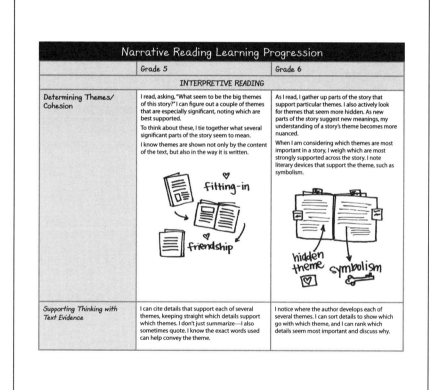

Narrative Reading Learning Progression

	Grade 5	Grade 6
INTERPRETIVE READING		
Determining Themes/ Cohesion	I read, asking, "What seem to be the big themes of this story?" I can figure out a couple of themes that are especially significant, noting which are best supported. To think about these, I tie together what several significant parts of the story seem to mean. I know themes are shown not only by the content of the text, but also in the way it is written.	As I read, I gather up parts of the story that support particular themes. I also actively look for themes that seem more hidden. As new parts of the story suggest new meanings, my understanding of a story's theme becomes more nuanced. When I am considering which themes are most important in a story, I weigh which are most strongly supported across the story. I note literary devices that support the theme, such as symbolism.
Supporting Thinking with Text Evidence	I can cite details that support each of several themes, keeping straight which details support which theme. I don't just summarize—I also sometimes quote. I know the exact words used can help convey the theme.	I notice where the author develops each of several themes. I can sort details to show which go with which theme, and I can rank which details seem most important and discuss why.

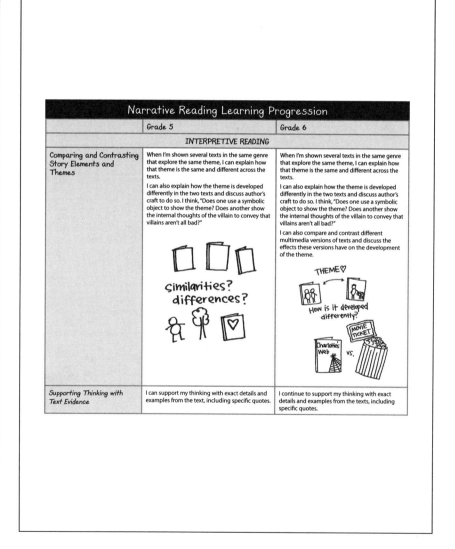

Narrative Reading Learning Progression

	Grade 5	Grade 6
INTERPRETIVE READING		
Comparing and Contrasting Story Elements and Themes	When I'm shown several texts in the same genre that explore the same theme, I can explain how that theme is the same and different across the texts. I can also explain how the theme is developed differently in the two texts and discuss author's craft to do so. I think, "Does one use a symbolic object to show the theme? Does another show the internal thoughts of the villain to convey that villains aren't all bad?"	When I'm shown several texts in the same genre that explore the same theme, I can explain how that theme is the same and different across the texts. I can also explain how the theme is developed differently in the two texts and discuss author's craft to do so. I think, "Does one use a symbolic object to show the theme? Does another show the internal thoughts of the villain to convey that villains aren't all bad?" I can also compare and contrast different multimedia versions of texts and discuss the effects these versions have on the development of the theme.
Supporting Thinking with Text Evidence	I can support my thinking with exact details and examples from the text, including specific quotes.	I continue to support my thinking with exact details and examples from the texts, including specific quotes.

For your link, emphasize that this kind of immediate revision demonstrates how quickly learners can raise the level of their work when they deliberately set out to do so. Send children off, encouraging them to use the other parts of the progression to revise other entries, and to have them in mind as they do their best work going forward.

CONFERRING AND SMALL-GROUP WORK

Today is one of those rare days when you may want to center your conferences and small-group work precisely around the work of the minilesson. It's just so important that children learn to evaluate their own work, set reasonably ambitious goals, and strive to improve quickly. You can predict that some children may need support with two aspects of this work—evaluating the specific things they are doing and not doing, and figuring out how to revise once they've set goals. Here's where student exemplars can be very helpful. We've provided some with the performance assessment or you may want to write one or two, using *The Thief of Always* as the text. Anything you can do to ground the work in something familiar will help. It should take about five minutes to write these. Remember, you are writing a child's response!

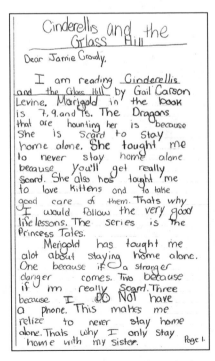
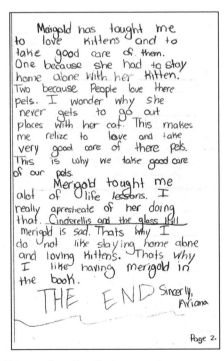

FIG. 10–1   Ariana explains how she learned lessons from her fantasy novel.

When you've gathered a few children who need some guided practice, take out a lower-level sample for them (lower than the one you did in the lesson) that is closer to the level these children are writing. Have the children practice evaluating this one, guiding them as needed to see what's missing—for example, specific quotes and details as text evidence. Together, come up with two or three things that the reader could add, using the progression, such as tracing more than one theme or supporting a theme with more evidence from across the story. Then bring out your exemplar that demonstrates those things, and help children underline and circle the important new parts. Finally, set them up to add on to their own entries.

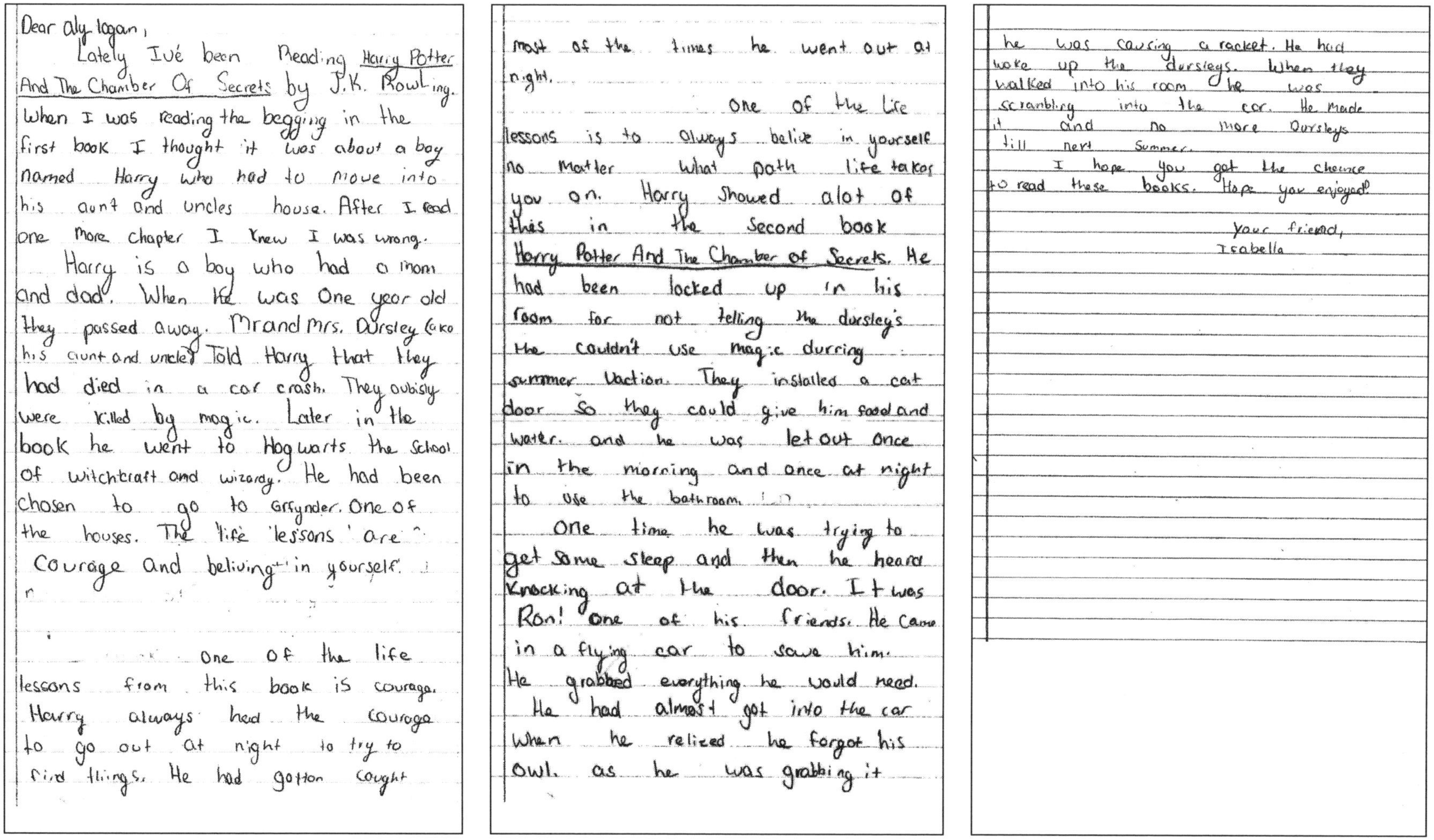

Dear Aly logan,

Lately Iué been Reading Harry Potter And The Chamber Of Secrets by J.K. Rowling. When I was reading the begging in the first book I thought it was about a boy named Harry who had to move into his aunt and uncles house. After I read one more chapter I knew I was wrong.

Harry is a boy who had a mom and dad. When He was One year old they passed away. Mr and Mrs. Dursley (ako his aunt and uncle) Told Harry that they had died in a car crash. They obisly were killed by magic. Later in the book he went to Hogwarts the School Of witchcraft and wizary. He had been chosen to go to Grfynder. One of the houses. The life 'lessons' are Courage and beliving in yourself.

One of the life lessons from this book is courage. Harry always had the courage to go out at night to try to find things. He had gotten Cought

most of the times he went out at night.

One of the life lessons is to always belive in yourself no matter what path life takes you on. Harry Showed alot of this in the second book Harry Potter And The Chamber of Secrets. He had been locked up in his room for not telling the dursley's He couldn't use magic durring summer Vaction. They installed a cat door so they could give him food and water. and he was let out once in the morning and once at night to use the bathroom.

One time he was trying to get some sleep and then he heard Knocking at the door. It was Ron! one of his friends. He came in a flying car to save him. He grabbed everything he would need. He had almost got into the car when he relized he forgot his Owl. as he was grabbing it

he was causing a racket. He had woke up the dursleys. When they walked into his room he was scrambling into the car. He made it and no more Dursleys till next Summer.

I hope you got the chence to read these books. Hope you enjoyed!

Your friend,
Isabella

FIG. 10–2   Isabella explains to her buddy Aly how her novel taught her about courage.

Mid-Workshop Teaching

We suggest that you use the mid-workshop teaching today to turn students to some playful work that will celebrate their mid-point in the fantasy unit. They did some challenging intellectual work today, and you want to hold onto that energy, while also holding onto their energy for fabulous fantasy. At this point, therefore, you might invite children to celebrate the mid-point of the unit by preparing a dramatic read-aloud interpretation of a scene to share with another club. Encourage them to think of this scene as a trailer—a way to highlight an important theme and to entice another club to read that book. So one club member might introduce the scene, and a few or all might perform it—and they want to choose something dramatic that will make others say, "Oh, I want to read that, too!" Children don't need a lot of time for this kind of work. Get them going, saying they'll have about ten minutes to prepare and two minutes to give their scene!

SHARE AND CELEBRATION

Set clubs up in paired groupings, so one club can present their book introduction and scene to another. Before they begin, tell the club who is watching that their job will be to say what most interested them in the book—what made them want to read it! Then enjoy watching your young dramatists ham it up. Meanwhile, you enjoy a sense of having done some serious and lovely work with your readers so far.

Yours,
Colleen and Mary

Using Information to Better Understand Fantasy Stories

IN THIS SESSION, you'll teach students that readers of fantasy refer to nonfiction texts and references to more fully understand the world they are reading about.

GETTING READY

✔ Prior to this minilesson, read aloud Chapters 20 and 21 from *The Thief of Always*.

✔ If you have a projector for your class computer, set it up before teaching this minilesson so that you will be able to show your online research to students (see Teaching).

✔ Before this session, gather nonfiction materials such as reference books, nonfiction trade books, and articles, and place in baskets (see Link).

✔ If you are able to provide Internet search access to your students, you will likely want to do so (see Link).

✔ Have your copy of *Mufaro's Beautiful Daughters* on hand (see Active Engagement).

✔ Download images and an excerpt of information on Great Zimbabwe. Two good sites are: http://www.bbc.co.uk/worldservice/africa/features/storyofafrica/10chapter1.shtml, http://www.metmuseum.org/toah/hd/zimb/hd_zimb.htm. Links are available in the online resources. You could also use the search terms "Great Zimbabwe history" (see Active Engagement).

✔ Introduce Bend III anchor chart, "How Fantasy Readers Use Elements from the Real World to Understand Fantasy (and sometimes vice versa)" (see Link).

TODAY IS THE FIRST DAY OF A NEW BEND. You are officially in the second half of the unit. Students very much have their fantasy sea legs. They are now ready to flex their minds a little to consider some ideas about fantasy that even the most dedicated fantasy reader is likely to have considered. Namely, in this bend, your readers will be immersing themselves in the connections between fantasy (stories based on things that could *never* happen) and fact (something that is meant to be true and provable). To kick off this work, you will be pairing reading fantasy stories with short nonfiction.

When the television show, *Game of Thrones*, based on George R. R. Martin's fantasy series, hit the airwaves, adults all over the world rediscovered their love of the fantasy genre. People who never loved fantasy found themselves falling in love with it for the first time. As the series has progressed, fans have wanted more between installments, and some have made the thrilling discovery that Martin, at least in part, has been relying to some extent on history to inspire his writing. For example, he has stated that Medieval England and the wrestling over the throne, especially during the War of the Roses, had a large influence. Knowing that his fantastical stories are, at least in part, based on fact, helps explain why they feel so real. And Martin is not the only fantasy writer to admit as much. Many fantasy writers will admit to sitting at their desks with piles of nonfiction references texts at the ready to help create geographic structures, flora and fauna, animal behavior, and architecture.

In this session, you will flip this idea a bit, encouraging students to lean on reading nonfiction as a companion piece to their fantasy reading. Students might be surprised by the suggestion; however, it is actually a quite natural counterpart to the work many fantasy authors do on the other side of the desk. For the nonfiction work in this session there are a few options available to you, depending on your resources. If you and your students have Internet search access, this would be a great time to employ it. Additionally, students could use nonfiction books from the classroom library, reference texts from the school or local library, and any articles you might be able to collect and print.

Using Information to Better Understand Fantasy Stories

CONNECTION

Explain that many fantasy writers use nonfiction to help them develop ideas for their novels.

"Jane Yolen, the author of *Merlin and the Dragons* and so many other fantasy titles, talks about how much research she does for her fantasy books. She has mentioned that she often has flower guidebooks and geography texts and other reference books around when she writes fantasy. She says that sometimes it's because she wants to get the fact as correct as possible. For instance, she might want be asking herself, 'Could flowers grow on this sort of cliff? If so, what would they look like?'

"Other famous fantasy writers use real history to come up with their stories. A fantasy writer for adults, George R. R. Martin has spoken about using The War of the Roses, a very old war that took place in England, as part of how he developed his fantasy series.

"It's not unusual for fantasy writers, those writers who probably have the biggest imaginations of all, to use real facts to help their nonfiction stories come to life."

 Name the teaching point.

"Just as writers of fantasy refer to nonfiction texts to develop the worlds of their stories, readers of fantasy can refer to nonfiction texts to more fully understand the world they are reading about. As readers of fantasy, you can use reference texts, online factual information, or other nonfiction texts to build a full image of the characters, settings, and events you are reading about."

TEACHING

Demonstrate how to research and use information from nonfiction texts to more fully understand the world evoked in a fantasy story.

"I thought this might be interesting to try in a book I've already read, *The Lion, the Witch and the Wardrobe*. I think the first step is to decide what topic I want to read more about. So I might think a bit about the book first." I held up my

In addition to giving students another opportunity to practice their nonfiction reading skills in a new context, this session also helps reinforce the felt knowledge of the author on the other side of the book they are reading. Thinking of the facts behind the fantasy reminds students, in yet another way, that authors have perspectives and make choices.

You might be surprised to see me reference The Lion, The Witch and The Wardrobe. *I chose to do so because I knew some students would be currently reading or will have read the text, further building the idea of a shared culture of literacy. Additionally, there is sometimes a need to change up the texts talked about in a unit just to keep from being redundant. However, if you would prefer to choose from your current read-aloud or one of the other picture books or short stories you have read, that would also be a valid choice.*

dog-eared copy. "I know this book takes place in the English countryside during World War II, and I also know that there are real animals and objects mentioned in this book, like lions, beavers, and Turkish delight. Learning more about these things might give me more insights into the book."

I looked to my laptop perched nearby and a few books I had pulled from the classroom's nonfiction library. These included two general books about England and a book about World War II, as well as a book on beavers and one on lions. "I think I'm going to start by reading about beavers. Mainly because Mr. and Mrs. Beaver were two of my favorite characters."

I said, "Students, you can keep track of my work by checking the big screen." I turned to my computer and typed into the search window, voicing over, "Beavers in England." When I clicked on the link, up popped a short article on beavers in Great Britain. I read a bit to myself, sort of in an audible whisper.

"Whoa! So this is saying that beavers have been extinct in England for 400 years. So that means . . ." I turned to look at the copyright date in my novel, "This book was written like sixty years ago, so they were definitely extinct then. And I am sure C. S. Lewis was well aware of that fact. But, he chose to put beavers in his novel. So this makes me think all sorts of things. Like, did he do it to show that Narnia was *really* another country, definitely not in England, because it had things that didn't exist in England? Not just fauns and witches and endless winters, but also extinct animals like the beaver?" I made a point to indicate I was reading and thinking more. "And also it talks about how industrious they are building dams. Which makes sense. Mr. and Mrs. Beaver in the novel are clearly hard workers, which fits with the facts about real beavers, too."

I looked away from my computer and back to the students. "My mind is overflowing with new ideas, just thinking about the facts I learned from reading a short article about beavers. I'm thinking about the choices Lewis made about including beavers as characters. But now I want to learn all I can about those other topics too. Like, about lions and the country of England and maybe even Turkish delight!"

Originally this lesson was written with England's climate as the nonfiction topic. The topic itself is less important than your legitimate interest in it and the likeliness that students might think of a parallel topic in their own fantasy novels.

In this lesson I demonstrate a quick Internet search. I could just as easily have looked at an article or a book, but if I have technology that I would like students to incorporate into their reading lives, I try to do so.

I looked up pictures and facts of castles to figure out where Wiglaf is living now. I learned that castles were cold and dirty! No wonder he is unhappy. I also learned that people did believe in dragons. They made TAPRESTIS WITH THEM.

FIG. 11–1   Christian researches medieval castles to learn about daily life for reading *Dragon Slayer's Academy*.

ACTIVE ENGAGEMENT

Set students up to revisit an earlier class fantasy read-aloud, alongside nonfiction.

"I thought we could try this with another one of our books, *Mufaro's Beautiful Daughters*." I held up the picture book to remind them of the story. "As you probably remember, this story is inspired by a Zimbabwean folktale, and it partly takes place in the old city of Great Zimbabwe." I pulled down the map to show them where Zimbabwe is. "From the art we can tell that there are some ruins. We could read up on those ruins. We could read up on garter snakes or gold or even royalty."

With the students, read an excerpt of a companion nonfiction piece, giving them time to discuss the new ideas they get about the fantasy piece by reading nonfiction.

"Let's go ahead and read a bit about Great Zimbabwe. As we read, let's think about what we're learning and what it's making us think about in the story." I read an excerpt from an online article about the ruins of Great Zimbabwe.

> *Great Zimbabwe's most enduring and impressive remains are its stone walls. These walls were constructed from granite blocks gathered from the exposed rock of the surrounding hills. Since this rock naturally splits into even slabs and can be broken into portable sizes, it provided a convenient and readily available building resource. All of Great Zimbabwe's walls were fitted without the use of mortar by laying stones one on top of the other, each layer slightly more recessed than the last to produce a stabilizing inward slope.*
>
> *Excerpt from http://www.metmuseum.org/toah/hd/zimb/hd_zimb.htm*

Before I even signaled to talk, students were atwitter. Discussions about the ruins and the stone, and their surprise that the story was based on a real place bounced from one student to the next.

"I think one of the things this is telling me, is that the real people who lived there were very intelligent to be able to build something like that. And the book has pictures of the ruins everywhere. Which makes the idea that the king in the story was so intelligent make so much sense," I overheard one student say.

"Wow, class, I need to stop you!" I waited for the buzz to stop before continuing. "I think it's fair to say that you can all see how knowing some of the facts behind *Mufaro's Beautiful Daughters* can really add interest and elevate our thinking in that book."

I chose to use this picture book because it was a familiar one to students, and also one they are unlikely to realize has a real-world connection. You could just as easily choose another picture book or short story your students are familiar with, but that has a clear nonfiction connection.

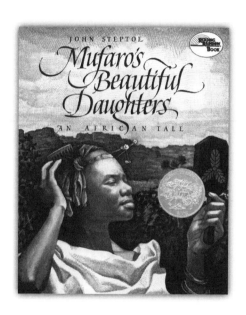

LINK

Remind students about the teaching point, as well as making clear that this is not something that can be done everyday as a fantasy reader.

"Readers, what I showed you today is by no means something I would expect you to try every day. But, I do think it's one of those things that would be fun and interesting to try occasionally. Especially if there's a book that you feel particularly invested in, wanting to understand as fully as possible. But, it's also possible that even just a quick flip through a related nonfiction book or a quick Internet search will do some interesting things for your reading. At the very least, you might picture things better, and at the most, you might be able to better understand characters, themes, symbols, or ideas.

"I'm starting an anchor chart for this bend. The first point summarizes what you just learned."

How Fantasy Readers Use Elements
from the Real World to Understand
Fantasy (and sometimes vice versa)

- Use information from nonfiction texts to better understand fantasy stories.

Give students a quick tip to help them navigate the logistics of balancing their fantasy novels and their nonfiction work.

As the students started to get up from the rug, I stopped them. "The computers in the back are available to your clubs if you want to do some quick research. Just make sure you don't head toward them if someone else is already on them. And, you will notice I placed a few new baskets of nonfiction materials on the shelf with your club books in the library. There are some articles I pulled, as well as some nonfiction texts I know might complement some of the reading you are doing." I pointed to the new baskets. "And, since you are such a curious bunch, I would not be surprised at all to see those baskets fill up as you find some new materials of your own to add."

Supporting Students to Find Appropriate Nonfiction Texts

WHILE YOU SHOULDN'T EXPECT that every student will run off immediately to the nonfiction shelves to do some complementary reading, you might want to be prepared to support the students who do. If you have clubs that are meeting today, you might want to stack the decks a bit and have pulled a relevant nonfiction text or two that you know is accessible for that club to read. You could encourage them to lay that text alongside their conversation to see if it brings any new layers of thinking.

Additionally, you might find you need to review some nonfiction reading skills for some students. Monitoring for sense, determining main ideas, and supporting ideas with text evidence might all be skills that require dusting off. If you still have charts hiding in closets from nonfiction teaching earlier this year, you might want to bring them out and remind students of the work they had done in high-interest nonfiction or content-area texts. "Remember how you used not just the words, but also the charts and illustrations to figure out what a text was trying to teach you? Well that's still true, even as now you are looking for information that will help lift the level of your fantasy reading. See this chart with the different flowers that grow at different elevations in Scotland? That information doesn't show up in the main text—and that's the information that will really help your reading!"

It is also important to be cautious in this work. You will want to make sure that even though nonfiction is fascinating, the children do not go too far afield from their fantasy reading. You will want to be sure that students understand that ultimately the goal is for the nonfiction reading to fuel some new thinking in their fantasy reading. In service of this goal, you might be prepared with some additional nonfiction texts to complement the text you modeled during your lesson or perhaps the class read-aloud. You might find it helpful to model examples of when nonfiction reading is lifting the level of the fantasy reading, "Oh, this definition and description of *dyslexia* is helping me to understand Percy Jackson on a whole different level."

But, examples where the reader goes off the rails—and then corrects herself—can be helpful as well. "Train stations in England can be rather busy places, according to this book. They are much busier almost everywhere than a lot of train stations here in New Jersey, where a lot of people have cars. I mean, I guess Grand Central Station in New York City is really busy—hey—wait a minute—I'm getting way off track and now I'm not even thinking of Harry Potter anymore!"

MID-WORKSHOP TEACHING   **Fantasy Creatures and Words Can Appear in More than One Book, by Different Authors**

"Readers, I'd like to stop you for just a quick minute." When all eyes were on me, I continued, "A few of you have made an interesting discovery. In addition to noticing how nonfiction texts can give you more information about your fantasy novels, you might also note that you can find more information about something *in other fantasy novels*. For example, this club is reading *James and the Giant Peach*, and it mentions something called a 'whangdoodle.' Stephanie remembered that she has read another fantasy novel, *The Last of the Really Great Whangdoodles*, and was using the things that author wrote about whangdoodles to add to the whole club's knowledge.

"When you come across a fantasy creature, you might want to do a little fast digging in your memory, or using other resources, to see if this is one created by this particular author. Or, if this creature is one used often in fantasy and might have a rich literary history. Sometimes knowing that literary history can give us some bigger things to think about when considering the significance of a word or object or creature."

Students Share Their Favorite Fact–Fantasy Finds

Invite students to share their discoveries from today's nonfiction research.

"Readers, I cannot believe how productive your reading time was today. When you were not immersed in your fantasy reading or work with your clubs, you were nose-in-a-book researchers, discovering fascinating facts that elevated your understandings and ideas. Can everyone who tried today's strategy show me a thumbs up?" I saw that almost every student had a thumb in the air.

"Since so many of you made interesting discoveries, I want to make sure everyone has a chance to share. Can you gather yourself in little clumps of three to five people? Just the people who are sitting right around you. Make sure no one is accidentally left out. When you've found your group, why don't you do a quick share of your favorite fantasy-related facts?" I gave the students a few minutes to share, while I listened in.

As the students spoke with each other, I was tickled to see how many of them had returned to the meeting area with not only the novels they were reading, but their nonfiction resources as well. There were guidebooks, history texts, articles, and magazines, sitting cheek by jowl with books featuring unicorns, elves, and talking furniture.

SESSION 11 HOMEWORK

 ## CONTINUE YOUR NONFICTION–FANTASY CROSSOVER WORK

Readers, for homework tonight, will you continue this nonfiction–fantasy crossover work? If you are able to jump online, then do some research to find out if something in your fantasy novel is based in fact. You might also want to look for geography information about the places in your novel.

Then see how those facts impact your understanding of your fantasy reading. Take a few minutes to jot down the facts you learn. Then do some exploration to see what new thoughts or questions that factual information leads you to develop about your fantasy novels.

Session 12

Using Vocabulary Strategies to Figure Out Unfamiliar Words

FANTASY LITERATURE, including fairy tales, has a long connection to special vocabulary and language. For example, the famous Brothers Grimm, who were linguists by training, stumbled upon the rich world of German folktales while studying language development. As self-professed word nerds, one of the main reasons we are such fans of reading fantasy is the rich vocabulary we experience every time we pick up a book. Whether the words are author-invented, archaic, or rarely used, a reader can't help but pick up new vocabulary when reading fantasy. The downside of this is that vocabulary can become the biggest stumbling block for some readers—especially if their vocabulary attack skills are not where they need to be. The good news, much like many of the things we tuck into this highly motivating unit, is that students are often willing to do the hard work required by the sophisticated vocabulary because they so badly want to understand what the author is on about.

In today's session, you continue with the notion that there is much to learn by bringing the "real" world into the world of fantasy reading. This session is slightly different from other sessions in this book because the minilesson is done more as a guided practice session. This means that the teaching and the students' practice will go hand in hand. Students will be reading and working on understanding the vocabulary of the poem "Jabberwocky" while you coach them. The poem was written by Lewis Carroll, many years ago, as a nonsense poem. It is meant to be hard to understand, which makes it a fantastic practice text for vocabulary work. Additionally, it is a fun text to read aloud. I encourage you to prepare for this session ahead of time by listening to someone reading the text aloud so that you feel comfortable with the more acceptable pronunciations. We personally like the reading done by Neil Gaiman, author of *Coraline*, available on YouTube: https://www.youtube.com/watch?v=XDLac7sAFsI.

Another important point is that today's minilesson might run a little longer than a typical minilesson because of the amount of reading and coaching. You might opt to shorten the share time or extend the workshop time, if that is at all possible.

IN THIS SESSION, you'll teach students that specific vocabulary plays an important role in everything they read, especially in fantasy novels. Students should use a whole toolkit of vocabulary strategies to figure out the meanings of unfamiliar words.

GETTING READY

✔ Review the "Word Work" strand in the fifth-grade Narrative Reading Learning Progression.

✔ Prior to this minilesson, read aloud Chapters 22 and 23 from *The Thief of Always*.

✔ To prepare to teach, preread and practice reading aloud the poem, "Jabberwocky." Be ready to display the poem using a digital device or using chart paper. Provide copies of the poem to students (see Teaching and Active Engagement).

✔ Display a chart, "As Fantasy Readers, Use Your Toolkit of Strategies to Tackle an Unfamiliar Word" (see Teaching and Active Engagement).

✔ Display and add to Bend III anchor chart, "How Fantasy Readers Use Elements from the Real World to Understand Fantasy (and sometimes vice versa)" (see Link).

✔ Make sure students have copies of the Narrative Reading Learning Progression for this session (see Share).

Using Vocabulary Strategies to Figure Out Unfamiliar Words

CONNECTION

Tell a story about a time when you were impressed by someone's expert vocabulary knowledge acquired through experience, such as by playing video games.

"The other day I was talking to Christian about Minecraft. I'm not so good at playing it yet, so I was picking up some tips. And so they were giving me some tips about Survival mode. Christian started talking 'mobs being spawned' in caves. And I was just so impressed by Christian using such fancy language, like 'spawn.' So I asked him how he knew that word. He said it was used in the game all the time and that if you played the game a lot, you started to figure out the word and you also started to use it a lot yourself." I noticed a good handful of students were nodding in agreement.

"I realized that playing video games and picking up vocabulary from video games is not so very different than learning and using new vocabulary words from fantasy books. After all, just as in video games, some of the language in fantasy books are made up just for the books (like *Muggles*), and other words are real words that are used a lot in fantasy, but are also used in real-world situations, like *squire* or *cavern*."

 Name the teaching point.

"Today I want to teach you that specific vocabulary plays an important role in everything you read, especially in fantasy novels. You need to pay close attention to words that are new to you, figuring out what those words mean by using your whole toolkit of vocabulary strategies."

You can engage kids by using examples that tap into pop culture in your connections. Students will find it intriguing that their teachers know something about kid culture. It makes it clear that their lives are very much a part of the classroom. Additionally, when you make these kinds of kid-culture references, you can posit yourself as the learner and the students as the experts.

TEACHING AND ACTIVE ENGAGEMENT

Explain that running across challenging vocabulary words in fantasy is common, but it can be intimidating.

"It makes a lot of sense why you might run across so many new vocabulary words in fantasy books. So much of what fantasy writers write about is made up out of their imaginations, so they need to make up new words to describe those invented things. And, even when things aren't made up, so many other fantasy stories take place in unusual or ancient locations which means they require a whole set of unfamiliar words, that while they're real words, are not words we use every day."

Share some familiar strategies for dealing with difficult vocabulary, positing them in the world of fantasy reading.

"As exciting as it is to run into these unfamiliar words, it can sometimes be intimidating. But, here's the thing: you already know so many different strategies for figuring out tricky words. Some of those strategies you learned this year, some you learned in the past. Let's take a look at some of the strategies that we know," I said. I revealed a chart and quickly went over each bullet point.

Introduce a poem or other text that is filled with tricky vocabulary, but is still understandable.

"I saw a lot of you nodding as I went over these strategies. Some of you might know of a strategy or two that is missing from this chart that we can add. I want to remind you that sometimes one strategy will work, but another one won't. Or sometimes you might need more than one strategy at one time to figure out a word. I thought we could take a look at a text together. A very famous poem written by Lewis Carroll, the author of *Alice's Adventures in Wonderland*, is written in a sort of nonsense language. But what I find fun about it, is that it's possible for a careful reader, one who has a toolkit of strategies to rely on, to figure out what a lot of the words in this poem likely mean. I'm going to read this poem to you, and I want you to follow along as I do."

I passed out copies of the poem to the students and then turned to a projected image of the poem as I read it aloud:

Jabberwocky

by Lewis Carroll

'Twas brillig, and the slithy toves
Did gyre and gimble in the wabe:
All mimsy were the borogoves,
And the mome raths outgrabe.
"Beware the Jabberwock, my son!
The jaws that bite, the claws that catch!
Beware the Jubjub bird, and shun
The frumious Bandersnatch!"
He took his vorpal sword in hand;
Long time the manxome foe he sought—
So rested he by the Tumtum tree
And stood awhile in thought.
And, as in uffish thought he stood,
The Jabberwock, with eyes of flame,
Came whiffling through the tulgey wood,

"Jabberwocky" can be great fun to read aloud, but it can also be intimidating, since there are so many nonsense words that don't seem to have a particularly clear pronunciation. You may want to listen to a reading of the poem if you are feeling nervous. There are many readings of the poem on YouTube. My favorite is the one by author Neil Gaiman.

And burbled as it came!
One, two! One, two! And through and through
The vorpal blade went snicker-snack!
He left it dead, and with its head
He went galumphing back.
"And hast thou slain the Jabberwock?
Come to my arms, my beamish boy!
O frabjous day! Callooh! Callay!"
He chortled in his joy.
'Twas brillig, and the slithy tove
Did gyre and gimble in the wabe:
All mimsy were the borogoves,
And the mome raths outgrabe.

I waited a minute as the students' jaws hit the floor. It was clear they were shocked, and a little thrilled, by how much unfamiliar language was being used in the poem.

Model using more than one strategy on a segment of the text to decipher unknown words.

"Now, I think I'm going to take the first stab at working out some of the vocabulary. And I think the first step I'm going to take is going to just get a gist of what's going on. I can tell that the first line is the beginning of a story, because it starts *was* and I know that stories can start that way. And there are words here in this first part that I know that are helping me get the gist too. Like *did*, *in*, *were*. So if I use those words, and sort of rely on my envisioning skills, I think I can tell that *brillig* is either a time or a season. And *slithy toves* are some sort of creature that do something or maybe move in some special way. Because *gyre* and *gimble* sound like moving words . . ." I stopped and showed that I was thinking, keeping my pen under the last line of the first stanza.

"And I feel like these last two lines, 'mimsy were the borogroves' and 'the mome raths outgrabe' are probably more creatures doing some things . . . I could substitute words that make sense. Let's see, like *flimsy* for *mimsy*, since it sounds alike. And *borogroves*, sort of sounds like maybe a butterfly or bird. So, 'All flimsy were the butterflies,' that could work. 'And the mome raths . . . ' seems like they're another kind of animal doing something. Maybe running or screeching . . ." I smiled and then mock wiped my brow.

Set students up to try the same work—read a stanza of the poem, using strategies from the chart to help decipher unknown words.

"So you all saw what I was trying to do. I was using most of the tools from my toolkit to work on understanding as much of the vocabulary as I could. Now, would you help me with the next stanza? Would you be willing to be brave and experiment a bit with our word-solving work?" A few of the students nodded. "Could you, with a partner, look over this next stanza. See which words you need to figure out, and try using your toolkit to help you."

The point of this exercise is not to actually figure out the definition of each nonsense word, but rather to model how a reader can use a plethora of strategies and a lot of perseverance to make sense of words that might at first glance seem impossible. If you feel that this text is too over-the-top challenging, you might opt for one that's more accessible.

The students turned to their partners, poems in front of them. I watched as some students immediately underlined or circled certain words and kept referring to the text as they talked.

"Well, *Jabberwock* is capitalized. So it's a name and based on the fact that whoever is talking is saying 'Beware,' it makes me think that it's a monster of some sort. Maybe a dragon or an ogre?" said one student.

"Don't you feel like *frumious* means either something dangerous or furious or both? Because that's what the word sounds like. And, because it's in the same section as the Jabberwock, it feels like this is all about dangerous things," said LaVon.

Give lean prompts and gentle coaching as students work, making sure to give students plenty of room to try and fail.

I voiced over as the students talked, "Don't forget to look across all the strategies. Remember, some won't work. Some will. Some words need more than one strategy."

The students talked on, requesting that they keep working through the rest of the stanzas, "Each one is getting easier as we read on," one argued. "We've got to keep going." So they did. In the end, most students came to some interesting conclusions about what the words could mean, and they jotted them in the margins of the poem.

LINK

Compliment students on their perseverance in working through the poem.

"I want to congratulate you on all the hard work you just did figuring out those unknown vocabulary words. It was impressive to see so many of you working together, using a few strategies, not just one, to work out what you thought the words could mean. This is exactly the kind of work fantasy readers do all the time. Maybe not to this extreme, but certainly, fantasy readers often find words that they don't know and need to figure out.

"Fun fact—some words, originally made up by authors or fantasy books, ended up becoming real words, used by people in real life. For example, the author J. R. R. Tolkien invented the word *tween*. And, another author named François Rabelais invented the word *gargantuan* in his book about giants. So this goes to show, that even if we think we're learning words for just one book, we might be learning them for life!"

Remind students of the teaching point, as well as other skills they know and can practice.

"When you go off to work today, you'll be reading and some of you will be meeting with your clubs. Clearly only one of the things you'll be doing is figuring out tricky words. You'll also want to be building theories, following themes, using writing to capture all of your thoughts . . . the list goes on."

If you take a moment to review the "Word Work" strand of the Narrative Reading Learning Progression, you'll see that children should be carrying forward a lot of strategies for figuring out new and tricky words. They've also been doing a lot of this work in nonfiction, especially in Unit 2, where they worked to read more complex texts. Get out those charts and examples as reminders!

"Let's add a bullet about vocabulary strategies to our anchor chart."

How Fantasy Readers Use Elements
from the Real World to Understand
Fantasy (and sometimes vice versa)

- Use information from nonfiction texts to better understand fantasy stories.
- **Use vocabulary strategies to figure out unfamiliar words.**

Use vocabulary strategies to figure out unfamiliar words.

Using the Language of the Literature When Having Club Conversations

IF YOUR CLUBS ARE MEETING ON THIS DAY, you might want to coach them toward using more sophisticated, text-specific language in their conversations. So many fifth-grade conversations can end up floundering in generalities and unexplained pronouns. However, wise teachers know that with a little coaching, students can elevate their language. Often, when that language is elevated, students elevate their thinking to match.

Depending on your students, you might decide to do a bit of light coaching toward using more exacting vocabulary. This might sound something like this, "When your club is talking about characters, you want to be sure to call them by name." Or, "I loved the way that Maria looked back into her book to find exactly the term the author used to describe the tool. Then all of you started to use that word too. Nice." Or, "When people are part of a community, they start to use the language of that community. A book club starts to develop a specific language that reflects the books they've read. I would expect the language in this club to be different than the club across the room. You might be talking about wizards, alchemy, and flax, while they might be talking about fairies, changelings, sprites, and gossamer. When we use a certain set of words that fit together like that, we call that cohesion."

Some topics for conversational vocabulary you might consider coaching into include:

- Characters
- Government
- Magic
- Setting
- Actions

It is worth saying that all of this should, of course, be done with a light touch, in a spirit of experimentation and risk taking. Students should not feel as if teachers are telling them that they need to choose the words they speak from a certain bank of words. This could have the opposite effect of making students hesitant to speak for fear they are not using the "correct" words.

Coach students to use specific literary vocabulary to describe character, setting, and mood. It can be helpful to have on hand some charts of words that are in the same meaning family, but that vary in intensity, such as the words *enraged, furious, angry, frustrated*, or *annoyed* to describe a character's feelings.

MID-WORKSHOP TEACHING
Remind Students to Carry What They Have Learned from Other Books as They Read New Books

"Readers, I am noticing that many of you are finishing up your second book with your clubs. Some have even finished your third! And that's not counting our class read-alouds and any picture books or short stories you might have been reading. I know you know this from other units this year, and in past years—and even from our writing workshop work where we've read *and* written about more than one text. But, I just wanted to remind you that readers make sure to hold on to texts from the past as they read forward. Especially when these texts have something in common with each other—as in this case, the fantasy genre. You want to be sure to carry all that you learned and practiced doing in one book into the next. You also might consider carrying any themes or other ideas from one text to another."

Making Checklists Part of Reading Workshop

Make students famous who used the checklist. Remind other students that using the checklist is something they can *always* do as part of reading workshop.

"Readers, can I get your attention?" I waited until the students' eyes were on me. "I was just speaking with a club who had pulled out their learning progression and were looking closely at how they did with Word Solving. Which made a lot of sense because that was what our lesson was one today. But, as they talked, Maria noticed that they had actually been doing a lot of envisioning work. Some of it was to help with their word solving—but not all of it. They decided that by looking back at their progressions they could make some great plans for their next conversation and set goals for their work."

I noticed that many students were now looking back at their learning progressions and nodding, some nodding and pointing out certain sections to each other.

SESSION 12 HOMEWORK

REVISTING METAPHORS—WHEN AND WHY AUTHORS USE THEM

Readers, in a few days we'll be spending some time thinking about metaphor and allegory on a large scale. But remember how earlier in the unit, you were thinking metaphorically about dragons and how they might symbolize conflicts faced by characters? Tonight, while you are reading, you should revisit some of that work. Read with an eye for when an author uses a metaphor. You might want to mark that page with a sticky note, or record the line in your reading notebook. Maybe think a bit about why that metaphor, why in this spot? Not so much that you are not paying attention to the rest of the story. But enough that you are starting to train your mind to notice those authorial moves a bit.

Session 13

Fantasy Characters Are Complex

ear Teachers,

No doubt your students have enjoyed immersing themselves in the unrealistic world of fantasy. Disappearing into a world where anything can happen is a wonderful escape from reality. You have also likely noticed that the third bend in this unit is dedicated to bringing a little bit of that reality back into your students' reading life. You students might balk at first, but they should know that a small dose of reality can make the fantasy that much richer.

In today's session, you might want to further mine this idea of the realism of fantasy by teaching students that, just as in life, characters in fantasy books are not all good or all bad. They are in fact, just like we are, rather complex.

MINILESSON

You might begin by telling a story about a reader in the classroom who explains how characters are never fully evil or fully good. Or, perhaps even better, talk about a friend who was more than one way. As you describe this reader's encounter with characters, or your relationship with a friend, you will want to emphasize that this is what life is really like. You might say something like, "Most of us know people who aren't all good or all evil. If we were really honest, as much as we *wish* we were all good, most of have some pieces of that goodness, balanced out by some negative bits. And if we want to get to know people in our lives well, or even know our selves better, we need to first start with the idea that people aren't all one way or another."

You'll then want to name your teaching point. Specifically, you'll be teaching your students that characters are complicated, and they are usually more than one way. Experienced readers are alert for the character flaws in the hero and the admirable traits in the villains.

You might want to say, "Readers, today I want to teach you that as the books we read become more complex, the characters also become more complicated. Just like real people, they are not just all evil or all good—they are nuanced. This means that powerful readers delve deeply into their characters' strengths, flaws, and motivations across the whole arc of the story."

You may want to remind students that they learned this very point in the Bend II anchor chart, "To Grow Ideas about a Character, Readers . . ." from the first unit of Grade 4, *Interpreting Characters*:

- Remember that characters are complicated. They might be one way in some contexts or relationships, another way in other contexts or relationships, or one way on the outside and another way on the inside.

You will then likely want to analyze a character from your read-aloud text, looking for signs that he or she is more than one way. If you are reading *The Thief of Always*, for example, you might want to point out that Harvey is actually a pretty complex character. He starts out selfish and kind of rude. Then he gets better, but still makes choices that are questionable. As the book continues, he becomes heroic, but he's never perfect.

This would be a perfect place to demonstrate another way to do some writing about reading. You could show your kids an emotional timeline you've made, of Harvey's development as a character across the book.

For active engagement, you might consider setting up your students up to analyze a different character from your class read-aloud. You would want to remind them of a character who is complicated, like Mrs. Griffin or Wendell. Depending on if you choose to use an emotional timeline or not, you might have students spend some time creating one for this other character. Alternatively, you might simply have them do some quick writing about the complexity of the character they are thinking of.

You would likely want to send them off remembering that fantasy characters, despite their magical worlds and strange powers, are just as complex and imperfect as human beings in real life.

CONFERRING AND SMALL-GROUP WORK

You might find in today's session that many of your students find the refocus on character a comforting one. It is highly likely most students will be naturally immersed in thinking about characters. However, today is also a good day to circle back to any teaching you feel students might need a refresher in, such as some work with fluency, monitoring for sense, or envisioning. For example, some students might truly benefit from being reminded about the importance of paying attention to objects and settings as possible symbols for them to interpret.

Additionally, you could take advantage of opportunities to teach students who are ready for teaching points you have planned for days up ahead. When you do this, those students not only act almost as "guinea pigs," but they also help you to refine your teaching.

Finally, if it has been awhile since you have had an opportunity to coach into club conversation skills, now might be a good day to do so if your clubs are meeting. Look for conversational moves, references to the text, their level of questioning, and/or reliance on their writing about reading. All can lead to fruitful teaching and celebration!

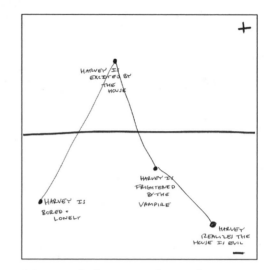

FIG. 13–1   The beginning of Harvey's emotional journey in *The Thief of Always*

Mid–Workshop Teaching

Again, you will want to choose the teaching point that makes the most sense for what your students are currently doing as readers and how the day's minilesson went. However, it's likely that many of your students might be interested in beginning to think of the additional layers of character development that fantasy writers have in their bag of tricks. For example, since fantasy writers can make up anything, they often play with characters' physical appearances. If a character is beautiful, is that because it mirrors what the character is like on the outside? Or is it somehow clashing with what they are like on the outside. Harry Potter's plain appearance disguised his power, but also let readers know that anyone no matter how they looked on the outside, could be a powerful world-changer. On the other hand, in contrast to characters like Harry Potter, Rictus's hideous appearance (and name) matched the kind of character he was. Everything from wings to fur to height to muscle mass can give readers more information to interpret.

FIG. 13–2   Julia reflects on characters being more than one way. ✸

SHARE

You might chose today to remind students to look at their checklists to see how they are doing with the goals they set earlier in the unit. Remind them that they have only a week or two left in the unit to meet those goals. If you do so, you might want to ask a couple of students to share their own goals and their plans for meeting those goals. Some teachers find it helpful to have a partnership model their thinking by having a conversation about their goals in front of their peers. Using that fishbowl model allows students who have a hard time being introspective an opportunity to get an insider's view. You might also opt to teach students to anticipate possible roadblocks for achieving their goals (not enough time to read, not liking the book, etc.) and how to get past those roadblocks. For example, do students know whom to ask, besides a teacher, for help when not understanding a text? Do they have an option of choosing a new book if a book is not working for them? These are problems, if they have not already been discussed, that could be a worthy use of a share time.

Homework

You might ask students to do a little more reflection into character complexity at home. Perhaps suggest they develop a way to keep track of complex characters. Maybe a newly designed graphic organizer? A way to sort and organize sticky notes that keep track of characters? Encourage students to think of the ways in which writing about reading can help add to the layers of their understanding about characters.

As is the case with other letters in this series, this letter has been written to make a few suggestions for possible ways this session can go. As always, if you feel that your students need something different all together, feel free to alter or skip as the need fits.

Enjoy!
Colleen and Mary

Investigating Symbolism

RECENTLY a niece who is in high school sent along a text with her English class assignment. She needed to annotate several pieces of literature with a variety of things. Most of it she was able to do with little struggle. However, when her teacher asked her to find symbols and explain what they meant, she was stumped, "My teacher has never taught me how to find symbols! She just told me what they were and what they meant." When she said this, we realized that this was the same for many adults we knew. Many of us tell stories of sitting in English class being told that the green light in *The Great Gatsby* means something. But we didn't always know why the green light mattered and not the candles or the picnic basket.

"We need to ensure that our students have the interpretation skills they will need for a lifetime of reading rich, complex texts."

Of course, this is not always the case, and we don't mean to suggest that it is. If your students were in a writing workshop last year that studied writing realistic fiction, they might very well have done work from the writer's stance of creating their own symbols. However, no matter what your students' past experiences with symbolism, it does underscore the fact that as students move on in school, they will face more and more challenging literature and be asked for higher and higher demands in their comprehension. We need to ensure that our students have the interpretation skills they will need for a lifetime of reading rich, complex texts.

The nice thing about symbolism, and one of the reasons it is taught in this bend dedicated to the intersection between fantasy and reality, is that symbolism is one of those

IN THIS SESSION, you'll teach students that fantasy readers try to figure out if repeated or highlighted images, objects, characters, or settings are a symbol of something else, and how this symbol might connect to a possible theme for the story.

GETTING READY

✔ Prior to this minilesson, read aloud Chapter 25 in *The Thief of Always*.

✔ A white board, chart paper, or something else to record student responses (see Connection).

✔ Find and prepare an enlarged or projected image of one or two artworks filled with symbolism. Two suggested images are *St. George Slays the Dragon* by Altichiero and *The Maiden and the Unicorn* by Domenichino. You may wish to use the Web Gallery of Art or a similar online art resource (see Teaching and Active Engagement).

✔ Be ready to display a chart, "Fantasy Readers Can Use Symbols as a Way to Interpret Themes" (see Teaching).

✔ Display and add to Bend III anchor chart, "How Fantasy Readers Use Elements from the Real World to Understand Fantasy (and sometimes vice versa)" (see Link).

fantasy elements that show up in students' daily lives. Knowing about symbols, such as the national flag, a peace sign, a particular color, also give them insights into their world and the culture they are living in.

In today's session, you will give students some background information about symbolism. You will then have them practice identifying symbols and interpreting their meanings by looking at a piece of art. You could just as easily choose to revisit the class read-aloud, a video clip of a fantasy movie trailer, or something else packed with symbolism. You might also decide to follow up today's session with one of those activities. If there's a rainy day and your school is showing a movie, you might suggest they show something from the fantasy genre. Then send the students to the movie armed with notebooks so they can jot possible symbols and their interpretations of them.

Investigating Symbolism

CONNECTION

Ask the students to consider what first comes to mind when they think of fantasy.

"Readers, I know we have spent a couple of weeks now eating, breathing, and dreaming fantasy. I just want to get a quick snapshot sense of what you think of when you hear the word *fantasy*. What is the first word (or words) that come to mind?" I gave the students a beat to think. "Now, call out what you were thinking. I'll record them on the board."

As students called out I wrote their responses on the white board.

> Dragons
>
> Unicorns
>
> Magic wands
>
> Castles
>
> Wizards
>
> Fairies
>
> Dark forests

Point out that most of what they called out were objects, characters, or settings that could also be seen as symbols.

"Wow, that is a lot of words!" I said, interrupting the melee. I capped my marker and looked over the list. "Hmm . . . I'm noticing something interesting here. That most of what you said are things that are objects, characters, or settings. Did you notice that, too?" Some students nodded.

"You know, what I find fascinating about that, but not surprising, is that so much of what sticks out for fantasy readers are these characters, objects, and settings that can often be interpreted as symbols. Symbols are perhaps one of the most memorable aspect of fantasy, as well as one of the tools fantasy readers use to get a stronger understanding of the stories they are reading."

Throughout this unit you will have likely notice that I warn against allowing students to look at any one element of fantasy as a scavenger hunt. This is something I learned firsthand, through trial and error, and teaching about symbolism is no different. It is great fun for students to spot symbols, we need to be consistent about making sure that they don't stop there.

Name the teaching point.

"Today I want to teach you that fantasy readers keep an eye out for repeated or highlighted images, objects, characters, or settings. When fantasy readers see these things, they pause and ask themselves, 'Could this be a symbol of something else?' and 'How does this symbol connect to a possible theme for this story?'"

TEACHING

Demonstrate how to find symbols, interpret meanings, and consider how symbols might fit with a bigger theme.

"Let's start first by saying that, like many cool things about fantasy, there are certain elements that go from story to story. Symbols are one of those things. So, often, we will see symbols, almost the exact same thing, meaning a very similar thing, in two completely different stories. For example, when a reader sees a crown, we know that it very likely is a symbol of power or royalty.

"Certain things you already expect to be a symbol because you've seen them before being used that way. For instance, a dove often symbolizes peace. Or a dark forest can represent the unknown. Unicorns are usually a symbol of innocence and goodness. Castles are usually a symbol of power (good or bad). In fantasy there are a lot of examples like this."

"Dragons are usually bad," Gabe interjected.

"That's not always true," Rosie responded. "It depends on the culture."

"You two raise a good point. Sometimes symbols can change depending on the context. Like in one story, rain could represent sadness. In another story, where there might be a drought going on, rain could represent hope or new life. The bigger point I'm trying to make is that the symbols in and of themselves are not what we're after. It's how they fit within the context of the story, and if there are other symbols in the story, how they fit together.

"Another great thing about symbols is that we can find them *everywhere*—not just in literature. Today I want us to practice finding symbols, interpreting what they could mean, and then thinking how they might fit into a bigger theme. I'm going to try this with a very old piece of artwork called *St. George Slays the Dragon*." I projected the painting onto the screen.

"So, as I look at this painting, a few symbols jump right out. I notice the castle almost immediately, which I think usually symbolizes power. And I notice that there is a man in fancy clothes on a white horse. He seems like he is the hero, maybe a knight. And I know white horses are a symbol of good. And look, just over his shoulder is a woman wearing a crown. I know the crown symbolizes power." I scan the image for a beat longer.

While this lesson employs demonstration at the teaching method, you could just as easily substitute that with guided practice or even inquiry. If your students need more scaffolding, you might opt for guided practice. If your students are old hands at art interpretation, you might opt for inquiry.

"And here, I see, I almost missed it, in this dark corner, the dragon. It's so small! I can tell that it symbolizes danger or something bad. And actually, now that I mention the light and darkness, I'm thinking that those could be symbols too . . .

"Looking across all these symbols, I see the hero who is slaying a dragon. The hero is in the light and is good, the dragon is in the darkness and represents evil. Somehow the hero is protecting not only the woman, but also the power she holds. And I think the castle sort of backs up that idea. Like the hero is protecting his whole nation in a way. I'm wondering, since the dragon is here, and it feels, sort of like the woman and the castle are representing power or the government . . ." I stop to scratch my head to make a real show of how hard I'm working. "Maybe the dragon is another country, or possibly another threat to the government. And maybe one of the themes that could be going through this paining is that governments can be threatened by outside things, but that they can win, as long as those threats stay outside."

I stopped staring at the painting and turned back to the students. "Readers, did you see how I first identified the objects, setting, and characters that seem like they could be symbolic? And then, I considered what those symbols could mean individually and then together. Then finally, I thought of how all of that could connect to theme." I quickly jotted down what I did on a chart.

ACTIVE ENGAGEMENT

Ask students to try analyzing symbols in a different painting or text.

"Fifth-graders, I am sure you are eager to try this as well. Shall we pull up a new painting to study?" They agreed. I projected a new painting.

"I'd like you to study this painting with a partner. It is called *The Maiden and the Unicorn.* You can use the chart to help you think through what it could mean." I barely said the title of the painting and the students were off and talking.

"She is a completely different person than the woman in the other painting. She's not wearing a crown," Julia said. "She doesn't even have shoes!" Sam added. I leaned in to that partnership, "Your move of using another text, in this case the other painting, to help you consider this one, is a great strategy."

"She's in the country. And I don't even see a castle."

"I think she's a peasant," another student added.

I stopped analyzing the painting here. I am well aware that there are many other pieces that could be construed as symbols, such as the people looking down from the castle. However, the point of my teaching here is not to interpret every little thing, but rather to model a piece of the process—just enough so that students have enough of a sense of how they could do it on their own.

I chose a simpler painting for the active engagement so that the work students do is more accessible and more likely to give them a successful experience. Also, even though the painting is simple, it has many possible layers of meaning, so students who are ready for higher-level interpretations can reach for that.

"Well, we know unicorns represent goodness and innocence. And the unicorn seems to really like the lady. So I think that she must be good and innocent too."

"Exactly! And if you connect it to the country, and the fact that she's a peasant, I think this whole painting is saying something about how the countryside is good and innocent. That maybe simple people are good."

LINK

Explain to students that the work they were able to do with the painting or text the class studied is the same type of work they can do with their fantasy books.

"There was a lot of great thinking going on today around the paintings that we looked at. But, clearly, we're not going off to read and talk about paintings. We are going to read and talk about books. Readers, whenever you are reading any text, whether it's a painting, a poem, a movie, or a book, you can look for symbolism and consider its multiple meanings.

Fantasy Readers Can Use Symbols as a Way to Interpret Themes

1. While reading, be prepared to find symbols.

   a. Symbols might be images, objects, characters, or settings

   b. They are repeatedly mentioned or highlighted

2. Consider what each symbol might represent or mean.

   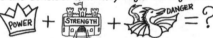 = Royalty or POWER

3. Lay those symbols and their meanings side by side and consider how they might fit together.

4. While pondering the relationship between the symbols, think about possible themes.

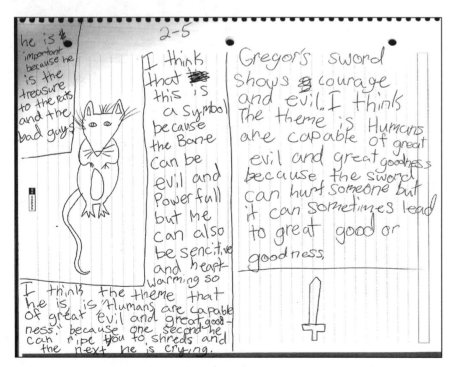

FIG. 14–1 Julia reflects on symbolism in *Gregor the Overlander*.

"Before you begin your work, let's add a couple of points to our Bend III anchor chart. One is from the previous session on fantasy characters, and the second bullet summarizes what we just discussed about symbols."

ANCHOR CHART

How Fantasy Readers Use Elements from the Real World to Understand Fantasy (and sometimes vice versa)

- Use information from nonfiction texts to better understand fantasy stories.
- Use vocabulary strategies to figure out unfamiliar words.
- **Understand that, similar to real people, fantasy characters are complex.**
- **Find possible symbols (images, objects, characters, settings).**
  - **Consider what each symbol might mean.**
  - **Think about how the symbols in a story might fit together.**
  - **Think about how the symbol(s) might connect to a possible theme.**

Understand that, similar to real people, fantasy characters are complex.

Find possible symbols (images, objects, characters, settings)

Settings Can Play a Special, Symbolic Role in Fantasy Stories

I GATHERED A CLUB that was reading *Harry Potter and the Prisoner of Azkaban*. I had noticed the last time I had heard these club members talk that they were not really discussing the role of setting very much in their stories. They were much more plot-driven. They talked about Sirius Black escaping and Scabbers going missing. Like many students reading sophisticated fantasy books, they seemed to be enjoying the setting, but not doing much work to interpret it.

"Hey friends, I've been impressed by so much of what this club has discussed about the events that happened in your book. I've wondered if perhaps you might be interested in switching gears a bit to talk about the various settings in the book and the possibility that some of the settings might be symbolic."

Maria jumped in right away, "Well, there's a whole bunch of settings in the book. There's the Dursley's house, Diagon Alley, Azkaban Prison, and Hogwarts. I think the Dursley's is sort of funny because it's safe for Harry, but he hates it. And the Prison is awful. It seems to represent evil."

"But more than evil," Paul interrupted, "because it's run by the Ministry of Magic. So it's sort of good, but it also does terrible things. I mean, clearly, the Dementors are terrible."

"And when they come to Hogwarts, Harry's other safe place, but one that he loves, it's like they represent bringing that evil with them," another student added.

"You guys are on a roll here," I said. "What do you think these settings are saying, so far, if you think of them as symbols and then consider the relationships among the symbols?"

Maria got a bright look in her eyes, "I think it's telling us another theme. That there are places where people are safer than others, but there is no truly safe place."

MID-WORKSHOP TEACHING
Special Objects in Fantasy Deserve Special Attention

"Fantasy readers, I know one of our favorite things about fantasy is the *stuff*. You know, the magic wands, time turners, magic books, and Turkish delight. These are the sorts of tangible things in the books that we read. I want to just remind you that these objects that writers have so carefully crafted to stand out to us readers are designed to be delightful and memorable for a reason. The writer wants us to stop and realize that these too could be symbols, worthy of stopping to interpret their meanings.

"When you come across an object that is mentioned a lot, or described in fine detail, you will want to stop and take note. You will want to ask yourself, 'Could this be a symbol? What could it be a symbol for? And how does it fit with the rest of the story?' For example, most of us noticed that in *The Thief of Always*, the presents the children receive every night at the holiday house are significant. It's mentioned that Lulu has so many, in part because she's been there so many years. What could these presents represent? How do they fit with the rest of the story's possible themes? Or do they suggest a new theme?"

Toggling Between the Small and the Large
Small Details and Big Ideas

Invite students to think about small, symbolic details—and then connect them to big ideas or themes.

"A few years ago I saw a famous writer, Junot Diaz, speak about writing. He said that even though he doesn't write fantasy books, he still loves to read them. He mentioned that one of the things he admired about fantasy books is their ability to toggle from one thing to another. He talked in particular about toggling back and forth between the macro and the micro—or the big and the small—the universal and the personal.

"As we work as readers of fantasy to pay attention to symbols, we are in many ways starting with the micro, or the small. And it is so fun and exciting to stay in those tiny details and ideas. However, we need to make an effort as readers to make a move to toggle back to the macro, or big ideas, and then, perhaps more importantly still, toggle back to the micro.

"So, as readers, we could try this right now with *The Thief of Always*. Let's think some more about the role of some small symbolic details in the book. Let's consider for the moment the role of the pond and the fish in the pond. And in the chapter we just finished where the pond has disappeared. Can you right now, turn and talk to the people near you about that pond and those fish? What do they symbolize? How does that fit into what we think is one of the bigger themes in the text? And then how does that theme give you more thinking about the pond and the fish?"

I gave the students some time to talk this out.

SESSION 14 HOMEWORK

 ### FINDING SYMBOLS IN YOUR OWN, EVERYDAY LIFE

Readers, on your way home today, or on your errands out and about, I would like you to keep an eye out for symbols. Where in the world that you live in, do you see symbols? What do they represent? Do any of them remind you of any of the symbols you have explored in fantasy? Why do you think that is? Feel free to sketch the symbols alongside your jottings. If you notice any connections between the symbols you see in your real life and the fantasy book you are reading, make sure to take note of that as well.

Interpreting Allegories in Fantasy Stories

IN THIS SESSION, you'll teach students that fantasy readers gain new insights into the real world by understanding and interpreting the metaphors and allegories that exist in fantasy.

GETTING READY

✔ Review the "Analyzing Parts of a Story in Relation to the Whole" and "Determining Themes/Cohesion" strands of the fifth-grade Narrative Reading Learning Progression. 🖐

✔ Before today's minilesson, finish reading aloud through the end of *The Thief of Always*.

✔ Prepare a chart showing the definitions of the words *metaphor* and *allegory* (see Teaching). 🖐

✔ Have a copy of *Mufaro's Beautiful Daughters* on hand (see Teaching).

✔ Choose and prepare to display an excerpt from *The Thief of Always* the shows metaphor or allegory. Also, if possible, have a few extra copies of this book available to share with students who need to refer to it (see Active Engagement).

✔ Display and add to Bend III anchor chart, "How Fantasy Readers Use Elements from the Real World to Understand Fantasy (and sometimes vice versa)" (see Link). 🖐

✔ Make sure students have copies of the Narrative Reading Learning Progression for this unit (see Mid-Workshop Teaching). 🖐

ONE OF THE VOICES that really resonated for us around fantasy has been Laurence Yep, author of the Dragon Series. Yep has spoken about how growing up in San Francisco's Chinatown and how he was bused daily to an affluent white suburb. He said he found that he really didn't like to read realistic fiction during that point in his life, but preferred fantasy, "because fantasy more closely mirrors children's emotional realities." In other words, the impenetrable castles, endlessly evil villains, and powerfully dangerous creatures of fantasy books can feel closer to the struggles, fears, and dangers children face everyday than what is found in realistic fiction.

In today's session, you will revisit the discussion of metaphorical thinking begun earlier in the unit and add on to it by showing students that all fantasy has an element of metaphor and allegory. Students will see that yes, fantasy is an entertaining genre, but it is also a genre that is a commentary about our real world. The corruption that comes from too much power, the difficulties that can come from being unique, even the invincibility that comes with love, are all life themes as well as themes that fantasy explores in a less direct way.

> *"Sometimes emotional realities are best explained and understood by the inventions of our imaginations."*

Today, students will take another step on the journey of learning about the connections between fictional literature and the real world. They will see how, even though in life, mere description can fail to adequately express our biggest life experiences, whimsical or poetic metaphor and allegory can capture it much more precisely. At first glance, this might seem like a bit of a stretch. Only a day or two we were talking about actual nonfiction texts as a connection to the real world. How might something metaphorical be considered even part of that reality? There are a couple of ways to consider that question. One is that, at this age, our fifth-graders very much have one foot still in childhood (they often still sleep with teddy bears and fear monsters under the bed) and one foot in adolescence. Their very lives toggle back and forth between reality and the life of their imaginations. The other answer of course, leans on Yep's concept that sometimes emotional realities are best explained and understood by the inventions of our imaginations.

Today is also the final day of this bend focused on the intersection between reality and fantasy. Tomorrow students will start the fourth and last bend, which returns them to the work of deep interpretation, this time with more experience and more knowledge under their belts.

Interpreting Allegories in Fantasy Stories

CONNECTION

Remind students of the work they did previously around metaphor.

"A couple of weeks ago, we talked about how characters in fantasy face dragons—both literal and metaphoric—meaning big dangerous things in their lives that they needed to battle. We talked about how we also might even have a few real-life dragons, and that fantasy helps us to face those dragons by showing how we can look at those struggles metaphorically.

"But, I'm about to tell you something that I know a few of you have already started to play with in your clubs. And here it is: since everything, absolutely everything, in a fantasy story can be and is often invented by the author, many fantasy authors take that opportunity to make sure most things have multiple meanings. A lot of these stories actually are teaching real lessons, and that makes them what we call *allegories*. But these metaphors and allegories aren't just another way to give us insights into the characters in our books. These metaphors also give us new ways to look at our own very real world."

 Name the teaching point.

"Today I want to teach you that fantasy readers can gain new insights into the real world by finding, understanding, and interpreting the metaphors and allegories that exist in fantasy. You can do that by noticing characters, objects, settings, and creatures that might have multiple meanings."

TEACHING

Define the literary terms *metaphor* and *allegory*.

"First, let's just take a minute to make sure we are all clear on what I mean when I use the terms *metaphor* and *allegory*," I said. I pulled out a chart I had prepared ahead of time.

"So metaphors and allegory can be a way for the author to comment on the real world, as well as for us, the readers, to decide if we agree or disagree with the author's take on that situation or issue."

◆ COACHING

You will notice that I am purposefully setting up this connection to be as matter-of-fact as possible. This is because many students, as well as many adults, overthink interpretation. Metaphor and allegory interpretation sounds much fancier than it is, and that can be intimidating. If, however, students see that this is just another task fantasy readers do, they will be more likely to approach it with lower expectations of difficulty.

Demonstrate spotting metaphor and allegory on a familiar text.

"It seems like the first thing I should do then, as a reader, is to look at a text with the expectation that something could, and very likely is, metaphorical or allegorical in a story. For example, in *Mufaro's Beautiful Daughters* we can look closely at some of the characters who appear in this book. Who could these people represent from our world?"

I turned to the part in the book when Manyara travels for a great distance from her home and comes across the old woman who gives her advice. I read that section out loud:

> "I will give you some advice, Manyara. Soon after you pass the place where two paths cross, you will see a grove of trees. They will laugh at you. You must not laugh back in return. Later, you will meet a man with his head under his arm. You must be polite to him."
>
> "How do you know my name? How dare you advise your future queen? Stand aside, you ugly old woman!" Manyara scolded, and then rushed on her way without looking back.
>
> Just as the old woman had foretold, Manyara came to a grove of trees, and they did indeed seem to be laughing at her.
>
> "I must be calm," Manyara thought. "I will not be frightened." She looked up at the trees and laughed out loud. "I laughed at you, trees!" she shouted, and she hurried on.

"This old woman seems to come out of nowhere, and her interaction with Manyara turns to be so important that it makes me think that John Steptoe, the author, is holding up a neon sign to the reader saying, 'Look at me! Interpret me!'" The students giggled.

"When we consider who these people could represent in our world, and how John Steptoe treats these characters in his book, we can begin to think about what he has to say about people like this in our world."

> **Metaphor:**
>
> When two things that are unlike are compared to make a point. Sometimes these things are not directly compared, but referred to.
>
> Her homework was an ogre waiting to devour her.
>
> **Allegory:**
>
> A story or other art work that seems to be about one thing, but is hiding a message, often a moral or political one.
>
> "The Emperor's New Clothes" is an allegory about power, vanity, and foolishness.

Make clear the trail from finding the metaphor or allegory and then interpreting possible commentary the author might be making about the real world.

I paused to show I was thinking. "Hmm . . . This old woman is treated very disrespectfully by Manyara. It feels a bit like an allegory of how older people are sometimes treated disrespectfully in our own world. Even though the older person might be wiser, the younger person might think less of them. And, the fact is, the older woman was right. Manyara's attitude and the fact that she did not listen to the older woman's advice got her into trouble. This makes me think that John Steptoe is using this as an allegory to tell us that young people would be wise to not dismiss the wisdom of older people.

"I for one, agree with his idea that we tend to treat the young and the very old not as well as we should. And that often people who think they're all too-cool-for-school treat these people the worst, much the way Manyara treated the older woman."

ACTIVE ENGAGEMENT

Guide students to practice identifying metaphor and allegory in the class read-aloud, then make the same leap into interpretation.

"Why don't we try this with another text? Let's take a look back at our book *The Thief of Always*. Let's with a partner, identify a place where the author might be using allegory or metaphor. Good places to look include images, settings, characters, objects, even plotlines. Then, after you and your partner have picked something that you are pretty sure is allegorical, see if you can determine what the author is saying about our world and whether or not you agree or disagree with it.

"Now, I'm only going to show you an excerpt from *The Thief of Always*. There is much more to this book than just this page. If you and your partner want to talk about another part of the text you find metaphorical or allegorical, please be my guest."

The sun came to wake him soon after dawn—a straight white dart of light, laid on his lids. He sat up with a start, wondering for a moment what bed this was, what room, what house. Then his memories of the previous day returned, and he realized that he'd slept through from late afternoon to early morning. The rest had strengthened him. He felt energetic, and with a whoop of pleasure he jumped out of bed and got dressed.

The House was more welcoming than ever today, the flowers Mrs. Griffin had set on every table and still singing with color. The front door stood open, and sliding down the gleaming banisters Harvey raced out onto the porch to inspect the morning.

A surprise awaited him. The trees which had been heavy with leaves the previous afternoon had shed their canopies. There were new, tiny buds on every branch and twig, as though this were the first day of spring.

"Another day, another dollar," said Wendell, ambling around the corner of the House.

"What does that mean?" said Harvey.

"It's what my father used to say all the time. Another day, another dollar. He's a banker, my dad, Wendell Hamilton the Second. And me, I'm—"

"Wendell Hamilton the Third."

As the students turned and talked, most students noticed the role of the sun rising and the role of springtime and new hope. They notice how the door to the House was open and that Harvey slid down a banister. All of these things feel like metaphors for how free and light Harvey feels now that he is not worried about his parents or what's going on. A few students commented on how springtime often signals new beginnings.

There are many excerpts from this book I could have chosen because almost any page a reader turns to is filled with metaphor and allegory. This becomes especially apparent to students after they have heard the entire book. I chose this excerpt because it has a nice, light tone and the references to sun and mentions of the House are lightly done, but easy for kids to grasp. However, if there is another excerpt that you like better, there is nothing particularly magical about this one.

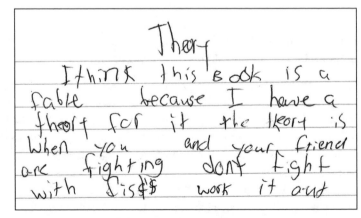

FIG. 15–1   Kylar thinks about how his story, *The Warriors*, acts as an allegory.

LINK

Remind students that the work they did today connects with the work they've been doing in the last few sessions—connecting the fantastical world to the real one.

"Readers, one of the things I think we're starting to really tune into is this idea that fantasy isn't all just about made-up imaginary stuff for our entertainment only. It's a genre that is showing us again and again that it has something to teach us about our own very real world and lives.

"Today when you go off to read, you might want to take some time to consider all the ways your novels are reflecting on our world."

I turned to the Bend III anchor chart that consolidated what students learned in this bend so far. I said to students, "Use our anchor chart as a reference. It will help you recall what you've learned in this bend. Remember that you can use these teachings now and for always."

ANCHOR CHART

How Fantasy Readers Use Elements from the Real World to Understand Fantasy (and sometimes vice versa)

- Use information from nonfiction texts to better understand fantasy stories.
- Use vocabulary strategies to figure out unfamiliar words.
- Understand that similar to real people, fantasy characters are complex.
- Find possible symbols (images, objects, characters, settings).
  - Consider what each symbol might mean.
  - Think about how the symbols in a story might fit together.
  - Think about how the symbol(s) might connect to a possible theme.
- **Interpret metaphors and allegories that exist in fantasy, and then use those insights to better understand the real world.**

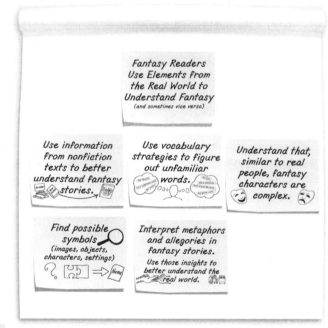

Teach Students to Assume that in Fantasy, Everything Has a Deeper Meaning

AS WAS THE CASE EARLIER IN THIS UNIT, you would be wise not to be surprised by students who have gone off on a scavenger hunt—this time to find metaphor and allegory.

This is still a good opportunity to teach into deeper interpretive work that will serve them well for years to come. One of the ways I find most helpful in guiding this work is to help students to notice when they might have questions about a choice an author might make and to use that question as an opportunity for interpretation. Have handy the "Analyzing Parts of a Story in Relation to the Whole" and "Determining Themes/Cohesion" strands of the fifth-grade Narrative Reading Learning Progression, which can be quite helpful here.

For example, I pulled up a chair next to Rosie who had her nose buried in *Harry Potter and the Order of the Phoenix*. I knew that her club was reading something else, so I was especially intrigued to see how she was balancing reading two vastly different fantasy novels. But, after checking in to make sure she was not getting confused going back and forth between the two books, I started to get the sense that she was not doing the same kind of thinking work in her independent book as she was with her club book. She was mostly just marveling at the events and magic in the story, but not saying much about her *thinking* about those things.

"I was wondering, Rosie, if you had been thinking at all about why the rebel group is called 'The Order of the Phoenix'?" I asked.

"Not really. I just thought it was a cool name," Rosie shrugged. "But, now that you mention it, the Phoenix is the kind of pet Dumbledore has. So maybe it's a code way for the group to say they're on Dumbledore's side."

"That could be," I allowed. "But I know that authors make choices for their books, but especially authors of fantasy who can invent creatures and use anything they want.

Rowling could have made anything Dumbledore's pet. But she chose the phoenix. Which is a special kind of bird. What do you know about the phoenix?"

Rosie answered, "It's a bird that catches on fire and burns up and turns to ash. And it seems like its dead. But then, a new version of itself is born from it's own ashes."

"Hmm . . . So that makes me wonder why Rowling would choose to call this rebel group 'The Order of the Phoenix'?"

Rosie said excitedly, "It makes total sense! They're wizards that were beaten down by Voldemort. Everyone thought they were dead. That they destroyed themselves. But, just when you think they're dead, they rise up from their ashes."

I complimented Rosie on her thinking and reminded her that as a fantasy reader it was tempting to just get pulled along by the story, but, if she took the time to ask herself regularly about the author's intentions she might find some hidden gems of meaning.

MID-WORKSHOP TEACHING
Checking on Goals Based on the _____ Checklist

"Can I get everyone to look up for a quick minute?" I asked. "I just wanted to remind some of you that as you are digging into your texts, you might actually meeting some of your goals you set for yourselves as readers. For example, I was just meeting with a couple of student who were looking at their learning progressions under the category 'Analyzing Author's Craft,' and saw that when they were thinking about metaphor they were also thinking about author choices in phrases as well as symbolism or a type. If you wanted to raise the bar a little more, you might scan your finger further down the sheet and notice that you could be thinking about other things as well."

Then I pulled out the two strands, "Determining Theme/Cohesion" and "Analyzing Parts of a Story in Relation to the Whole," from the student learning progression. I laid these next to Rosie's novel and reading notebook and suggested, "I think if you, and perhaps your club, used these now, you'd be able to consider your best thinking and how to raise its level. One way to do this is to use phrases like 'the author probably included this point in order to …' and 'this part is important because …'. I left Rosie whispering with her club readers as they pored over their notebooks and rubrics.

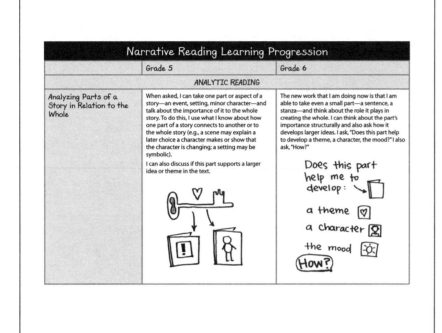

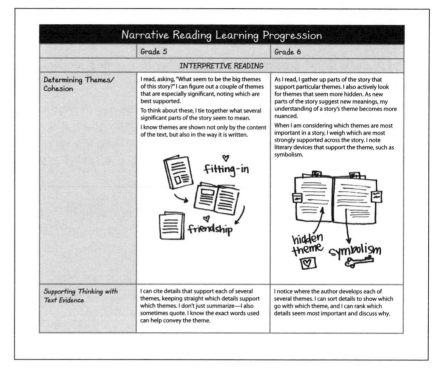

Strengthening Club Members' Work

Remind students that club members help each other to become stronger by asking questions and challenging each other's ideas.

"I know many of you had conversations with your clubs today that centered on thinking of possible metaphors and allegories in your novels and what the author might be saying about the real world. I know others of you had conversations about other ideas you're developing. The work you are all doing to stay in the realm of ideas and not just retelling your books, while also making sure to stay true to the text, is not easy work to do and it should be congratulated.

"I also wanted to share one observation I had about the thinking you were sharing—you are a very agreeable bunch! People were sharing all kinds of ideas—some of them fantastic, some of them far-fetched, some of them a little in between. But no matter what idea was being shared, most of you were simply listening to the idea and nodding, maybe asking a clarifying question or two and then moving on.

"I want to remind you that your job as a reader and as a club member is to think and to help grow other people's ideas as well as your own. That means, if an idea needs to be tested, questioned, or argued, we need to remember all that we know about disagreeing politely, and then put those skills to the test. We can make a point of asking our club members, 'Why do you think that?' or 'What part of the text made you get that idea?' We can also say, 'I'm not sure I agree with you. Can you explain more?' or 'I have a very different interpretation of that same part of the text. And here's why.'

SESSION 15 HOMEWORK

 CONTINUE TO READ THROUGH THE LENSES OF METAPHOR AND ALLEGORY

Readers, I know many of you are fired up by just how much can be discovered and understood by reading a text with the lenses of metaphor and allegory. Tonight for homework, I want you to continue to read with that lens, this time taking the time to mark a particular section of your text that stands out for you. When you find that section, can you take a few minutes to jot your thoughts on what that metaphor or allegory could mean, and perhaps even why you think it might be important to the whole of the text?

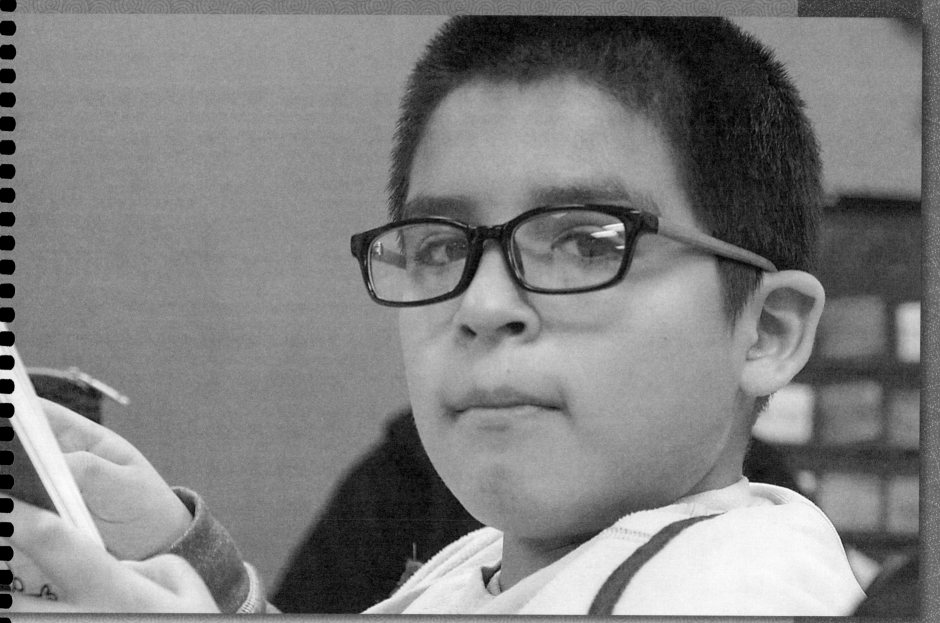

Paying Attention to How Cultures Are Portrayed in Stories

IN THIS SESSION, you'll teach students that fantasy readers pay close attention to how cultures are portrayed in stories—the culture in which the story takes place, as well as other cultures. They also consider how characters, settings, and plotlines may vary across fantasy stories from different cultures.

GETTING READY

✔ Have a copy of *The Thief of Always* on hand (see Teaching).

✔ If you know students are mostly reading books from one culture, you might consider having books from a variety of cultures available during the active engagement portion of this lesson (see Active Engagement).

✔ Students bring a book to the meeting area that their club is reading or just recently finished (see Active Engagement, Conferring and Small-Group Work, Share).

✔ Display Bend III anchor chart, "How Fantasy Readers Use Elements from the Real World to Understand Fantasy (and sometimes vice versa)" (see Link).

✔ Introduce Bend IV anchor chart, "How Expert Fantasy Readers Connect Fantasy and the Wider Literary Canon" (see Share).

TODAY YOU BEGIN THE FINAL BEND OF THIS UNIT. In the last bend, you asked students to make a connection between fantasy and reality. In this bend, you will be asking students to make a connection between fantasy and the wider world of the literary canon. As has been mentioned elsewhere in this book, today's fantasy written for children has its roots firmly in a rich tradition of literature that reaches back as far as the *Epic of Gilgamesh.* Students who learn to read fantasy well are learning a whole host of reading skills, and at the same time, having a blast as they prepare for more complex and serious reading in high school and college. The archetypes, language, and interpretive work they discover while reading *The Lightning Thief* or *The Girl Who Circumnavigated Fairyland in a Ship of Her Own Making* is likely the precursor to the reading work that awaits them in archaic, challenging, and culturally influential texts written for adults.

In today's session, you will kick off this work by teaching students the role of culture in fantasy stories. Since fantasy has a long history, it stands to reason that fantasy crosses a variety of cultures and shows up in a variety of forms. Looking across fantasy stories, readers can find blue unicorns from China, djinn from the Middle East, and trolls from Europe. Though many of the books available to your students might be more Western leaning, you will likely want to make sure students are exposed to stories from other cultures, as well. Short story anthologies, picture books, and fairy tales can do in a pinch. However, even if you are not able to get access to much in the way of cultural variety, there is still value in showing students how culture is intertwined with story. Close readers can spot cultural references, as well as get a window into the culture of the author or the culture of the world the author describes, whether or not the culture seems to be front and center in a story.

One of the main purposes of this lesson is to give students another tool for interpretation by looking at another layer of text. However, perhaps more importantly, you are showing students that their world is a wide one, with a huge variety of cultures. Story belongs to everyone, across all cultures.

Paying Attention to How Cultures Are Portrayed in Stories

CONNECTION

Tell a story about a student, or another reader you know, who realizes that cultural differences might have an effect on fantasy stories.

"Yesterday, Gabe's club wanted to share something they noticed about the different books they were reading. They said . . . ." I interrupted myself to look at the club members for a beat. "Jump in if I'm not telling this story right," I said to the club. They smiled. "They said they noticed that dragons were depicted differently in different kinds of fantasy novels. Like, they noticed in some of the books written by authors of Eastern cultural descent that dragons were wise and often good, if not particularly friendly. And that in most of the books they read by authors of Western cultural descent, dragons were more evil and cruel."

The students from the club nodded. "This got them to thinking about culture and how so many fantasy stories seem to be very connected to cultures and traditions. Some of them are very old, and some of them are more related to our current world.

"Then, Gabe decided to research more about Eastern and Western cultures and histories to see if there might be other kinds of cultural differences—not just for dragons. He learned that there was a type of war called the Crusades (1095 to 1291) that took place in Europe and in parts of what is now known as the Middle East. He started to wonder if there was any relationship between how dragons were included in stories symbolically. Like maybe, because Eastern tradition held dragons in such high esteem, that Western tradition included them in stories as the enemy as a way to symbolize their dislike of each other." I paused to let this all sink in. "Yep, they did all that cultural thinking because of dragons."

Many years ago, I went to an exhibition of Eastern fantasy and folktale art at the Brooklyn Museum. I was surprised to see the many similarities between Western and Eastern archetypes and stories. Yes, there were differences that come from geographical and cultural differences. However—and I know I shouldn't have been—I was dumbfounded by the number of similarities. Cross-cultural fantasy study is a fun rabbit hole to explore.

Name the teaching point.

"Today I want to teach you that expert fantasy readers not only pay close attention to the cultures the stories they are reading come from, but they also pay attention to how other cultures are portrayed. They also take note of how similar characters, settings, even plotlines vary across fantasy stories from different cultures. By paying attention to those things, readers can learn more about their own and other cultures."

When choosing books that represent a variety of cultures, especially ones that represent cultures that are different from my own, I make a point to study the author's background. With very few exceptions, I prefer to gather books written by authors who are from the culture they are referring to, since these are likely to be the most accurate culturally and emotionally as well as factually.

TEACHING

Explain that story literature, whether fantasy or not, has a lot to teach us about culture, and readers can use the opportunity to learn more.

"I think it's important to say, from the outset, that all art, all literature, does teach us something about the culture the text is coming from. This is true in all texts that we read. What is especially interesting about looking at culture in fantasy stories is that since everything or anything can be made up in fantasy, including the ways people dress, the words they use, the foods they eat, the homes they live in, and even they way they act, these books have a unique way of giving a window into culture. Whether this is our own culture, or one that is new or less familiar to us."

Ask students to consider alongside you the class read-aloud text, through the lens of culture.

I held up a copy of *The Thief of Always*. "Let's try this with a book we know really well." A few students exchanged knowing glances. They loved talking about this book any chance they got. "I think it helps to consider culture if you know something about the author. I know that Clive Barker was born in England and lived there for almost forty years before writing the *Thief of Always*. So we know he's English, the same as C. S. Lewis, the author of *The Lion, The Witch and The Wardrobe*. I know some things about English culture already, and Western culture, which America is a part of. Let me think of some of the other things I can say I noticed or learned about the culture Clive Barker is writing from."

I made a show like I was thinking, and Christian, as I was hoping he would, jumped in, "Well, the holidays are part of a culture. And the holidays the House does are not ones that every person does. Like Halloween and Christmas."

"You are exactly right," I said. "The holidays do let us know that the culture of the book is firmly grounded in the West. And the facts that holidays are so important to the children—so important that they are used as bait to lure the children in—tells us a bit about children's culture as well, don't you think?"

"Our culture is a little like that," Stephanie said. "We really care a lot about holidays here in our culture."

"And maybe Clive Barker is perhaps sticking a little criticism too, about our culture. Because he might be saying that maybe holidays shouldn't be that important. That maybe regular old days should be valued more."

ACTIVE ENGAGEMENT

Invite students to revisit their own texts or another text, looking for what can be learned about culture.

"Readers, I'd like you to give this a quick try with your clubs right now. Get close together with your club members, grab your latest book, and try your hand at thinking about culture in that book. You might want to start, if you know, by thinking about the author's background. You might want to consider family relationships, character actions, food, even objects and how they are treated. See if any of these things give you insight into the culture or cultures in your book, and perhaps even insights into your own culture."

If your children have been in our Units of Study over the years, they may have studied fairy tales and folk tales in third grade. In that study, students would have looked at Cinderella stories, and how the characters are portrayed across cultures. It's amazing how many versions of Cinderella there are! It's also fascinating to see what makes her beautiful or admirable in different stories. Here, as you invite students to consider how their fantasy stories might reflect cultural influences, you could remind them to think about fairy tales and legends as well.

The students scooted over to their club members and began to talk. I crouched next to the club who was currently reading *Haroun and the Sea of Stories* by Salman Rushdie. "Well, we know he's from India," declared one student.

"Yeah, and the whole book is like, definitely from a different country. I mean, it's a made-up country, but you can tell with so many things that it's a different culture. It's definitely from Salman Rushdie's culture. There's genies, for one thing. And stories seem *really, really* important. Maybe even more important than in our own culture," Stephanie added.

LINK

Compliment the students on the work they have done around stories and culture.

"The work you just did discussing your books with a focus on what there is to learn about culture is a very grown-up thing to do. There are adult readers who read things and just race through, never stopping for a moment to consider the culture the story could be coming from and the influence that might have on how the story goes. Yet, here you are, fifth-graders, doing work that some people do their doctoral thesis on!"

Remind students that culture isn't the *only* thing to think about. They should also remember that there are always other big things to think about when fantasy is involved.

"Whether you are reading or talking today, I hope that you keep in mind that culture is definitely one thing you can learn about and think about in fantasy books. And you also know other things you can do, such as read fantasy alongside nonfiction texts, perhaps to supplement your cultural knowledge. You can work through challenging vocabulary. You can pay attention to quests and thematic patterns. You can do so many things!

"It might help you to refer to our Bend III anchor chart," I said, gesturing toward the chart.

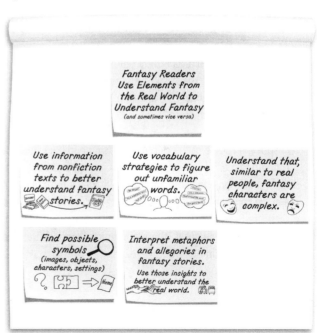

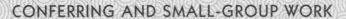

Using Text Features to Help Readers Build Background Knowledge

OFTEN, when children read fantasy or historical fiction texts, they skip the material at the front of the novel—the maps and charts—because they want to start the story. Yet these features can help readers develop background knowledge that may be important to make sense of the characters and the plot. However, very few readers think about the text features in a fantasy novel. If students do think of text features, the thinking is light and very rarely do I find students poring over maps and character family trees with any sort of regularity.

I pulled up next to a club composed of avid readers, which was fantastic—but in their voraciousness, club members sometimes missed great things in the books they were reading. Over the last few weeks, I had noticed that most of the books they chose were chock-full of text features. Yet, I saw very few students spend more than a few cursory seconds looking at them, and had never heard mention of the features in their conversations or seen evidence in their writing about reading jots.

"So, in the book you're currently reading, *The Spiderwick Chronicles*, there is a map right in the front of the book. I just wanted to let you know that text features, like maps, illustrations, timelines, and family trees are there to help you, just like the text features in nonfiction texts."

As I spoke, a couple of the club members flipped back and noticed the map, seemingly for the first time. "If we just start with the map, and think about what we talked about in the minilesson, maps are another great way into thinking about culture. After all, on maps we can get a sense of the part of the world this fantasy story might take place in, the land and water formations, maybe some important buildings, roads, bridges, landmarks. In some cases, the map depicts a world that's totally made up, with not basis in anything in our world!"

I guided the students to notice a few things about the map, all things that are mentioned by the text of the book, but perhaps were not noticed with any sense of lingering before now. One of the students piped in, "By looking at the map I see the creek and the trees and just how few other people live around the family. I mean, I knew that, but looking at the map helps me to see it in a new way."

I stood up to go. "That's nice work. I want you to remember that when books or other texts have text features, they are there for a reason. Oftentimes in fantasy books they are there to help the reader, but they also can give additional information that isn't included in the text. This information can help you develop crucial background knowledge."

MID-WORKSHOP TEACHING
Turning to Nonfiction to Investigate Historical or Cultural References

"I just wanted to share with you a quick observation that I think you might want to know about. La Von and his club are reading *The Lightning Thief*. And they knew that while the book was centered on American culture in general, they also knew it was talking about ancient Greek culture in particular. But they didn't feel like they know enough to talk too expertly about it. So they took a tip from the work they did a couple of days ago, and they headed to the nonfiction section of the classroom library to leaf through some books on Greece and Greek mythology. What a resourceful idea!"

Gleaning Historical Insights from References in Fantasy Books

Lead a discussion on cultural theories and understandings gleaned from reading fantasy books.

I gathered the students in a circle, along the perimeter of the meeting area. Some students were perched on chairs or tabletops to allow everyone to fit into the circle. When I knew I had everyone's eyes, I began to talk, making sure to set the tone of respectfulness I wanted the students to carry forward.

"I know from listening to some of your conversations and looking over some of your notes that many of you have been thinking about the idea of 'culture.' You've been talking about how the fantasy books you are reading can and often do reflect on the cultures that they represent. I thought it might be good for some of you to share your thinking with us."

Margaret jumped in, "My club is reading the *Dragon Slayer's Academy* series. And a lot of what it talks about is definitely from medieval European cultures because of the castles and stuff." A few students nodded. "But, that wasn't the part that really got us interested. We noticed that there's a character named Eric, who turns out to actually be a girl whose real name is Erica. But, when she first went to the school she couldn't get in because she was a girl. And that made us think hard about this culture. It's basically saying there are some things girls *can't* do, just because they're *girls*."

La Vonn said, "That's sort of the same, but not exactly the same as how in *The Lion, The Witch and The Wardrobe*, the girls weren't supposed to fight in the big battle. Only the boys were. Even Edmund was supposed to fight before Susan, even though he was a traitor and Susan was older. That says a lot about that culture."

"But, it's different now, right?" another student said. "Those books are talking about a culture from olden times."

Margaret jumped back in, "Well, in some ways, yeah. But in other things, like football, there's no girls who can play in the Super Bowl!"

"Okay," I interjected. "So one cultural thing some of us noticed in our books were the roles of girls and boys or men and women. Is there anything else?" I barely finished speaking before several more students' hands shot up.

"Great work! To sum up today's learning, I'm starting a new anchor chart for Bend IV."

You'll see that we refer to historical settings as reflecting different cultures and places around the world (or simply down the hall) today. Many children have grown up embedded in their own familiar culture. Books can bring them into the lives and cultures of others.

Whenever I speak with students about culture, I make sure there is a clear understanding that speaking about culture, our own or someone else's, must be done with the utmost respect. Establishing a sense of respect for all cultures is essential, even if not all cultures are represented in the room. All people's lives are worthy of respect, I want students to understand, even those that are very different than our own.

How Expert Fantasy Readers Connect
Fantasy and the Wider Literary Canon

- Pay attention to how cultures are portrayed in stories:
  - The culture in which the story takes place
  - Other cultures
- Consider how characters, settings, and plotlines may vary across fantasy stories and across different cultures.
- Use text features, such as maps, timelines, and illustrations, to better understand a story.

SESSION 16 HOMEWORK

 ## TEXT FEATURES: THINKING, CREATING, WRITING

Readers, as you probably already noticed, many fantasy books have text features like maps and illustrated diagrams and other things. Some books do not, but one could imagine how they might be useful. Tonight for homework I would like you to consider doing one of the following things:

- If your book has text features, choose one to spend a few extra minutes studying after you are done with your planned reading. See what you can learn about the setting, characters, story, or culture from studying that text feature. Then take a few minutes to jot down your thinking about that.

- If your book does not have text features, consider ones that would have been helpful if the author had included them. For example, if there are a ton of characters in your book, you might consider creating a family tree or other character chart. If there are many events unfolding over time, you might consider creating a timeline. If the setting plays a particularly important role, you might sketch a map. Then jot a bit about what you did.

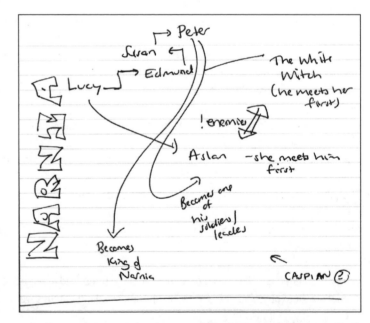

FIG. 16–1 LaVon tries sketching a relationship map to keep track of characters, and he pastes it into his book as a new text feature.

Session 17

Identifying Archetypes

S INCE OUR COLLEGE YEARS of reading *The Iliad* and *The Odyssey* we have been fascinated by the continuity and cross-cultural role that archetypes play in texts. Kids understand archetypes also, and find them fascinating. Many young readers predicted that Dumbledore would have to die in *Harry Potter*. They knew that the hero must face off against the villain on his own. Which meant that something had to remove Dumbledore, the most powerful wizard in the world, to allow Harry to fulfill his destiny.

Thinking and learning about archetypes is important for many different reasons. Archetypes help students make predictions or anticipate how stories are likely to go. They also allow students to do more nuanced thinking into books because archetypes can be a shorthand of sorts into the world of a story ("Oh, he's the teacher-figure. Good, she'll get the facts she needs now."), allowing readers to consider the significance of different characters, settings, and plotlines for bigger ideas like themes and author's purposes.

In today's session, you will teach explicitly into archetypes, using a guided practice model. If your students have a lot of experience with archetypes, you might find this lesson is best done with a lot of student input. If your students have less experience, you might find yourself doing more front-loading of information to allow them to use that information later. There are far too many archetypes to possibly teach each and every one. While archetypes are fun, they are easy to get caught up in, to the detriment of finding the deeper meanings of stories.

IN THIS SESSION, you'll teach students that expert fantasy readers use what they know about archetypes to help make predictions, inferences, and interpretations about stories.

GETTING READY

✔ Before this minilesson, choose and prescreen a video clip that uses one or more archetypes the students will be familiar with. We suggest a short commercial from United Airlines. Prepare to show a video clip to your students. A link to this video is available in the online resources, https://vimeo.com/7158709 (see Teaching and Active Engagement).

✔ Prepare a chart entitled "Some Archetypes You Encounter in Fantasy Books." You may also choose to create this chart with your students during class (see Teaching and Active Engagement).

✔ Be ready to create a T-chart with your students listing archetypes from the video (see Teaching and Active Engagement).

✔ Display and add to Bend IV anchor chart, "How Expert Fantasy Readers Connect Fantasy and the Wider Literary Canon" (see Link).

✔ Students will need their learning progressions, club books, and sticky notes (see Share).

Identifying Archetypes

CONNECTION

Tell a story about a time when knowing about archetypes was fun for you.

"When the first Harry Potter book came out, I was the first person I knew who read it. But, after reading the first book, I knew, *knew*, how the whole series was going to go. Or at least most of the major plot points. I was so confident in what I knew, I wrote down my predictions on a piece of paper in front of my friends. We sealed it in an envelope and did not open that envelope until the last book came out many years later. And I was right about almost everything!"

The students were atwitter. "Now, before you think I have some sort of magical powers, let me assure you, the only magical power I had, and still have, is that I read a lot of fantasy books. So, because of that I know about archetypes. That means I know that there are certain types of characters, plots, and settings that show up in many books and follow a familiar pattern. These archetypes, like the hero and villain, the rescue story, and the peaceful kingdom seem to go the same way most of the time."

Name the teaching point.

"Fantasy readers use what they know about the genre every time they read. Knowing about and expecting archetypes can help readers go beyond simply noting characters, plots, and settings and move into making astute predictions, inferences, and interpretations. They can do this by using their knowledge as a type of shortcut to analysis."

TEACHING AND ACTIVE ENGAGEMENT

Ask students to brainstorm common archetypes they know from literature.

"To get started in this work, let's take a few minutes to brainstorm with our partners about archetypes we already know. What are some of the archetypes? And how do they typically go? For instance, one archetype is the *hero*, and we know that heroes are mostly good, but they also tend to be loners and surprisingly, some would rather *not* be heroes. Now see if you and your partner can list a few more archetypes," I said. As the students talked, I listened in, primed the pump as needed and then recorded a handful of things the students were mentioning on a class chart. After a few minutes, I brought the class back together and showed the chart.

◆ COACHING

If your students are typical, you will likely need to emphasize this point again and again, that knowing about archetypes is not merely a fancy-sounding scavenger hunt. There is work to be done, and work that is helped along, when a reader brings archetypes into the discussion.

If you know going into this lesson that your students will not have much knowledge about archetypes, feel free to prepare this chart ahead of time and then simply go over it with your students. If your students know some things, but not enough to fill out a whole chart, you might want to coach some students to add more.

Explain that archetypes can be used as a tool to help fantasy readers do more thinking work.

"I'm sure there are tons more archetypes that I haven't included on the chart that you might want to add when you have some free time. But I think this is a good start."

I turned back to the students, "One of the things that's nice about archetypes is that they show up in similar forms in many different stories. So they are sort of a shortcut way to signal to the reader about this character or plot or setting. So readers can say, 'Hmm . . . I've read something like this before. So I already know a lot. I can make a prediction here or develop an interpretation here because I'm already a few steps ahead.'"

Set students up to watch a video clip that is rich in archetypes.

"Let's try this all together. I'm going to show a video to you. We're going to watch it twice. The first time I want you just to identify the archetypes: the characters, plotlines, or settings that you recognize from other fantasy stories."

I played the video for the students. The stop action animation shows a father kissing his sleeping son good-bye as he heads off to travel for work. Then, the son dreams his father flies away on a magical bird, lands at a round table, vanquishes a dragon, and is crowned king. The next scene shows the father returning home and giving the boy a toy dragon.

Record the archetypes students noticed on a chart.

When the video was over, I asked the kids to share with their partners what archetypes they noticed in the video. I then jotted those down on a T-chart:

Archetypes You Noticed	What the Archetype Made You Think
• Dad as hero • Other knights–Dad's companions • The dragon	•

As I prepared to show the video again, I said, "Of course, it's not enough to just identify the archetypes. This isn't a scavenger hunt where you get prizes just for finding things. The real value in archetypes is allowing them to be a thinking shortcut—letting them make you think bigger thoughts because you carry all of what you know from other examples of this archetype as you encounter this new story."

Some Archetypes You Encounter in Fantasy Books

	The Hero *Harvey, Arthur, Nyasha, Elizabeth, Harry Potter*	*A good character who is often lonely and would rather not have to be a hero. The hero has to complete his or her quest alone. Usually wins.*
	The Villain *Mr. Hood, Manyara, Dragon, Voldemort*	*A bad character who is often surrounded by other characters he or she is mean to. Wants to be in charge of everything. Usually loses.*
	The Wise Person *Mrs. Griffin, Merlin, The Old Woman, Dumbledore*	*A very smart character who usually helps the hero by teaching him or her.*
	Companions or friends *Rictus, Lulu, Ronald, Nyoka, Hermione*	*These are people who are friends with the hero or villain. They mostly stick to the hero or villain, however some of them can be false friends.*

I chose the United Airlines commercial mentioned in this lesson for a few different reasons. The first reason being that it included a few different archetypes in a very short period of time—only one minute—making it very easy to have repeated viewings. I also loved the arc of a complete story that it made. On a purely aesthetic note, I really liked the use of stop motion animation with paper puppets. If, however, you either do not like this video or would prefer not to use a commercial, there are plenty of short clips available online that will do similar work to this video.

After a second viewing of the video, record the students' thinking about the archetypes they found.

I showed the students the video again, noticing that they couldn't keep from whispering during the second watching.

When the video was over, I uncapped my marker and said, "So let me start with my thinking. I noticed that the father became the hero of the story. And that made me think about heroes in general. How maybe to the boy the father is a hero for going to work and coming home. How he looks up to him. And since I know heroes tend to be lonely, and also tend to not want to be heroes, I think that fits into what I think is probably true for a lot of parents who have to travel. That they miss their kids, and they would rather not leave them behind, but they have to." I jotted a few notes on my chart to record my thoughts.

If you have time or you feel your students could benefit from more than two viewings, you should certainly make the decision to do so. You might even decide a select group of students would benefit from previewing the video so as to be more fully prepared to interact in this lesson.

Archetypes You Noticed	What the Archetypes Made You Think
• Dad as hero • Other knights–Dad's companions • The dragon	• Dad is the boy's hero. He's just as conflicted as other heroes are on their quests.

"Can you talk to your partner about one or two of the other archetypes that are still up on the chart? What do they make you think? What ideas are you getting? As you do this work, remember to think about what you know from other stories about similar situations or archetypes, and let that knowledge spark some new ideas for you."

I circulated as the students shared their thinking with each other. "I was thinking that the dragon might have been a bad guy. But, I think it might have also been a symbol, because it's been a symbol in a lot of the books we read," Julia said.

"I agree," Rosie said. "I think the dragon might mean different things to different people though. I think for the dad, the dragon represents the work he has to do. That it's really hard work, but he needs to do it for everyone to be happy. But for the boy, I think the dragon is adventure. And he really likes dragons. His dad knows that, so he brought him one."

After listening to a few more students, I jotted more of their findings on the chart.

There are also archetypal themes, settings, and structures for fantasy novels. Here, we stick with archetypal characters, but we list others on a chart of common archetypes found in the online digital resources. We provide a preview on the next page.

LINK

Reiterate that archetypes are a launch pad to stronger thinking.

"Readers, what I love about what you did today was that you were able to take what you know as experienced fantasy readers, and apply it to a whole new text. And one of the ways you did that was by identifying and analyzing archetypes. You were able to make predictions, inferences, and some pretty dazzling interpretation by using archetypes as a launch pad.

"Another thing that is so great about archetypes is that you'll see them everywhere. Not just in fantasy stories, but also in realistic fiction, poetry, even pop music! And each time you run into them you can say, 'I am so ready to think deeply about this, because I am already halfway there!'

"Today, when you go off to read and talk with your clubs, I want you to continue to challenge yourself to not only get lost in the story, but to develop some new theories and ideas about your stories. You can do this by leaning on archetypes, but you can also do this by thinking about quest structures, complex characters, and noticing symbols.

"Before you go off, let's add a point to our Bend IV anchor chart. Refer to this chart as you work today, and as you work through the rest of this bend."

ANCHOR CHART

How Expert Fantasy Readers Connect Fantasy and the Wider Literary Canon

- Pay attention to how cultures are portrayed in stories:
  - The culture in which the story takes place
  - Other cultures
- Consider how characters, settings, and plotlines may vary across fantasy stories and across different cultures.
- Use text features, such as maps, timelines, and illustrations, to better understand a story.
- **Use their knowledge of archetypes to make predictions, inferences, and interpretations about stories.**

Use their knowledge of archetypes to make predictions, inferences, and interpretations.

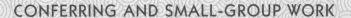

Fantasy Readers Go beyond Archetype Scavenger Hunts by Looking across Texts

DESPITE THE REPEATED MENTIONS for students not to get caught up in an archetype scavenger hunt, it is likely at least one club or a few students have gotten caught in that rut. It's an easy one to get caught in because it can feel good to find and label things. Depending on the level of reading a student is currently doing, it might be a great step forward away from simply retelling a story. It is also possible at the lowest levels of fantasy text that there is not much deeper thinking to do aside from simply identifying the archetype.

That said, for a good chunk of students, you will likely want to move them away from simply identifying archetypes and into using them as tools to strengthen their thinking. One good way to do this is to have students pull out texts or their notes on texts that they have already read. By touching each text and naming archetypes that appear

in some form in more than one book, we can guide students to then see if there are thematic connections as well. "There is a wise teacher who sacrifices himself in both *The Lion, The Witch and The Wardrobe* and *Harry Potter*. Do you think there might be a connection between those books thematically?" you could ask.

You'll also find that some of your readers are ready to think across a lot of stories because they have read so many by now—your lower level readers especially, who may be on the twelfth Dragon Slayer Academy book! For these readers, you might pose an interesting new challenge, which is to see if any archetypes other than character archetypes appear in their books—like good vs. evil as a theme, or the dragon's forest or magical pool. Getting children to investigate these archetypes is one way to get them thinking analytically, and to see that the authors of their books are part of a longstanding genre—one which your students are enticingly expert on!

MID-WORKSHOP TEACHING
Thinking about Unexpected Archetypes

"Fifth-graders, can I get your eyes?" I waited until everyone looked up. "A few of you have commented that some of the archetypes you are studying are different in some ways than other archetypes in other stories. In other words, maybe all of the books you've read so far have had princesses being sweet and helpful and kind, but the book you just picked up describes fairies as mean and sort of annoying. When that happens, you know that archetype stands out because it is so different from everything else you've seen. There's no doubt that the author knows that it's different too. So, what a wise fantasy reader will do is to ask him- or herself, 'Why did the author play with this archetype? What message or theme is the author trying to send me by making me pause and say "Hmm?"'"

	Good versus evil Thief of Always, Harry Potter, The Lion, the Witch & the Wardrobe	A story where the hero must face the villain, usually for power.
	Rescue stories The Paper Bag Princess	A story where someone or something gets taken and must be rescued.
	Castle The Lion, the Witch & the Wardrobe, The Paper Bag Princess	A building where someone powerful lives.
	Forest Mufaro's Beautiful Daughters, The Paper Bag Princess, The Lion, the Witch & the Wardrobe	An area with a lot of trees and animals, usually a bit dangerous and sometimes magical.

Using Checklists to Raise the Level of Writing about Reading

Readers can reach toward their goals by using tools and revising their work with the help of those tools.

I ended work time a bit earlier than usual to allow time for a longer conversation in the share. I asked the children to bring their learning progressions and their club books with sticky notes to the meeting area. When everyone was gathered I said, "I noticed a few clubs today trying to elevate their thinking by turning to the learning progression as they talked. And I thought that was a fantastic idea. However, what really impressed me about these clubs is that they didn't just use the checklist to identify what they were doing well and name their current level. They reminded themselves to use the checklist to revise their jottings.

"But that wasn't all! They also helped each other to revise at least one of their jots to make it better—to make it the level each reader wanted to be. By doing that, they were able to have a really strong model to take back to their book and try to make their future thinking just as strong.

"Right now, will you compare your best jotting with a partner's? And partners, use your learning progression to make suggestions for how to take this work up even another notch!"

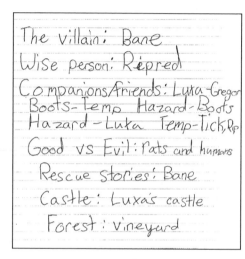

FIG. 17–1 Julia reflects on the archetypes in her novel.

SESSION 17 HOMEWORK

USING THE LENS OF ARCHETYPES TO EXAMINE PARTS OF YOUR OWN LIFE

Readers, for homework tonight, look at your world with archetype lenses. Examine something that's part of your life—soccer practice, band rehearsal, video games, TV commercials—all through the lens of archetypes. What archetypes do you see in the world outside of fantasy stories? And once you identify some of these archetypes, how do they make you think about your life?

Once you've recorded those examples, spend a few minutes thinking about your current or recent reading in fantasy books to see if you notice any through-lines between or among various archetypes. Jot or sketch everything so you'll be ready to share with others.

Reading Across Texts with Critical Lenses

IN THIS SESSION, you'll teach students that one way readers analyze a story is by using critical lenses, such as being alert to stereotypes and gender norms (or rules).

GETTING READY

✔ Review the "Critical Reading" strand by the Narrative Reading Learning Progression ✋

✔ Have on hand some of the book covers and possibly some film clips or images you've downloaded of classic fairy tale heroes and characters (see Connection, Teaching Conferring and Small-Group Works, and Mid-Workshop Teaching).

✔ Also have on hand any texts you might want to refer to while studying these topics, such as excerpts from *The Thief of Always*, *The Paper Bag Princess*, *Mufaro's Beautiful Daughters*, or other texts.

✔ Display and add to Bend IV anchor chart, "How Expert Fantasy Readers Connect Fantasy and the Wider Literary Canon" (see Share). ✋

JUST A FEW DAYS AGO, students were beginning the interesting work of considering how their fantasy books can be a window into the cultures they represent. Of course, as adults we know that any book, not only fantasy books, can be windows into culture. And some of your students will no doubt have already made that discovery for themselves. The work today builds on some of the discussions your students have been having around culture, but this time moving into the realm of critique.

This is important work to address head on, because the fact is, one of the prevailing concerns parents, other educators, and even some children, have about the fantasy genre (fairy tales and anthropomorphic stories fall under this category as well) is that stories in this genre can wittingly or unwittingly perpetuate stereotypes about cultures, peoples, and genders. One only needs to look at the more well-known classic pieces of children's literature to see these norms at play: Wendy takes care of the children while Peter Pan goes on adventures, the ugly character is the evil one, the poor character also happens to be the one who does not like to work. The list can go on and on. Recently, however, many children's book authors work actively to counteract these broad generalizations and stereotypes that many theorize have had a negative impact on children's sense of selves, as well as their sense of the value of other people. Readers these days are seeing more powerful heroines and multifaceted male heroes, as well as more emphasis placed on kindness and balance than on power and riches.

However, you cannot rely on a carefully curated library to be sure your students are not exposed to images and storylines that adults and kids might find objectionable. This is, of course, near impossible to do. But, perhaps more importantly, you will want to teach your students how to hold their own moral compass in hand and use it to make decisions about the texts they encounter. You will want students to ask themselves questions such as, "Do I agree or disagree with the way the author is portraying this character?" "Who holds the power in this narrative, and how do I feel about the message that is being told through that dynamic?"

In today's session, you might prepare by digging deep into your own childhood texts to find examples that are worthy of study. You might want to be sure to find examples that run the gamut from worthy of some challenging critique, to texts that have shown themselves to be pretty critically impervious of offense.

> *"You'll want to teach your students how to hold their own moral compass in hand and use it to make decisions about the texts they encounter."*

You might also want to bear in mind that whenever teachers delve into the realm of social criticism, you need to be clear of your goals. I tend to be one who believes that students must draw their own conclusions. This is because I certainly do not want my own biases and assumptions to trump those of students. But perhaps more importantly, telling students my opinion does not help students to form their own opinion or learn how to do their own critical thinking. A wise teacher spends most sessions like this with an ear tuned for possible future teaching points, as well as a pocketful of questions to ask students so as to keep them doing the heavy lifting.

Today you will guide students to reconsider stories and images they are familiar with by using various critical lenses. You will also teach students about the role of master narratives and counternarratives in literature, which are two important concepts that they are likely to carry into their reading lives for years to come.

Reading across Texts with Critical Lenses

CONNECTION

Describe characters you like in the read-aloud, and compare them to other favorite characters.

"Do you remember when the movie *Frozen* came out? It was a smash hit, which I'm sure you remember. But, what you might not realize is that it was so very different from other fairy tale or fantasy movies that we have gotten used to seeing. The story had characters that very much acted in ways we are not used to seeing in movies or literature. There were heroes and villains to be sure. And there were quests and magic aplenty. However, there were some ways that characters broke everyone's expectations. Expectations people might not have even known they had.

"That got me to thinking about our read-aloud. I've been rethinking my favorite parts of *The Thief of Always*. I find myself thinking about favorite characters, and what I like and don't like so much about them. And sometimes, these character traits seem to be related to traits I've seen in other characters. It's a little bit like what we discussed a couple of days ago, about archetypes. But it seems a little different as well—it's about stereotypes, too. I'm just pondering how the characters in the novel fit with my expectations of young male and female characters. And how some books, a lot more than maybe I would wish for, perhaps use stereotypes instead of simply archetypes, as characters."

 Name the teaching point.

"Readers, today I want to teach you that one way readers analyze a story is with critical lenses, such as being alert to stereotypes and gender norms (or rules). One way to do this work is to consider characters' actions and appearances."

TEACHING

Demonstrate analyzing a character in terms of how he or she fits stereotypes and gender norms.

"This is fascinating work, readers. Let me show you a little bit about how it goes. First, one way you can analyze a character, is to compare that character to other characters, by his or her appearance. I just showed you how I thought about the Disney characters, for instance, and realized that all those female characters reinforce a stereotype that girls have to look like Barbie dolls to be important, A stereotype is a typical way of thinking about things—that girls have to be beautiful or that boys have to be strong, for instance. Stereotypes can be really damaging, because they make

For this lesson, I often have available, from the Web, some images of current supermodels, of Disney heroines, of characters from movies and novels. You could also include Hermione from Harry Potter *and Bella from* Twilight. *You'll notice that, universally, they are slim, graceful, with clear features, and usually long hair, like LuLu. Do the same for the male heroes, and you'll see a parallel representation emerge. The message seems to be, "You can be brave, as long as you are beautiful." If a character has a physical disability in a fairy tale, for instance, that damage is meant to symbolize a damaged soul. That kind of repeated aligning of difference with something damaged is something we want to question by reading through critical literary lenses. Beauty does not, actually, mean automatically that someone is good or brave.*

individuals feel as if they don't fit. Also, some stereotypes are negative, and that's not fair. So I'm happy that LuLu doesn't fit the stereotype of 'beautiful blond,' with her looks. I'm not completely happy that she is blond and has beautiful eyes. It would have been cool to have a girl who maybe wasn't so stereotypical in her appearance. But at least she doesn't care about her beauty.

"Another way readers analyze a character is by his or her actions. Readers ask themselves, 'Does this character act in ways that are unusual?' In particular, you can look for how a character reinforces or breaks with gender norms. Gender norms are the rules associated with being a girl or a boy. These are invisible rules that aren't written down, but that we all seem to know. One of my favorite stories is *Oliver Button Is a Sissy*. It's about this boy who wants to tap dance, but his father and his classmates all think that boys shouldn't dance, boys should play football! In fact, before we go any further, think for a moment about an idea you have, or used to have, about what boys and girls are allowed to do, and then share with your partner."

I walked around the class, listening in.

After a moment, I said, "Friends, I heard you say things like boys aren't allowed to wear dresses. Others said that girls are supposed to be polite and to take care of people. Some of you said that girls aren't supposed to fight. A lot of you said that boys learn not to play with dolls. Friends, there is nothing inevitable about any of those rules. We learn them from the books we read, the films and television shows we watch, and the people who surround us. So, one thing I like about LuLu is she breaks with a traditional gender norm that girls should be polite and pretty. She is really strong, and she fights! In fact, I think there is no way Harvey could have beat Mr. Hood without LuLu's help!"

FIG. 18–1 La Von thinks about the gender roles in his books.

ACTIVE ENGAGEMENT

Give your students a chance to practice this work, reminding them of some characters and stories that might get them started.

"Readers, do you see how I thought about what characters look like, and what they do, to think about how they break with or conform with stereotypes and gender norms? Let's give you a chance to try this work. You could keep going with *The Thief of Always*, or you could turn to the characters in the stories you are reading. I know that the readers of *Deltora Quest* will be eager to talk about Jasmine and Lief, and how they mix up traditional girl-boy roles. And what about Eric/Erica in *Dragon Slayer Academy*? Isn't she the best 'knight' in their school? I want to listen to that conversation!"

As students talked, I listened in, making sure to give tips to push their thinking when appropriate. "I often find it helpful to compare characters, to talk about more than one, when I do this work," I said. "Give it a try, really thinking hard about how the characters' appearances and actions fit with or break with stereotypical roles and norms."

Teachers, you could decide to extend this teaching by also showing how characters fit into certain norms of relationships and other identities. Do all the girls and boys end up dating, or are other possibilities shown? Do nontraditional family structures get honored? You could also look at characters' fates—who gets to survive?

LINK

Tell your readers that they can read critically whenever they encounter text or stories, including television and film.

"Readers, we are really in the fastest and most intense part of this whole unit on fantasy literature. There are so many things we have learned over the past several weeks that have helped us to be incredible readers of this genre. Now, as we are at our most expert level, we are ready to really be critical of the ideas, characters, and situations that are presented to us in our books, but also in other texts, like movies and television shows. We want to keep an out for the types of messages we are receiving when creators of stories represent characters in stereotypical ways. We don't want stereotyped characters to get in the way of knowing that all people can be good and all people can make bad choices. But that looks or culture or economics are not what make people that way. It is the actions that they take and their inner selves that let us know that. And those qualities can come in all sorts of packages!

"Now go off to read! Remember to be extra alert to how different characters are represented—those with disabilities, those of diverse ethnicity and culture, those who make personal choices about how to live."

I make a point in this link of reminding students of the focus of today's session, but also of to point out that they are steadily growing more and more expert in the genre. I want students to understand that expertise makes the work go faster, but also become more complicated as well.

Looking For Characters Who "Break the Mold"

MANY OF YOUR STUDENTS will have a lot to digest after today's minilesson. Some students will be ready for even more. The students ready for more are likely the ones who have already brought up the idea of stereotypes during read-aloud discussions and book club talks. For those students, you might decide to introduce the idea of how stories tend to go. For this work you might want to gather a few clips of Disney movies or classic fairy tale picture books. Perhaps even some ads from magazines that show "girl toys" and "boy toys." You will also want to pull a few examples of counternarratives that the students are likely familiar with, such as *Frozen*, *Shrek*, and *The Paper Bag Princess*.

You might then say something similar to what I said to Gabe's book club after I had gathered them on the rug, "Some of you probably know that in our culture, there are some predictable ways that stories tend to go. If I were to start a story out by saying, 'There once was a kind, poor boy who worked very hard . . .'" you could probably tell me the story ends with the boy working so hard that he is able to find a good job or get an amazing opportunity that allows him to not be poor anymore. Or if I were to say, 'There was a pretty young lady and a handsome young man. The young lady needed help, so the young man helped her and . . .'"

"They fell in love and lived happily ever after," Stephanie finished for me.

I smiled. "That's exactly right. Those stories, the ones we are so used to that we could finish them, are so powerful because they have become the way we expect those kinds of stories to tend to go." I displayed some of the images I had brought to the rug with me. The students nodded as they looked them over.

"But, the thing is, not all texts follow the way stories go. Some shake things up and do something disruptive and unexpected. Those stories go against what is expected.

Some examples of that include one of the texts we talked a lot about—*The Paper Bag Princess*. They help give readers another option for how stories can go—and in turn help us to imagine another way our own *life* stories can go. Not every pretty young girl marries her handsome prince and lives happily ever after—or even wants to. When you read stories, not just fantasy stories, these could be realistic fiction or even nonfiction, you want to keep an eye out for where the author lands in terms of the type of story he or she is putting out there. Does the story follow the way most stories like this have gone? Does the girl "get a prince" at the end? Or does she go off to find more dragons?"

MID-WORKSHOP TEACHING
Comparing and Contrasting with a Critical Lens

"Readers, I'll make this quick," I said. "I can tell from the buzz in the room that there is a lot of critical thinking going on. I want to congratulate those of you who are taking everything you have read in this unit and holding it up to the light of a critical lens. One way you can help add layers to that work is to think about texts in contrast or comparison with other texts you know.

"And you don't need to limit yourself to just the written texts in the classroom right now. When you are talking and thinking about the books you are currently reading, you can also think of the books, and movies and television shows you have experienced before. Sometimes by placing one text up next to another one you can see things you have never seen before."

Celebrating the Revisions Students Make in Their Thinking

Ask students to share what they used to think—and how their thinking has changed.

"Readers, I think so many of you used to think one thing about either the books you are reading, or about certain ideas that are out there about the way people are *supposed* to be or act. I think there was a lot of revision of thinking happening today. Woohoo!

"To celebrate that, I'm going to ask you to fill in this sentence, 'I used to think _____, but now I think _____.' If it might help, go ahead and jot your thinking on a sticky note. Otherwise, just make a mental note. We're going to do a popcorn share. Just call out what you're thinking when you're ready."

At my signal, the students began to share:

"I used to think that my book was very fair. But now I think that only the boys get to do anything exciting so now I'm thinking it's not as fair as I thought."

"I used to think that it was a good thing that poor people in books got a chance to be rich if they worked hard. But now I think it's weird that I never see rich people working hard to stay rich."

"I used to think that *Frozen* was really great because it was not about romance. And now I still think it's a great movie, but now maybe I wish that not all the girl characters had to be skinny and beautiful."

"Students, I heard some excellent insights! Now before you go off to your next class, let's hang onto what you just learned by adding a couple of key points to our Bend IV anchor chart."

How Expert Fantasy Readers Connect Fantasy and the Wider Literary Canon

- Pay attention to how cultures are portrayed in stories:
  - The culture in which the story takes place
  - Other cultures
- Consider how characters, settings, and plotlines may vary across fantasy stories and across different cultures.
- Use text features, such as maps, timelines, and illustrations, to better understand a story.
- Use their knowledge of archetypes to make predictions, inferences, and interpretations about stories.
- **Analyze a story by using lenses, such as being alert to stereotypes and gender norms (rules).**
- **Figure out if a story is a master narrative (expected) or a counternarrative (disruptive, unexpected).**

Analyze a story by using lenses, such as being alert to stereotypes & gender norms.

Figure out if a story is a master narrative (expected) or a counter narrative (disruptive, unexpected)

THE RESCUE   W—E A KNOWLEDGE QUEST

SESSION 18 HOMEWORK

 ### READ SOMETHING NEW, USING AN EYE FOR ARCHETYPES

Readers, tonight for homework, I'm going to ask you to do some work that connects to yesterday's thinking and helps us to prepare for tomorrow's work. Can you, when you're reading tonight, make a point of reading something that is *not* your fantasy novel for a few minutes. It can be an article. It can be a poem. It can be a realistic fiction novel. And can you read with that eye for archetypes we were using just a day ago? If or when you find any archetypes in those other kinds of literature, can you make a quick note? Or if you see character "breaking the mold," will you note that? We will be using those notes first thing in the minilesson tomorrow.

The Lessons We Learn from Reading Fantasy Can Lift Our Reading of Everything

IN THIS SESSION, you'll teach students that they can apply their fantasy reading skills, such as interpretation and cross-text study, to help improve their skills in reading other genres.

GETTING READY

✔ Students bring their homework from last night to the minilesson (see Connection).

✔ Gather and display all the charts the class used during this unit, including the anchor charts for Bends I through IV (see Teaching).

✔ Baskets of books or other texts from a variety of genres for students to explore (see Active Engagement).

A S WE DRAW EVER CLOSER to the conclusion of this unit, You want to make sure to squeeze every last bit of opportunity it offers. In this case, you want to feed off the energy your students have around this genre and allow it to begin to power their reading for the rest of this year and perhaps throughout their future years.

In today's session, you will teach students that the plethora of skills they have been gathering and honing over the weeks are not purely for the reading of fantasy. In fact, much like cross-training helps athletes reduce injury and keep them in tip-top shape for other sports, fantasy is a type of cross-training for readers. It works a variety of muscle groups in unexpected and thrilling ways, allowing students to find skills and talents they didn't even know they had. I suggest that you pull a few baskets of books representing a variety of genres to give students on the spot practice with this.

You will also notice, that unlike most of the other minilessons in this unit, this lesson is very lean. There are a few reasons for that. As the days of dedicated fantasy reading draw to a close, you'll likely want to maximize the amount of time your students have to read and think and talk. Additionally, you are very likely at this point, to have several ideas of things you would like to use to embellish this lesson to tailor it to your students' needs. That said, the most important point to hit in this lesson is the concept that they are more experienced and skilled readers than they were just a few weeks ago. You want them to understand that they can use those skills for now and for always.

Today's session is an important one because it is a transference lesson, yes. But, it is also important because it actively shows students that the things we love can often help give us new insights and improve upon other things in our life. A great lesson to learn young!

The Lessons We Learn from Reading Fantasy Can Lift Our Reading of Everything

CONNECTION

Ask students to share what they noticed about archetypes across their various forms of reading.

"Readers can you gather with your clubs to start, and share some of what you noticed about archetypes across your days of thinking about them?" The students scooted toward their club members.

As the students shared, I noticed, as I was hoping, that there was a wide variety of experiences and mediums that the students were describing which contained archetypes. There were song lyrics, commercials, sports uniforms, billboard advertisements, and even some mentions of favorite sitcoms and other shows on television. The buzz in the classroom was loud, but very much a focused and productive buzz.

I brought the class together, and before I even said a word, La Von had his hand in the air. "I looked for archetypes," he said. "There were archetypes everywhere! I mean seriously, I felt like I couldn't even go to bed without seeing another archetype. I watched a basketball game and there were archetypes on the uniforms! I had no idea there was so much fantasy everywhere!"

"That is exactly right. And, just to add to the craziness, it's not just archetypes that are everywhere. There are so many things we learn to do as readers, so many things we learn about, when we read fantasy."

Name the teaching point.

"Today I want to teach you that by strengthening fantasy reading skills, readers can actually improve their skills in reading everything. As experienced fantasy readers, you can now use your skills of dealing with difficulty, interpretation, and cross-text study with almost everything else you read, including realistic fiction, poetry, even nonfiction."

Throughout this lesson and the entire session, you might notice a "loosening of the reins," and even more use of we as we try to make sure students feel as if with their new expertise and knowledge they are most definitely part of this new type of literary world.

TEACHING

Have students take a virtual tour of the charts from the unit, reminding students of all they have learned and asking them to share with a partner.

"Take a look around at all the charts we used during this unit. (I had just added a bullet to our Bend IV anchor chart.) Remind yourself of some of the things you learned and did as readers in the last few weeks." I gestured to the charts I had displayed across the front of the classroom. Seeing them all lined up like that was impressive.

ANCHOR CHART

How Expert Fantasy Readers Connect Fantasy and the Wider Literary Canon

- Pay attention to how cultures are portrayed in stories:
  - The culture in which the story takes place
  - Other cultures
- Consider how characters, settings, and plotlines may vary across fantasy stories and across different cultures.
- Use text features, such as maps, timelines, and illustrations, to better understand a story.
- Use their knowledge of archetypes to make predictions, inferences, and interpretations about stories.
- Analyze a story by using lenses, such as being alert to stereotypes and gender norms (rules).
- Figure out if a story is a master narrative (expected) or a counternarrative (disruptive, unexpected).
- **Apply their fantasy reading skills to reading other genres.**

Apply their fantasy reading skills to reading other genres.

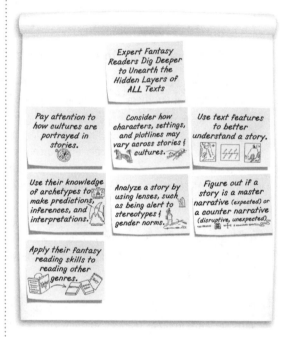

"Why don't you and the people sitting next to you study all these charts and take a little trip down memory lane and discuss all the things you know as fantasy readers?"

I listened in as the students talked about character complexity, thematic threads, and deciphering tricky vocabulary. I was admittedly a little impressed by not only all they had learned, but how well they were able to spot all they had learned.

Let students know that they can take these skills on the road.

"Now, as I'm sure you already imagined, it's not enough to just learn how to do these sorts of amazing things in fantasy. As an experienced reader, you want to be able to lean back on your past reading experiences and pluck the skills you have earned from all those experiences with text. You can pick up any text in the world, an article, a comic book—even a textbook—and apply some of your fantasy readying skills to it. Because, the truth is, and you already know this from our other units this year, once you have learned a skill in one area, you can apply that skill to anywhere it can work."

ACTIVE ENGAGEMENT

Introduce baskets of texts from a variety of genres for students to explore, using their new fantasy reading muscles.

"You might have noticed that there are five baskets sprinkled around the meeting area, one in each corner and one in the middle. You are going to scoot in a minute to the basket that is closest to you. Each basket has texts that represent a different genre.

"I'm going to ask you to gather with the people who are nearest to the very beginning of that basket to read excerpts from those texts. Then, using some of the skills you learned during this fantasy unit, read the text. When you're done reading, see if you can talk through the skills that you used that you first honed as readers of fantasy."

The students scooted off to the baskets. I had placed a few copies of *Number of the Stars* in one, with sticky notes on the first page. I had placed copies of texts from different genres in other baskets: the picture book *Each Kindness*, an article from the class magazine subscription for *Time for Kids*, sheet music from the students' recorder class. In the last basket I had placed several copies of Gary Soto's poetry anthology *Canto Familiar* with a poem marked with a sticky note.

Coach students as they read, calling out to the larger group occasionally.

I watched as students read for a few minutes, as they did I voiced over, "Don't forget to look back at our charts to remember some of the skills you know."

I then listened carefully as students shared what they did and what they learned. "I totally didn't know what this word was," confessed one student, holding the magazine. "But then I remembered all that work around looking for parts of words you might know, and I was able to make a pretty good guess."

Gabe chimed in, "I know this part of *Number the Stars* really well. But I had never looked at it thinking about archetypes before and wow! I totally see villains and heroes and companions that I never saw before!"

"This picture book is *full* of symbolism," Maria declared. "The toys, the clothes, the water!"

These were the texts I had on hand with three or more copies. There is nothing inherently special about these texts other than the fact I had multiple copies and they represented a variety of genres. Comic books, textbooks, even workbooks could work. What's important is that they offer some challenge that allows students to practice their reading skills as they read the beginning only.

In sessions such as this, one of the biggest challenges is to be everywhere and hearing everything, while at the same time not being too obtrusive so that students feel free to let loose with their thinking. One trick I employ to make sure I listen, but don't overstay my welcome is to squat next to each group of students. It is hard for me to stay in that position for too long—so I am up and on to the next group in no time!

I gathered the students back together, "So much going on out there with your reading! Thumbs up if you were able to apply one of the strategies you've learned from your fantasy reading." I looked back at a sea of thumbs.

LINK

Set students up to finish their fantasy reading and then segue into other genres.

"Of course, many of you are finishing up or just finished up your fantasy novels yesterday or today. In that case, you might be moving out of reading fantasy books and into other kinds of reading. If that's the case, you might be trying the strategy of applying what you learned in fantasy to other genres.

"For the rest of you, you might want to instead read today with your mind on your books. If you do notice yourself using a strategy and doing some work that feels particularly good, you might want to mark that place with a sticky note, or record it in some way. That you can remember to use that strategy with another genre as soon as possible."

Wrapping Up: Final Discussions, Flash Essays, Compliments

TODAY will likely be the last day you meet with any clubs about their work together. Tomorrow will be the wrap-up and celebration day. So, depending on how many of your clubs are meeting today, you might choose from a few different options:

- Travel from club to club, helping them to draw their reading of their current book to a close, as well as reminding them to have a final discussion about the stack of books they read together during this unit. You might encourage them to bring physical copies of the books and place them at the center or their club, or else encourage them to review their sticky notes and reading notebook entries to remind themselves of their thinking. You could prompt them by saying, "One thread that went through all the books was . . ." or "One way the books were very different from the other was . . ." or "If we were to sort these books into piles based on themes or ideas . . ."

- Encourage clubs to save some time at the end of their conversations to write flash essays of their thinking about reading fantasy with their clubs. Invite them to draw conclusions about the specific books they read as well as about the genre in general.

- Take a victory lap. Listen in to each club long enough to hear something to compliment. Then share that compliment with that club.

No matter what you decide to do, remember where you are in this unit—almost at the end. This is not the right time to take up any big ticket items that might take several days to resolve. It *is,* however a good time to take lots of notes begin considering your conference and small-group teaching points for your next unit.

MID-WORKSHOP TEACHING
Not Taking Fantasy Reading Skills for Granted

"Readers, as I'm looking around, I'm noticing a lot of you are close to the end of your books or have just finished them." A few students groaned good-naturedly. They were not ready for this unit to end. "And, I was pleased to see how many of you are already picking up new texts in new genres to take your fantasy reading skills on the road. Congratulations on that!

"However, I also want to remind you that you are not done with being fantasy readers. That for as long as you live and as long as you choose fantasy books, you will be practicing old reading skills and learning new ones. You don't want to become 'take it for granted' readers who just sort of sleepwalk through their books, missing all the amazing things there are to learn. You know that while you might very well be an expert fantasy book reader right now, as you grow older and explore new levels of texts, new topics, and new authors, there will be so much more to learn, so many ways to outgrow yourself."

Helping Students Set Their Own Reading Course

Gather students to circle the classroom library. Give them a virtual tour of the texts contained there.

"Readers, come join me in the library," I called, as students wrapped up their work. The children gathered around, some sitting on the floor, some perched on chairs they dragged over.

"I thought it was only fitting that on the day before our final fantasy reading celebration we come here to take a sneak peek at the reading that is still left for us to do this year, and perhaps even over the summer. I wanted to point out that there are so many books and magazines and other texts to read here. Some are fantasy." I pointed to a few baskets with single copies of fantasy novels. "But we have lots of other things here too. We have club sets of all kinds of books. We have incredible biographies, riveting mysteries, mind-bending poetry." As I talked through each type and genre in our library, I lifted up baskets and highlighted shelves. I could tell the students were seeing our library with new eyes.

Explain to students that today is a good day to start making their next set of reading plans.

"As you wrap up your fantasy book club work, you will be wondering what comes next. And to be sure, we still have a lot of learning and growing to do here in fifth grade. But I also want to remind you that you want to set your own reading course. You want to make your own independent reading plans. Are you going to go on a personal quest to read all of the books in a fantasy series you discovered in this unit? Are you going to stick with your club, maybe finishing up your club's reading list? Maybe exploring a new genre? There are so many things to choose. The choices are almost limitless.

"Before we head off into the rest of our day, can you gather with a few people who are sitting near you, and just imagine some possible reading plans for life after fantasy? You might even start your conversation by saying, 'One thing I really enjoyed about reading fantasy is. . . . I'd like to carry that through to my next reading project by reading. . . .'"

REVIEW YOUR JOURNEY AS A FANTASY READER

"Tomorrow, as you know, is going to be our last day of this fantasy unit, as well as our celebration. Tonight for homework I want you to prepare for this day. I would like you to go through all your old jots on sticky notes and old notebook entries, which stretch back from the beginning of the unit. I would like you to gather up your reading logs, club notes, any artwork you might have created—any artifacts of your journey as a fantasy reader in this unit including your learning progressions. If you have time, you might reflect a bit on what you've done so far as a reader of fantasy and how far you've come as a reader from where you were just six weeks ago."

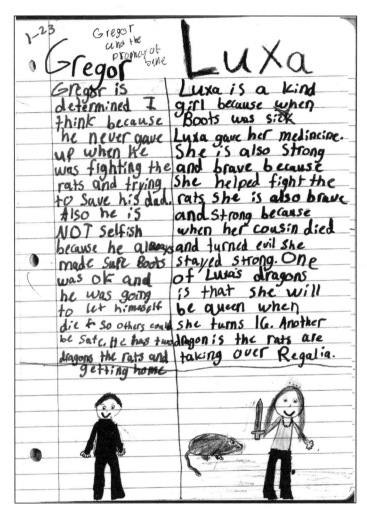

FIG. 19–1 Morgan thinks about characters' traits, complications, and dragons.

Happily Ever After

*Celebrating Fantasy and Our Quest
to Be Ever Stronger Readers*

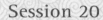

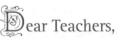ear Teachers,

Our favorite part of every fantasy story is the ending. But even more so when we know the ending is a happy one. So, congratulations on completing this unit on fantasy book clubs! We hope that you find this final day a happy conclusion to a joyous unit.

Today is the day to celebrate all of the exhilarating and exhausting work you and your students embarked upon weeks ago when you began this unit in fantasy book clubs. It is the end of the story of your learning together, and hopefully the beginning of a new journey the students will begin, carrying everything they learned about reading and the genre of fantasy.

Just as has been the case in all of the sessions in these books, there are many pathways you can choose for your students to best match their needs and preferences. In fact, we might argue that in today's session there are even more choices, simply because the goal of today's instruction is to help guide students on another quest—this one, a reflection quest. A quest to look back at their work in the past weeks, admire how far they have come, and then make plans for where they still want to go.

You might decide to forgo the choice described in more detail below and instead create another celebration of your own design. You might also decide to choose from one of the following ideas:

- Invite students to dress up as their favorite fantasy characters. Students mix and mingle with other characters, having book talks and making recommendations as they imagine their character might.

- Have students go back to notebook entries, sticky notes, learning progressions, even class-created charts from the beginning of the year and revise them with their newly expert eyes. How might they go back and imbue all of their learning on to those original documents?

- Encourage clubs to do Reader's Theater of key scenes from their fantasy novels, being sure to leave time for each club to explain the significance of the scenes they chose to dramatize.
- Create artistic realizations of key themes, concepts, or ideas from this unit. Students can paint, sketch, or even create photographic stills that give fellow readers a window into the most important take-aways from this unit.

You could also, as is suggested in this letter, create a whole-class experience, one final quest if you will, that builds off of a whole-class experience, designed to remind students that as readers become more expert on any given genre, it behooves them to carry those skills into their next endeavors, as well as to continue to build and enjoy their fantasy reading lives (if they so choose).

If you choose this option you will want to do a little preparation ahead of time. Ideally you will gather artifacts from your work in this unit. This might include charts, video clips, famous quotes, samples of student writing, imagery, or anything else that will remind your students of the journey they took with you. Additionally, you might want to group these artifacts together into stations or centers so that students will be able to move from table to table.

If you are feeling especially ambitious, you could suggest to other colleagues in the same grade who also taught this unit that this might be a fun, gradewide celebration. If this is the case and you and your colleagues were more or less aligned, instead of students visiting stations within the classroom, students could move from class to class.

WHOLE-CLASS EXPERIENCE

You might begin today's session by meeting your students at the classroom door. Perhaps you've hung a sign on the door that says, "Welcome, reading heroes and heroines. Enter if you are prepared to attempt your final quest." Or, you might simply greet the students at the door with your most serious face and declare, "The day has dawned on the final trial of your fantasy reading know-how. When you cross this threshold you will be leaving the fifth-grade hallway and entering into the realm of fantasy reading challenge, conversation, and reflection."

Explain either orally or through signage that students are to gather with their clubs to embark on their journey. This is a journey fashioned off of many final chapters in fantasy books or final scenes in fantasy movies. The scene occurs after the heroine has completed her quest and in a moment of reflection and celebration, either literally or figuratively looks across the big moments she experienced, her trials and tribulations, her companions and her bested enemies. In movies, these moments sometimes show up as montages, and other times as flashbacks interjected between pans of familiar faces in the crowd. In the

Lucy,

I feel that this Genre means many things to me. One day, fantasy may mean that I am reading about a characters life, while the next, I may feel like I am escaping reality and becoming the character myself. Fantasy sometimes connects to situations that I experiance in my own personal life, which sometimes causes me to make decisions like the character did. I think that fantasy teaches myself and many others, certain skills and strategies. I used to think that a characters quest was simply the obstacle they are undergoing, but I learned that characters commonly have a intenal quest. Such as, helping on the quest, searching for someone or something, learn something new, etc.

Sincerely,
Maya.

FIG. 20–1 Maya thinks about why she reads fantasy and how it affects her life.

television show *Survivor*, it was the moment when the finalist walked through the torches of their fallen comrades before heading to the final vote.

Except this time, instead of visiting comrades, students will be revisiting key lessons, ideas, and conversations. These could include:

- A copy of one or all of the whole-class read-alouds with your sticky notes with prompts left in the book, as well as any charts that were created as part of those conversations. You might place a card next to the book suggesting the club revisit the text, reminding themselves of conversations they had about the book, and anything new they would add to those conversations, or using their learning progressions to have a "fresh" conversation about the book.

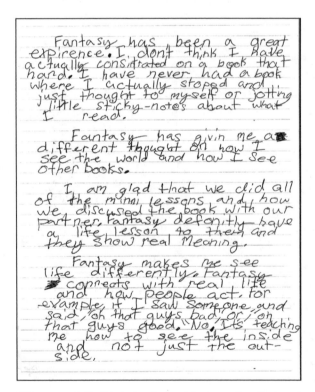

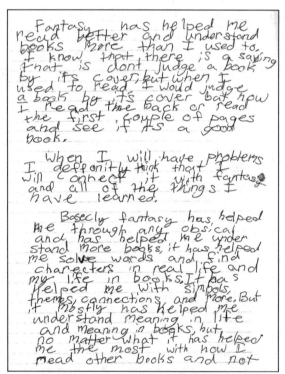

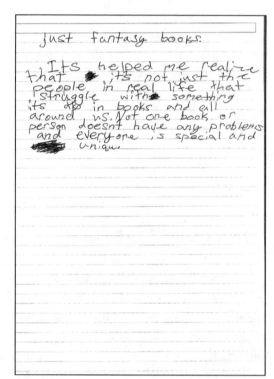

FIG. 20–2 Julia thinks hard about how reading fantasy has changed her.

- A display of the most popular books students read in their book clubs. These could be divided into club-specific baskets, or else display the array of books that were read during the unit by all students. There might be a card displayed on the table directing students to sort through the books and rank them from their least to most liked. Encourage them to think of other ways to rank the books (scariest, hardest, strangest).
- A computer with video clips the students might have viewed during the unit, cued up to be watched again. There could be a card asking students to rewatch the video clips, this time with the eyes of expert fantasy viewers, carrying everything they know about interpreting the genre to their discussions.
- A gathering of student-created sticky notes and notebook entries. You might ask students to look over these artifacts and create their own. Or you might also ask them to choose one artifact to build off of, perhaps having a juicy conversation or writing a longer piece.

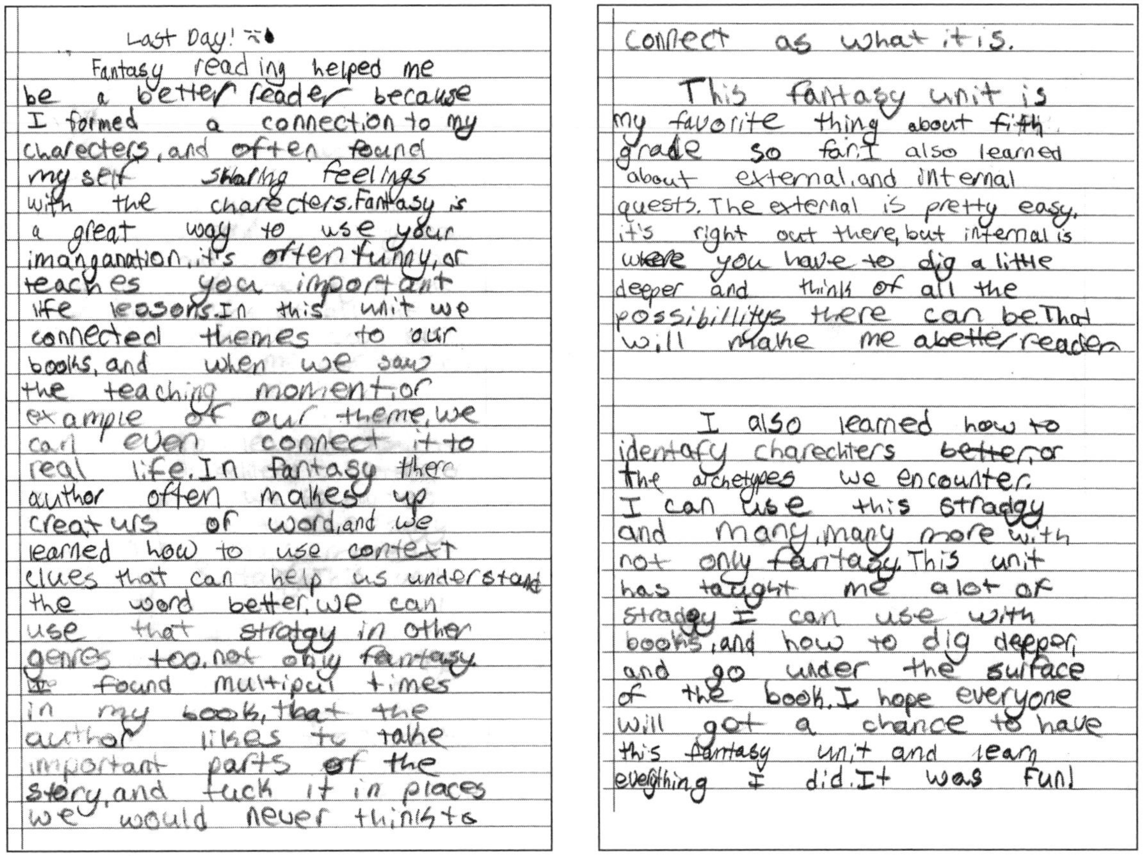
Last Day! :(

Fantasy reading helped me be a better reader because I formed a connection to my charecters, and often found my self sharing feelings with the charecters. Fantasy is a great way to use your imanganation, it's often funny, or teaches you important life lessons. In this unit we connected themes to our books, and when we saw the teaching moment or example of our theme, we can even connect it to real life. In fantasy there author often makes up creat urs or word, and we learned how to use context clues that can help us understand the word better, we can use that stratgy in other genres too, not only fantasy. I found multipul times in my book, that the author likes to take important parts of the story, and tuck it in places we would never think to connect as what it is.

This fantasy unit is my favorite thing about fifth grade so far. I also learned about external and internal quests. The external is pretty easy, it's right out there, but internal is were you have to dig a little deeper and think of all the possibillitys there can be. That will make me abetter reader.

I also learned how to identafy charechters better, or the archetypes we encounter. I can use this stradgy and many, many more with not only fantasy. This unit has taught me a lot of stradgy I can use with books, and how to dig deeper, and go under the surface of the book. I hope everyone will got a chance to have this fantasy unit and learn everything I did. It was fun!

FIG. 20–3 Aly thinks about how reading fantasy helped her to develop thematic connections. (Notice the "sad face" at the top of the page!)

- A collection of images, either artworks viewed in earlier lessons or else artwork associated with books the students read in read-aloud or in clubs. Students might be set up to study the artwork through the lens of archetypes, but they could also be asked to create their own, new fantasy-expert lenses. They could focus on objects, settings, or individual characters.

- A short stack of copies of class charts from the unit alongside a few markers and blank paper. In this area, students could be asked to look back at those familiar charts and either revise them or else create new charts that they feel would be useful for either their own future fantasy reading or else for next year's fifth-grade readers.

- A station that asks students to leave behind their favorite artifact from the unit, along with an index card describing the artifact and what it tells other fantasy readers about that student's journey in reading fantasy.

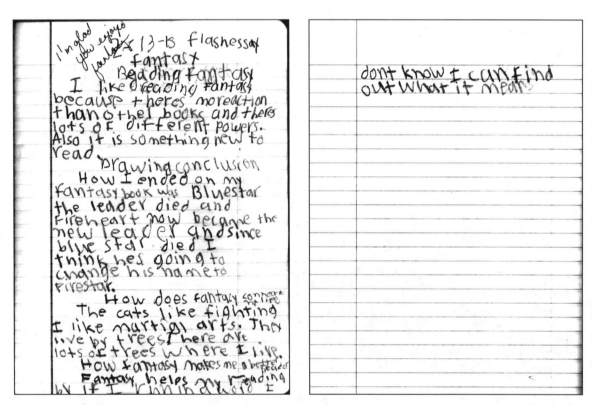

FIG. 20–4   Fantasy was a new genre for Malachi. The Warriors series converted this reader! 👏

- A station with samples of the reading checklists and an instruction to talk through what they accomplished from the checklist and what they plan to work toward in the future.

You could arrange these materials in baskets on tables, or else simply set them up around the perimeter of the room. To lead the students from station to station, you might decide to create a trail in the classroom, lined with charts, anchor texts, and student work that leads from one activity to the next.

As clubs move from station to station, you will want to actively coach into their thinking, writing, and conversations. You will want to prompt them with, "At the beginning of the unit you thought . . . ? And now?" Or, "Wow, that's great thinking! Did you always think that way? Talk us through how you came to this conclusion."

Depending on how involved your stations are, students might move every 10–15 minutes or so. When you get a sense of the students drawing to a close, you will want to reconvene your class in the meeting area.

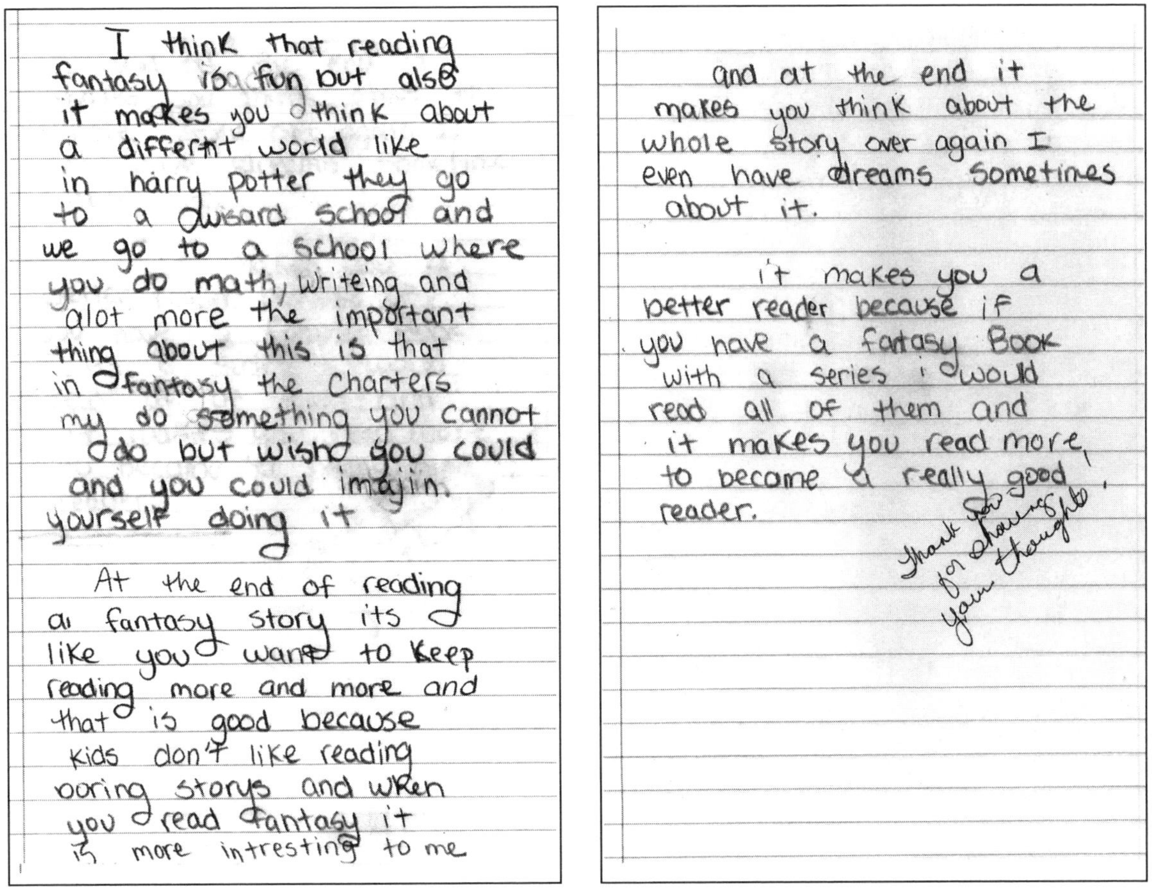

I think that reading fantasy isa fun but also it makes you think about a differnt world like in harry potter they go to a dwisard school and we go to a school where you do math, writeing and alot more the important thing about this is that in fantasy the charters my do something you cannot do but wishd you could and you could imajin yourself doing it

At the end of reading a fantasy story its like you wanr to keep reading more and more and that is good because kids don't like reading boring storys and when you read fantasy it is more intresting to me

and at the end it makes you think about the whole story over again I even have dreams sometimes about it.

It makes you a better reader because if you have a fantasy Book with a series i would read all of them and it makes you read more to become a really good reader.

thank you for sharing your thoughts

FIG. 20–5 Addi shares how fantasy fulfills her wish to be magical, and how it makes her want to read.

REFLECTIONS

When your students have completed their station journey, you will want to give them some time to put all of the pieces together. Depending on your students, there are a variety ways this can go. You could unroll a large piece of butcher paper and begin with a big thought or question about the unit written across the middle, such as, "Reading fantasy has taught me . . ." Students could then have a written conversation, responding to each other's comments with comments and questions of their own.

Alternatively, you might ask the students to bring their reading notebooks or a piece of paper and a clipboard to the meeting area to ask them to write their individual reflections down. This could be done as a freewrite, or else even as a letter to their future reading selves. If this is the last or close to the last unit in your school year, and your students will be heading off to middle school next year, you might encourage them to write a list of the most important things they learned from this unit that they do not want to forget in middle school. These could be about reading in general, fantasy in specific, but could also be about the life lessons students learned during this unit.

Or course, the easiest option is to simply have one last grand conversation about fantasy with the students. You could start them with the sentence, "I used to think . . . about fantasy, but now I know . . ." and let them take it from there. You could simply begin by sharing your experience of the unit and your learning and asking the students to share their own stories.

Whatever you decide to do, the most important thing is that students are given an opportunity to revel in their growth and celebrate each other's company on this learning journey.

All our best,
Colleen and Mary